When
GOOD
KidsGo
BAD

Effective Solutions For Problem Behaviors

Steven T. Olivas PhD, HSP

Copyright © 2012 by Steven T. Olivas, PhD, HSP
Published by
Premier Publishing & Media
Premier Education Solutions
3839 White Avenue
Eau Claire, WI 54702

Library of Congress Cataloging-in-Publication Data

Olivas, Steven T.

When good kids go bad : effective solutions for
problem behaviors / by Steven T. Olivas. -- 2nd ed.
p. cm.

Includes bibliographical references.

ISBN 978-1-936128-13-6 (pbk.)

1. Problem children. 2. Discipline of children.
3. Child psychology. I. Title.

HQ773.O45 2012

155.4--dc23

2012008794

www.pesi.com

When Good Kids Go Bad provides an effective marriage of evidence-based practice and clinical experience. For the novice (parent or professional), it's an excellent introduction to an array of challenging behavior problems and effective principles and methodologies for behavior management and behavior change. For those with more experience, it's a reminder of why these kids behave the way they do and is a refresher course on practical strategies and tactics we may have neglected. And all delivered with humor in a light and readable style that makes it easy to absorb!

-Peg Dawson, EdD
Author of Best Selling *Smart but Scattered*

About Dr. Steve

As a psychologist in private practice, Dr. Steve has worked with children, teenagers, and their families since 1991. He truly enjoys the spontaneity, creativity, and honesty of this population. Through this work, he has developed an extensive practice helping teachers, schools, and school districts, both to help manage individual clients and to conduct staff development and trainings.

Dr. Steve earned a B.S. and an M.A. from the University of Wisconsin (Whitewater Campus) and culminated with a Ph.D. in Counseling Psychology from the University of Oklahoma.

All of that after a somewhat auspicious start to his academic career, during which he earned several infamous distinctions at St. James Elementary, Mukwonago High School, and a brief stint at Marquette University. He has tried his hand at improvisational comedy, has written a weekly column in Nashville's local newspaper, and has cohosted a popular radio show. Currently, he is lamenting the death of his dream to play for the Chicago Cubs ... but he remains hopeful that Heather Locklear will someday call.

Dr. Steve currently lives in Tennessee with his wife, Heather (not Locklear ... but close). He also has two children who, with any luck, will someday have nutty kids of their own.

Table of Contents

Chapter 1
Introduction to the Real Issues
The Truth on Why You Need This Book

Sometimes the Divine Hand of Creativity will, with an audible *THUNK!* on the top of my head, command true brilliance to fly forth from my fingertips like magma from Mt. Vesuvius. Other times (and I fear this is one of them) I sit here, staring dumbly at the blank computer screen and flashing cursor, until my hands are moved to put forth all the ideas springing from my mind.

First, thank you for picking up this book. I have done my best to impart pearls of wisdom gleaned from my clinical and professional experience. I have spent a number of years as a psychologist in private practice, as a public speaker around the country, as a college professor, and even a couple of stints as an improvisational comedian. Through it all, I think I have learned a thing or two.

My reason for writing this book was really twofold: One, as a part of my seminar work with therapists, nurses, social workers, parents, teachers, and administrators around the United States, I have been asked over and over if I have a book based on the materials I teach. The answer had to this point always been a reluctant "no." I wanted to produce a book that speaks *with* you and not *at* you. While this book does not add anything groundbreaking to the seminar, it does put the material in a format to which you can return many times for reflection.

Second, I tried to bridge the gap between the three worlds that your kiddos touch; namely, home, school, and the therapy office. Too often, a book like this focuses on only ONE of these worlds, but unless all of the adults in the child's life are marching in stride, we will not maximize our potential effectiveness. Making sure that the therapist, the teacher, and the parents can share a common methodology prevents the bright kids from wriggling through the loopholes!

If you would indulge me a final rationale for writing this book, I wanted to put a product out there that changes the pace and tone of most books on this topic. While troubled kids bring certain seriousness into their homes, our offices, and of course, the schools and classrooms, many are truly bright, creative, and remarkable to deal with. Some of the most interesting and entertaining kids I have seen in therapy have been viewed as terrors! But rather than come from a position of dire seriousness or dry data regurgitation, I wanted to assist in building change and long-term relationships with these children—while simultaneously offering some skills for short-term management.

The book is divided into three main sections. The first section helps to provide a framework within which I discuss treatment and management. I go over the labels (or, diagnoses) we hang on troubled kids, with special attention paid to differentiating among four labels that have tremendous overlap: *depression, anxiety, ADHD,* and *bipolar disorder.* (PTSD, too, although a specific discussion of the profound effects of trauma lies outside the scope of this book.) I also add a bit about medication—if for no other reason than to introduce some of the more common medications and to offer something on the effects and side effects you can expect. Part I also begins to offer ideas for relationship and behavior management with the children to help transition into the rest of the book.

Part II focuses briefly on the set up. I cover some basic "rules for engagement" and lay the groundwork for more specific interventions. Of course, all throughout Parts I and II, I offer some specific strategies. It would be nearly impossible to completely withhold during these parts! But before launching into the final segment, I thought it would be nice to orient everyone toward a certain number of common denominators of *any* good management strategy.

And lastly, Part III focuses entirely on concrete ideas to effect positive behavioral change. I know that many readers have been exposed to a number of good ideas with regard to behavioral change, so I don't know if the strokes of insight presented here are completely new to you. Consider these some of the basic ideas for management tactics. This information comes from material I have taught over the years combined with a healthy dose of great ideas I have heard from folks just like you whom I have met while doing my seminars.

Let's tee it up and kick this book off. Killer instinct is required—helmets and shoulder pads are optional.

Part I

Understanding the Kids in Your Life

Chapter 2
A Brief History of Behaviorism
If Skinner Had a Greek Dog

To begin our discussion of dealing with troubling behaviors, we should at least get an understanding of the basic principals of behaviorism. I use these terms throughout the book, so I want to make sure that all of us are on the starting line together. To begin our discussion, we have to go way back … to ancient Greece … "Old School" style to the teachings of a fellow named Aristotle.

Not to say that Aristotle started the ball rolling toward behaviorism per se, but he did come up with an important concept pertaining to motivation. And let's face it—figuring out a kid's motivation will help us to choose behavior management strategies. In other words, *"What makes these kids do what they do?"* and more importantly, *"Can I help them achieve their goals in more acceptable ways?"*

Enter Aristotle. He came up with a concept that was so simple, it was actually rather profound. He said that motivation for ALL human behavior boils down to the same *prime mover.*

According to this brilliant thinker, if he asked why you chose to do a certain behavior, you would give him an answer. Then, if he questioned *why* that answer was important, you would give another answer. He would ask *why* again, you would answer again, and so on and so forth down the line. The place at which you would eventually arrive—the place at which Aristotle could no longer question *why*—would reveal that prime mover. That place, according to Aristotle, is *happiness* (Aristotle, from *The Nichomachian Ethics,* p 195–196; Morgan (Ed), 2001). Aristotle philosophized that happiness was the motivator lurking behind our decision to conduct ALL behavior.

Let's make this more applicable to your life. If I were to ask you *why* you are reading this book, you would probably answer something along the lines that you wanted to learn some things about kids and behavior change. If I were to ask why that is important to you, you would say something about wanting to become a more effective adult to those kids. Again, I would ask why that is important. We would follow this chain down to its logical conclusion, and eventually we would arrive at the place Aristotle said was the starting point for decision-making: Eventually, you would come to the conclusion that you did it *to be happy.*

Actually, today we still utilize Aristotle's idea in psychology, but we attribute it more to Carl Rogers and Abraham Maslow than to Aristotle. You see, Aristotle's way of thinking pervaded for a l-o-n-g time, but there stepped onto the scene in the early 1900s a fellow named Sigmund Freud, and all seemed to go batty for a while. Freud was a bit dark when it came to his theories about human nature and motivation (to say the least!). In simple terms, while Aristotle felt that happiness motivates all human behavior, Freud felt that the two motivators were sex and aggression (Freud, 1949).

Freud believed that each of us has a bubbling cauldron of sex and aggression in our unconscious mind, and that this cauldron is called the *id* (Freud, 1949). The id is big and hairy, has giant teeth hanging out of its mouth and one eye in the middle of its sloping forehead, and drags its knuckles behind it when it walks. Freud was not a generally happy fellow, if you know what I'm saying. But, while he was vastly important in shaping the way we think about the unconscious, people today tend to *pooh-pooh* his ideas about the role of sex and aggression to motivate behavior.

So, about 20 years later, onto the scene stepped Rogers and Maslow. You all remember Maslow's hierarchy, right? You memorized it for the final exam in your Introduction to

Psychology class and then immediately forgot it because you didn't think you would ever have to use it again.

Oh, tell me I'm wrong!

Anyway, if you recall, on the tippy top of Maslow's hierarchy sat the pinnacle he felt we all strive to hit: *self-actualization* (Maslow, 1943). Bearing in mind that psychologists like to use big words to explain simple concepts to make us feel smart when people don't know what the heck we're talking about, "self-actualization" just means "realizing one's potential," which you could equate with *happiness*. Maslow got us back to basics ... back to Aristotle. He and Rogers taught that we are all pushed to climb up that hierarchy, that we are all motivated to become all that we can be and achieve the ultimate prize: happiness.

So let's assume that happiness motivates all human behavior. Apply that same principle to some of the difficult (or angry, or tough) kids in your life. They, too, are motivated by happiness, Aristotle would say. But, the world may have dealt a very different hand to them than what was dealt to you or me. So, the way they attempt to achieve happiness may be profoundly skewed from what we consider to be "appropriate behavior." These kids may never achieve a state of joy—rather, for them "happiness" may be defined internally as *coping* or merely surviving in the world in which they live. These kids may have learned to adapt to their lives in ways that are functional where they come from but are causing all kinds of problems in your office, or in the neighborhood, or in a school setting.

For example, let's examine the student from a very chaotic household. He has learned that, in order to get his needs met, he has to act out. His "voice" has to be louder (metaphorically speaking) than the din that surrounds him. So, he throws wild temper tantrums to achieve an end for himself. At home, this is functional behavior. He tantrums, his parents give in, he gets his needs met.

But now, this same child enters school. A similar scenario arises, but rather than being functional in the school setting, it is remarkably disruptive.

What is the task of the adults in the life of this kiddo? To reteach methods for getting needs met but in a way that is adaptive to this particular setting, or any setting outside of the chaotic home. The nice thing about behavior is that it can be taught, untaught, and retaught, but these processes take a lot of time and energy on the part of those who step into the role of therapist, coach, or teacher!

So let's leave Aristotle behind and fast forward about 2,000 years … to the birth of psychology as a discipline.

Around the turn of the century, there was a fellow named Pavlov who was hard at work in the former Soviet Union. All of you probably remember him, as you were taught his concepts early in the semester of your Intro to Psych class. He was, as you may have already surmised, the guy who became famous by working with dogs. (We'll talk about another "dog guy" later, as well as the "cow lady!") In actuality, Pavlov was not a psychologist. He was, in fact, an investigator of natural sciences and was interested in studying the salivation patterns of dogs (Pavlov, 1927).

Pavlov had quite an impressive laboratory, with rows of dogs in cages all along tiled aisles. Also working in the lab were assistants who were in charge of caring for and feeding the dogs. To accomplish this, they would, of course, walk up and down the aisles doling out food and attention. As they walked, their heels and soles would make *click-click-click* sounds along the tiled floor.

After some time, Pavlov noted something of interest starting to happen. He noticed that the dogs began to salivate when they heard the shoes *click-clicking* along the tile. Thus was the origin of behaviorism—classical conditioning (Pavlov, 1927).

But there was a fundamental issue with classical conditioning that made it difficult to translate into anything useful for anyone reading this book today. Classical conditioning deals only with behaviors over which we have absolutely no control! Pavlov's theory only had to do with reflexes, which are behaviors that occur automatically. Pavlov's theory comes into play when we see some scrumptious food advertised on TV, and our mouths begin to water—yup, just like the dogs in the lab! When it comes to advertising, Madison Avenue loves to go all Pavlovian on the consumer, because it works.

Let's shift to the United States. Here, we get the train rolling toward the behavioral theory that applies to changing behaviors over which we *do* have conscious control. The fellow who opened the door to this line of thinking was actually one of the very first psychologists in the United States, E. L. Thorndike.

Thorndike was looking over Pavlov's work one day, and it occurred to him that we needed something more. He wasn't too sure what that something more was, but as with most advances in science, he had to start somewhere. So, he developed another concept, which, like Aristotle's "happiness" theory, was profound in its simplicity—*the law of effect* (Thorndike, 1905).

What is this strange law of effect?

Thorndike postulated that if we do something and something good occurs ... we are more likely to do it again.

You can guess the other side of the coin—if we do something and something bad occurs, we are less likely to do it again.

Pure genius! Well, actually, looking back, it isn't all that profound. But consider the context: Thorndike's law of effect was important from a historical perspective because it opened the door for a guy whose work was pivotal to managing and changing voluntary behaviors, a fellow whose theory you have all used (probably more than you realize), B. F. Skinner.

Even if you don't recognize the name, you will immediately recognize the key terms of his theory (Holland & Skinner, 1961):

Positive Reinforcement - Positive Punishment

Negative Reinforcement - Negative Punishment

These concepts may seem very simple at face value. Or, they may make you cringe, as they can be somewhat confusing, thus making them favorite exam questions of college professors everywhere. In either case, let me take a moment to define these terms, as I use them throughout this book.

Positive reinforcement is probably the easiest of the four concepts to understand, as the words all seem to make sense together. Plus, it is the concept we are encouraged to use most often, so I am guessing most of us are familiar with this one. Positive reinforcement means to GIVE something GOOD in order to increase the incidence of a particular behavior.

The child acts well, you give something he or she likes, the good behavior increases. Not too tough conceptually. Examples of positive reinforcers are as varied as the children for which we use them. Tootsie Rolls®, words of praise, good grades, smiley faces, and play time are all good examples.

Let me say a word about using *time* as leverage for positive reinforcement or negative punishment (described below). Depending on the developmental level of the kids with whom you work, you may manipulate lunch time, recess time, computer time, free time, lab time, face time, bedtime… We like to use time for two critical reasons: a) It tends to work, and b) we don't have to mess with huge chunks of time to make our point understood. I'll give a school and a home example to illustrate the point.

School: Let's say you teach third grade. If you make an 8-year-old problem child sit at your side for 10 minutes during recess while his buddies are out playing kickball, he is driven bonkers and you have made your point. Of course, with some of the issues the students bring to the table (chronicled in Chapters 4 and 5), it may take multiple repetitions of this approach or more advanced methods of behavior modification to have an effect. However, the 10-minute time out will have an impact on most kids in a typical classroom.

Home: The element of time as leverage works well with your own kids. If you send your child to bed 10 minutes early, it makes an impact, particularly if he or she has brothers or sisters who are going to *razz 'em*. Time is very important to kids. Heck, time is even important to kids who are too young to tell time! Use it, and behold the wonder!

Okay, time alone will not be enough of a motivator with some of your atypical kids to make a notable difference. But even with the atypical children (and when incorporating any advanced plan), you still need to deal with the reinforcement of the good and the punishment of the bad with smaller, day-to-day issues. It takes time and patience.

Oh, and let's not forget the biggie—the positive reinforcer that brought all of you into the helping professions: *money!* I am quite certain that most of you chose your profession because you wanted a job that would allow you to retire at 45 with a yacht, private jet, and second home in the South of France…

Right.

Let's cover the other three aspects of Skinner's theory (Holland & Skinner, 1961). We first covered positive reinforcement. Second, we have a concept that most folks use incorrectly. Here, I provide you with the correct usage of *negative reinforcement,* and then you are free to go forth and use the term any way you choose.

To begin, if I were to ask you the definition of *negative reinforcement,* you would most likely come back with some version of, "Well, if a child is acting out and I scold him, his bad behavior may actually escalate. That seems like negative reinforcement." In other words, most would believe that negative reinforcement boils down to inadvertently reinforcing a negative behavior.

At face value, this makes a good deal of intuitive sense. Acting out is negative, scolding is negative, and obviously what you are doing is reinforcing, so negative reinforcement seems to have all bases covered.

This is a pretty common misperception. The term *negative reinforcement* messes with our heads a bit because it sounds like an oxymoron (i.e., how can reinforcement be negative?). Well, as used by Skinner, the terms *positive* and *negative* do not pertain to *good* or *bad* per se. Rather, they refer to *giving* or *taking away*. When we use the word positive, it means to give. Remember that positive reinforcement means to give something good in an effort to increase good behavior? Same deal with negative reinforcement: It means to TAKE AWAY something BAD in an effort to increase good behavior.

Example: Did you, or perhaps someone you knew, have a mom who would nag at you when you were a kid? I can see a few of you nodding vehemently—some with anger, some with abject sadness—as you look back on your childhood or teen years. As an aside, I also know the secret many of you are carrying from these formative experiences: Now *you* have become a parent who nags! But no matter … the circle of life makes human beings somewhat predictable—and a little fun to mess with from time to time.

Back to Mom: What did she nag you about? Nine times out of ten, the answer people shoot back is, "Clean your room!" Ah, yes, you can almost hear Mom's voice echoing through the corridors of your mind as you are lost in the nerve-grating reverie of your high school home life.

What would happen to Mom's nagging behavior once that room got cleaned? Well presumably, she would withdraw the nagging once she met her goal of having you clean your room.

That is negative reinforcement—*taking away something bad in an effort to increase good behavior.*

But here is the rub: If you have a mom who nags, are you really motivated to make her happy? No, probably not. Nagging tends to bring out anger in kids. Therefore, negative reinforcement is never as powerful a tool as positive reinforcement—not that it has no place in the reinforcement hierarchy. In fact, many classroom teachers use negative reinforcement really well; for example, telling students that if they meet all of their goals this week there will be no homework Friday or that if everyone does all of the chapter questions, there will not be a quiz. You get the picture.

Now to punishment. *Positive punishment* is another brain twister, as those two words do not seem to belong in the same neighborhood much less right next door to each other. Following the logic laid out earlier, *positive* must mean to give something, and that is exactly what we have here. Positive punishment is GIVING something BAD in an effort to decrease a particular behavior. And the clearest example of this is a good old-fashioned spanking.

While typically frowned on by mental health professionals these days, many of us grew up with a mom or a dad (or both!) who would give a spank once in a while. I grew up in Wisconsin, and we called it a *lickin'* in my neck of the woods. Furthermore, the worst type of lickin' was a *talkin' lickin'*. That was where your dad would explain to you exactly why you were the recipient of said lickin' while he was perpetrating the act. From the perspective of most of my friends, we just wanted to get the lickin' over with and could really have done without the explanation.

Sidebar: Corporal punishment appears to work for parents, because from their point of view, it is remarkably *negatively reinforcing.* For example, say two brothers are beating each other up in the living room. Dad walks in and swats them both, the infernal racket stops, and calm is restored. In Dad's mind, the punishment worked—and worked well. He can sit down and read the paper in peace. But let's pan up the steps and take a peek into the bedrooms of the siblings. You can picture one of the brothers, maybe 7 years old, sitting on his bed with short legs dangling over the side. His face is a mess of tears, and shame, rage, and embarrassment are taking over. His mind is filled with thoughts of hatred and revenge.

In the short run, corporal punishment does work well—but it is the long-term consequences that we mental health folks fear. Other forms of discipline work as well or better than spanking and don't present a risk of physical or psychological harm. Further, all of that energy is going to stream out at some point, and parents will have a different animal on their hands when that happens. I know that many kids get spanked, and for most of them, they'll be fine. Those are the kids who are generally well behaved and only get paddled once in awhile. But those aren't the kids this book is about. This book is about the kids who get into trouble all of the time, and if those kids have parents who spank, the spankings could get out of hand over time. We frown on corporal punishment for these kids in particular, because the storehouse of negative energy building inside of them becomes massive.

The final piece to this puzzle is negative punishment, and that is the tactic that I guarantee most of you use for behavioral management. Negative punishment is TAKING AWAY something GOOD in order to decrease a behavior. Here again, time can be a wonderful motivator for most kids. Time, privilege, stuff, grades … all of these can be used effectively as leverage in negative punishment.

That wraps up the history and definition of terms of behaviorism used throughout this book. Also, this supplies the "nurture" part of the nature/nurture dyad that shapes "normal" behavior in the well-functioning human beings we are today. Look around you the next time you are roaming the hallways. Marvel at the "normal" people that surround you. In Chapter 3, we will offer explanations for abnormal behavior. Buckle up and be sure to stretch before proceeding. It is going to be a wild ride!

Chapter 3
Physiological Roots of Abnormal Behavior
Is It Just Me, or Am I the Only Normal One in Here

As we begin the discussion of what may cause negative, or abnormal, behavior, let me provide some structure for you. First, we examine a few *physiological* possibilities. These include an overview of the brain, the sympathetic nervous system, gender issues, and hormones. I cover the emotional and *psychological* possibilities in Chapter 4 when I begin to describe diagnoses that can contribute to the behavior that makes people stare lovingly at the Home Depot® whilst driving by, thinking about how nice it would be to work there instead of in your office.

Understanding the Brain

Let's talk about the "nature" part of the nature/nurture equation. Chapter 2 was all about the shaping that takes place once we are up and walking around … but what about the codes written right onto the hard drive in our head when we are delivered to Mom's front porch in that little kerchief tied around the stork's beak, and what about things that percolate beneath the surface of our awareness?

Pretty Freudian, right? Maybe, but as a point of fact, looking at the neurological underpinnings of behavior and behavior change is exactly the direction in which our profession is currently headed. Understanding neural connections, mirror cells, and structural differences in the amygdala, hippocampus, and frontal lobe structures (such as the anterior cingulated cortex) is under investigational scrutiny to demonstrate how talk therapy and relationship skills—as well as insight and awareness—can actually change your brain! Pretty cool stuff. I start with a basic explanation of neuropsychology. It is remarkably simple because I am not all that bright of a guy, but it is comprehensive enough to effectively describe the parts of the brain affected by our interventions and the way in which we create effect when implementing those interventions. To help me out, I employ the words and metaphors of two internationally renowned experts in psychology: Harville Hendrix, Ph.D., and Stephen King.

First, let me explain the brain as Harville Hendrix does. There are probably 10 or 12 ways of thinking about this, but I like the way Hendrix lays it out in his book *Getting the Love You Want* (Hendrix, 2007). Refer to this picture to help orient you while I discuss.

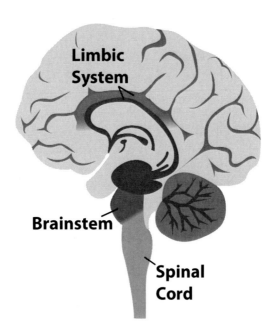

To begin, Hendrix points out that there are three distinct levels in our brain. We are most interested in changing the neural connections in the middle portion, but the upper and lower areas are also quite important. So, let's review from bottom to top.

The lower part of the brain is the fist-like lump that sits atop the spinal cord. Hendrix has a few names for this part: "old brain," "ancient brain," "reptilian brain"—you get the picture. For our purposes in this book, I refer to this part as the brainstem.

The brainstem has exactly ONE purpose and function; namely, to keep us alive. It makes sure the heart keeps beating, the lungs keep breathing, the food keeps digesting … all of the things we don't have the time to think about all day. I return to the humble brainstem in a moment. First, I want to talk about the target for most psychological interventions, the midbrain.

The midbrain covers the brainstem like a blanket over a hard-boiled egg. (Bad simile—forget I said that!) More importantly, the midbrain holds a structure called the amygdala, and that is where several things that are remarkably important to our discussion are housed. The amygdala is where emotions live. It is where novelty lives. It is where some motivation lives. Unfortunately, it is also where trauma and addiction live, and it is also home to the group of fellows that Stephen King calls the "boys in the basement."

Explanation may be necessary …

At the end of the book *Bag of Bones* (King, 2008), Stephen King offered the reader a bit of insight into his process of writing the novel. During his discourse, he talked about a time when a reporter asked him about where he gets his ideas. Having fielded this question about 75 million times throughout his career, King had a flash of creativity: Instead of answering with his pat reply, he decided to say that it was like there were boys living in the basement of his mind. So, if he got stuck on a plot point or needed to tie ideas together in a creative manner, he would stop thinking about it and go for a walk. And even when he wasn't thinking about it, *the boys were!* When the boys came up with an idea, they would send it up the coal shoot until it popped into King's conscious awareness.

Talk about Freudian! Stephen King channeled Sigmund's notion of id, ego, and superego when he delivered this thought, but all of us can relate to the notion. For example, have you ever heard a song on the radio while you were getting ready in the morning but could not for the life of you remember who sings it? Eventually, you stopped trying to figure it out, but then, totally out of the blue, while you were stuck in traffic and trying to wolf down a breakfast burrito, the name of the singer popped into your mind.

King would say that this is the work of the boys.

I bring this up because it is a clever anecdote, but also because it bears relevance to a discussion of bad behavior and interventions to curb said transgressions. More specifically, trauma, particularly early trauma, messes with the way the boys make decisions, and so does addiction. In fact, the radar antenna of the boys in the basement gets downright skewed when exposed to addiction or early trauma. Some problematic decisions, then, are not based on reason or logic; for example, as Hendrix so eloquently put it, it is quite optimistic of you to think that you have any conscious control over who you fall in love with!

Helping kids and teens overcome traumatic early experiences or addictions requires time and patience because we have to deal with the boys and their thinking process. I say more about trauma and addiction later. First, let me finish off our discussion of the brain.

The upper part of the brain is where personality and thinking live. It can be called the frontal lobe or the executive center. It sits about the midbrain/limbic system and is what separates us from lower life forms. The executive floor of the brain is important to consider because it is at the mercy of the lower floors. In other words, our brains were built to have motivation run uphill, but in therapy or through behavioral intervention and/or relationship building, we are trying to effect change in the *opposite* direction: from the top down.

Here is an example of bottom-up motivation: If you have ever been swimming and found yourself under water for a bit too long, you have experienced the panic of needing to breathe. Your brainstem jumps into the driver's seat and shoves everyone else into the back seat. It grips the limbic system and overrides all other functioning: For the next few moments, the limbic system is commanded to feel fear and nothing else. The brainstem decides that it wants adrenaline pumping to the muscles, because all systems are focused on activation. The brainstem hijacks the frontal lobe and commands the upper brain to think about nothing except getting the heck to the surface.

What the brainstem wants, the brainstem gets.

Same with the limbic system. When addiction takes over, it makes the person think in ways that defy common sense. The addict knows that there are consequences but either ignores them (the Freudian concept of denial) or convinces himself or herself that his or her actions make perfect sense. The devil is whispering into the ear of the addict, and logic goes out the window. When the boys are out of whack, they hijack the upper, executive functions and take over reason.

As I said earlier, adults in the lives of troubled kids are trying to affect the limbic system through the penthouse region of the brain. It's not impossible, but this method requires far more patience and perseverance than a bottom-up change.

Enough neurology for the time being. I revisit the limbic system briefly when I discuss psychotropic medications and talk about specific addictive processes, but let's move ahead. It is useful to introduce a genetically programmed system that can impact behavior: the sympathetic nervous system.

The Sympathetic Nervous System

Psychologically speaking, the mechanism behind shyness or gregariousness lies in the *sympathetic nervous system*. In fact, procrastination operates under this same mechanism. What the sympathetic nervous system does (and kudos to those of you who already know this) is to activate the *fight-or-flight* response in us. The fight-or-flight response, of course, gets us amped up and ready to rock and roll when we need a burst of energy to either flee or put up our dukes.

For the sake of simplicity, follow me on this next metaphor. The fight-or-flight response is triggered in each of us by a little switch in our brain. When the switch gets flipped, we get ready to rock. Our hearts beat faster, our palms sweat a little, our hands shake, our adrenaline flows, and our breath gets rapid. Have you ever been cut off in traffic and had that little sympathetic *"charge"* shoot through your body? Most of us have had that experience. But let me ask you this: Does your body like that feeling? Probably not! In some cases, it can actually *hurt*. It may feel like electricity moving through you or a tingling in your legs and arms, or it may force you to catch your breath, but whatever the case may be, it tends to be uncomfortable. Tension is created during the sympathetic response, and the majority of us experience this as anxiety.

All of us have that little switch, but we differ in the amount of arousal it takes to flip it. For some, it takes very little arousal to activate the fight-or-flight response. When kids whose switches are easily flipped approach a new situation or a new group of kids, their body activates. Their heart pounds, their hands sweat—they get *tense*. Of course, these kids do not like this experience, so they learn to back away to reduce the tension. Over time, they learn to avoid approaching such situations in the first place because of the stress they create.

On the other hand, I am sure you all know kids who are little thrill seekers. They are the children (or grown-ups!) who will dive into a situation first, then ask questions only after they are neck-deep in some sort of mess they can no longer get out of. Well, these folks also have a sympathetic nervous response, but it takes a *lot* of arousal to flip that switch in their brain. As a result, they do not feel the anxiety or tension that the shy kids do. They are freed up to approach and experience without anxiety.

Now, a word to procrastinators: You operate under basically the same rules as the shy and/or the thrill-seeking kids. Procrastinators do their best work when they feel as though their back is against the wall. If it is not the night before the project is due, they are not sufficiently motivated to sit down and focus on the problem at hand. The "motivation" they talk about has to do with flipping that switch. For procrastinators, it takes a lot of arousal to flip the switch that activates the sympathetic reaction that will shove them headlong into the *action* phase.

Folks who need to get a project done 3 months before it is actually due (procrastinators typically want to strangle these folks because they make them look bad) actually operate according to the same principle; it just takes a lot less arousal to flip that switch, so they feel the anxiety much earlier in the process.

So procrastinators, you can tell your moms, dads, bosses, and spouses that you are not lazy or bored or disinterested—you were born this way! And tell them Doctor Steve said so!

Gender

Let's move away from internal physiological processes for a moment and discuss a more overt determiner of behavior: gender. One's gender can play a role in behavior; specifically, bad behavior. Now technically, the correct term is *sex* rather than *gender*, as *sex* refers to your being physically a man or a woman, and *gender* refers to the emotional or psychological level of masculinity or femininity to which you identify. However, after the whole Freud discussion, I think it may be less confusing if we use the term *gender*.

To kick off this segment, ask yourself whether boys are the same as girls. Or, how about this one: Are men the same as women? Please remember that throughout this book I speak in *generalities*. All of us can think of exceptions to the rules, but the rules are there for a reason: They tend to work in most instances.

We live in a society that is trying to force-feed us political correctness, whereby everyone is supposedly the same, bearing the exact same strengths and weaknesses. Unfortunately, the data just do not shake out that way. Boys and men, girls and women do have relative strengths and weaknesses. Some are more evident earlier in life, some later; some are nature based, and others nurture; and some are horribly offensive to speak of in polite company (e.g., Do men really parallel park better than women? Do women really multi-task better than men? Does either gender have any *clue* why a lousy 34-cent bag of peanuts is no longer included with a standard coach-fare ticket?).

There are indeed *brain-based* differences in boys and girls, men and women. And before we even get into how this impacts the kids in your life, I have medical images from Harvard University that attempt to show some of the subtle differences between a man's brain and a woman's brain. These are a bit technical, but please forgive my brief sojourn into the ultra-scientific.

The Female Brain

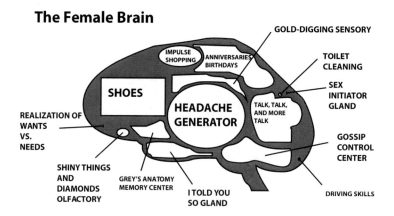

GOLD-DIGGING SENSORY

IMPULSE SHOPPING

ANNIVERSARIES BIRTHDAYS

TOILET CLEANING

SHOES

SEX INITIATOR GLAND

HEADACHE GENERATOR

TALK, TALK, AND MORE TALK

REALIZATION OF WANTS VS. NEEDS

GOSSIP CONTROL CENTER

SHINY THINGS AND DIAMONDS OLFACTORY

GREY'S ANATOMY MEMORY CENTER

I TOLD YOU SO GLAND

DRIVING SKILLS

FOOTNOTE: The " Put Oil into the Car" and "Be Quiet During the Game" glands are active only when the "SHINY THINGS AND DIAMONDS" Olfactory has been satisfied or when there is a shoe sale.

Figure 1

The Male Brain

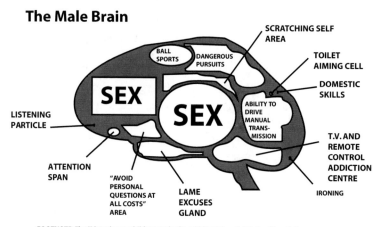

SCRATCHING SELF AREA

BALL SPORTS

DANGEROUS PURSUITS

TOILET AIMING CELL

DOMESTIC SKILLS

SEX

SEX

ABILITY TO DRIVE MANUAL TRANS- MISSION

LISTENING PARTICLE

T.V. AND REMOTE CONTROL ADDICTION CENTRE

ATTENTION SPAN

"AVOID PERSONAL QUESTIONS AT ALL COSTS" AREA

LAME EXCUSES GLAND

IRONING

FOOTNOTE: The "Listening to children cry in the middle of the night" gland is not shown due to its small and underdeveloped nature. Best viewed under a microscope.

Figure 2

Sorry to blow your mind, but I strive to be as medically up to date, balanced, and politically correct as possible. Actually, I'd like to thank the awesome website www.extremefunnyhumor. com for supplying a version of those pictures.

Let's back it down a step and talk on a more neurological level (hard science for the layperson) about how boys and girls may be different in their strengths and weaknesses, both in the home, and, perhaps more saliently, in the classroom.

First, here's an easy one: From a physiological perspective, girls have an advantage in the classroom when it comes to the way their ears and eyes take in a situation. In a nutshell, girls view situations more globally than boys. Boys' sensory apparatuses are built more to focus on one thing at a time (Cahill, 2005). You hear all the time that boys and men are more visual than girls and women. There is some credence to that, as what a boy is looking at is where his attention has the best shot of landing.

In the classroom, the implications are pretty straightforward. If you've got a girl in the back of the room who is being distracted by something and you are at the front of the room teaching, she is more than likely able to take in what she is looking at *and* what you are saying. But, if you've got a boy in the back of the room who is looking at something and you are in the front of the room trying to teach, you might as well be on another planet— he's into what he's into and it will be very difficult for him to follow what you are saying. Thus, it's particularly important for boys to have their eyes on the teacher, because whatever they are looking at is probably on what they are concentrating!

Rather than celebrating our differences, we are goaded into trying to ignore or deny them. However, boys and girls have different strengths that affect how they develop and learn. For example, which babies tend to talk first, boys or girls? Who tends to read first? Write first? Girls, girls, and girls. And that is not to say that boys do not have relative strengths when they are little tykes. Which babies tend to walk first, boys or girls? Who tends to crawl first? Run and jump first? Boys, boys, and boys. In a nutshell, girls' brains are developing in a direction geared toward communication, and boys' are developing more toward action. These differences are nature based, as they take place before we even have a chance to intervene and influence. I address our external influence later.

When it comes to applying this concept to school, think about who is going to have an easier time when they hit school age. If you said "girls," give yourself a gold star! Girls are going to have a bit of an edge when it comes to school stuff, particularly at an early age. They are going to be better at reading and writing because these activities belong to a skill set they have had more time to practice. Plus, their brains are developing more rapidly and in a more complex manner with regard to these areas than are those of boys (Maccoby & Jacklin, 1974; Medical Education Online, 2011).

As a result, girls score better on standardized reading and writing tests than boys (Viadero, 1998, National Assessment of Educational Progress, 2011). This difference begins to even out between fourth and sixth grades, but remnants persist throughout life. Women tend to be better in areas of language application—particularly as it pertains to emotional material.

When it comes to nature, boys are a bit behind the eight ball in a couple of other areas that make school more of a challenge for them. One is with ADHD. (See Chapter 4 for a full description.) While numbers are a bit fluid due to changes in children over time and different methods of collecting and analyzing data being employed, the ratio of boys to girls who are diagnosed with ADHD is about 4:1 (APA, 2002). Furthermore, the ratio of boys to girls who are sent for an ADHD referral is about 6:1.

I round out this discussion by noting that the ratio of boys to girls when it comes to autism spectrum disorders is also overwhelmingly slanted toward (or against, depending on your perspective) boys. Boys have a far higher rate of autism spectrum issues than do girls (Yapko, 2003). Here is one more fact for you: The rate of students with learning disabilities (LDs) is higher for boys than girls (National Health Interview

Survey, 2003). Girls have a distinct advantage when it comes to operating within the parameters set forth by our school systems.

Add to that the fact that we are socializing our boys and girls differently, and we have the emergence of some true gender differences, some of which may be interpreted as acting out behavior for our boys. What do I mean by that?

Take the points I made previously and summarize them this way: Due to developmental and neurological strengths of girls with regard to communication and a higher incidence among boys of ADHD, LD, and autism spectrum, boys feel more frustration in the classroom than girls. Sounds straightforward enough, but let's look into how boys and girls handle problem solving and frustration differently.

To begin, let's backtrack and switch focus from nature (brain development) back to nurture (how the world around us influences the growth of our kids). We begin by examining a classic study describing how grown-ups interact with little ones (Hargreaves & Colley, 1986). Do we, as adults, talk differently to boys and to girls, and if so, how? I know we try not to and may even try to convince others that we are absolutely gender blind when we are in the presence of a toddler. While this may be so for a really small subset of us, the majority falls into the "guilty as charged" category.

It seems that when adults speak to little girls, they tend (on average) to use more words and softer tones of voice, and their words tend to be more relationship or communication oriented. When adults talk to little boys, they tend to use fewer words, their tones tend to be a little harder, and the words tend to be more action oriented.

Think about how adults *play* differently with boys and girls (Hargreaves & Colley, 1986). I think you can probably intuit this part, but let me fill in the blanks for you. The data seem clear on this issue, and I summarize the findings in my own words: We as adults tend to play with our boys like dogs and with our girls like cats.

You dog people know how you play with dogs! You pull their ears, flip them over, and make them bite their own paws. Now, think about how we play with cats. We are more gentle, don't make sudden movements, and get overly invested in little toy mice that, if alive, would be the scourge of the kitchen. Making a sudden move around a cat sends it shooting to the top of the refrigerator, where it will sit for 2 weeks, giving you the stink-eye.

There have been a number of studies that demonstrate this pattern. One famous study (Wood & Eagley, 2002) took a group of toddlers and had adults interact with them. Then they took the children away and brought them to a different group of adults; only this time, the kids were dressed as members of the opposite sex.

Guess what happened? The adults played rougher with the kids they perceived to be boys and more gently with those they perceived to be girls.

Boys interact on a more physical level with others and particularly with each other. Plus, in general, they are not taught the more subtle social skills of identifying emotions within themselves or others. Therefore, even problem solving becomes more of a physical act for boys. Remember, girls are learning language skills more rapidly than boys. Girls just have more school-acceptable tools in their arsenal when they need to solve a problem.

So, we've touched on how boys and girls problem solve in different ways. There are also gender differences in how kids handle frustration—regardless of whether they are labeled as troubled. Even among your well-behaved kids, boys tend to be more frustrated in school and have fewer skills to handle those frustrations. The net result is more activity and more "acting out" on the part of the boys. This natural tendency—and trust me, I recognize that there are exceptions—often tests the patience of teachers who may (due to frustrations of their own) jump to conclusions about the boys that may or may not be clinically accurate. This conclusion jumping is even more likely to happen if the teacher is feeling stressed, depressed, or overwhelmed or is nearing burnout (see Chapter 6).

I know it seems like I have spent a fair amount of space in this chapter ripping on the boys, but that is certainly not my intent. Merely, I am trying to show how some school issues may be a function of normal differences between boys and girls. Let me try to salvage some masculine dignity here before moving ahead with the chapter and point out that men have bigger brains than women!

(Editor's note: While Dr. Steve is correct in stating that the average size and weight of a man's brain is larger than the average size and weight of a woman's brain [Dekaban & Sadowsky, 1978], we here at the publishing house felt it prudent to provide further clarity on this point. The human brain is made up of two kinds of matter: grey matter and white matter. Grey matter is the part of the brain that, simply put, is involved in thinking and higher-order functions. White matter is a fatty substance that acts as insulation. So, while men have bigger brains, women actually have more grey matter [Allen, et al., 2003]. Women's brains are built for speed and multitasking, and men's brains are built for battle. Men are better able to sustain a blow to the head because they have more packing material up there!)

Now that I have restored some balance, let's get back to the point. I have eluded to emotions a couple of times this chapter. For now, suffice it to say that emotionally, girls have the advantage, and boys are hampered by a phenomenon called the "Boy Code" (Kindlon & Thompson, 2000).

Picture this if you will: A 10-year-old boy is playing little league. He stands in the batter's box, waving the bat menacingly in an attempt to fool everyone watching into believing he is not afraid. The pitcher rears back and, as hard as his fifth grade arm can possibly throw, lets the pitch fly with all of the laser-sharp accuracy of an airplane missing its wings. The pitch, with a thud that could be heard from outer space, sinks into the batter's rib cage like a baker's fist into a mound of bread dough. Can the batter cry?

Heck no! This little guy has learned early Rule #1 of the Boy Code: show no pain. Or to quote a famous movie line, "There is no crying in baseball!" For that matter, the Boy Code states that you show no pain, hurt feelings, sadness, embarrassment, shame, etc. All negative feelings have to be protected by a shield. What is this shield? Think about the emotions that boys *are* taught they are allowed to show. More than likely, the pain the batter is feeling—and make no mistake about it, he feels *pain*—will be concealed behind a shield of anger.

Anger is an emotion boys are allowed (dare I say, *encouraged?*) to show. When I deliver seminars to men's groups, I always open with the same line: "Men have three basic emotions—happy, angry, and horny. Every other feeling state is protected by one of these three shields."

And it's true. Boys learn early on to not show pain. The hot little radioactive nugget of pain in that batter's gut will be protected by anger so he will not cry. Fight back tears, sure; but he'll put on a little show that may include yelling something ugly toward the pitcher, challenging him, or at the very least giving him the stink-eye on his way to first base. Then, while standing on first, he will wear a good, stern look to once again convince the crowd that he is not a sissy. He is not hurt.

No one is better at defining and reinforcing the Boy Code than other boys. Boys police each other closely to maintain the status quo when it comes to the rules of emotional expression. Parents, though, are not immune to this reinforcement, with dads typically worse than moms at honoring the Boy Code (Ruble, 1988).

In any case, the Boy Code dictates that boys learn to deal with pain through anger. And the hotter that radioactive nugget of pain sitting in his belly, the thicker the shield of anger will have to be to protect it. Now think for a minute about the kids you work with who come from a train-wreck of a home. The nugget of pain they carry with them is *burning white hot,* so they have to encase it in a lead box called anger, and they do a fine job of it! Anger, toughness, or carrying a chip on one's shoulder can result from some sort of spin-out in the home. I address this in more detail in the next chapter.

Hormones

Shifting gears to discuss a final physiological culprit in behavior, hormones are naturally occurring chemicals in the body that play a role in growth, maturation, mood, and various other daily functions. And yes, they can have a profound impact on behavior. Think about how hormones sometimes play a role in how you, an adult, feel. How you feel plays a role in how you behave, doesn't it? Of course!

In our kids, there are three hormones we see as having the most impact in bad behavior. The first is a drug that (once again) our boys are saddled with: testosterone.

Girls and women have testosterone in their bodies, just as boys and men have estrogen in theirs. But throughout their lifespan, boys and men have higher circulating levels of testosterone than girls and women. Higher levels of testosterone are related to higher levels of aggression and a higher activity level (Simpson, 2001). More testosterone makes your motor rev just a little hotter. This side effect of testosterone is evident across all species, not just humans.

Applying this to overt behavior, we have seen cases where elevated testosterone levels in boys take on the appearance of ADHD, as this elevation tends to make them more hyperactive and more impulsive. The physiological signs to look for are not 100% clear cut, but typically, high testosterone affects boys rather than girls and is particularly noticeable when it occurs in prepubescent boys, resulting in their being a little bigger than their same-age classmates. Or, you may have a fourth or fifth grader starting to grow facial hair, who appears to be revving a little hotter than peers. With these kids, getting a medical workup is vital, as we can deal medically with a hormonal issue rather than hanging a psychological diagnosis on the child.

I cover the other two hormones in the following paragraphs, but first, I want to issue a general heads-up when it comes to psychological diagnoses for children: Almost every psychological issue in kids—particularly prior to the completion of puberty—*looks like ADHD*. In the next chapters, I talk about the diagnostic process and differential diagnoses, but suffice it to say that hyperactivity and impulsivity are symptomatic of nearly every diagnosis and, as it pertains to the current discussion, hormonal fluctuation.

The second hormone that can have a profound impact on behavior is thyroxine.

Thyroxine is a hormone that governs metabolism—or more metaphorically, it controls your thermostat. If kids have *hyperthyroidism*, abnormally high levels of thyroid hormone, they will (once again) appear to have ADHD (summarized in Stein and Weiss, 2003). Their metabolism will be buzzing like a hummingbird (thermostat set too high), and they will be very prone to hyperactivity and impulsivity. These are kids who will eat two or three lunches in the cafeteria but never gain an ounce. We had a teacher with one of these students in her room tell a practitioner in my private psychology practice that she has to take her student out and, "… run him like an Alaskan Husky dog" just to burn off the excess energy so he could sit down and focus in the afternoon.

Again, these are not bad kids, but the accelerator to their motor is stuck to the floor due to hormones.

As an aside, the way thyroxine tends to affect adults is usually in the opposite direction. For the most part, grown-ups don't complain much about extra energy and the ability to keep weight off. Where we see thyroid affecting adults who come through our practice is when they have *hypothyroidism*, low levels of thyroid hormone (thermostat set too low). This condition looks, feels, and presents like depression. These adults tend to be a little heavier than those around them and complain that no matter what they do, they simply can't lose an ounce. Their metabolism, due to low hormone levels, is slogging along rather than operating at a normal speed.

A quick test of thyroid function can be done with a pencil. I first heard Dr. Oz teach this technique on *Good Morning America* and have told folks of it ever since. It is really simple: Take the pencil and place it vertically at the outer corner of your eye. If there is eyebrow hair growing to the outside of the pencil, you are fine. If there is no hair outside of the pencil (and you are not having issues with over-plucking), you may want to get your thyroid levels checked.

Lastly, let's examine how the hormones associated with *menarche* can mimic a psych diagnosis. And for those of you without the same Word of the Day calendar I have sitting on my desk, *menarche* refers to the first menstrual period in a girl's life.

This issue became apparent to me after we had had a number of referrals to our office by mothers who wanted their daughters evaluated for bipolar disorder. The girls were in the same general age range: middle school plus or minus a year or two. Having never been an 11-year-old girl myself, I did not have a point of reference. But I did come armed with the knowledge that bipolar disorder does not typically spring out of nowhere when a girl hits puberty.

As it turns out, when a girl hits the runway leading to menarche, there is a good chance that her hormones have not quite found their rhythm in the cycle. This actually is pretty common, but some girls can have intense fluctuations in hormones, leading to some unpredictable and at times downright nutty behavior! The symptoms have some common denominators if there is an imbalance that warrants attention, and these include unexplained crying spells, anger outbursts, feeling "high" some days, and truncated periods of depression. Until a girl's body hits its stride with her cycle, she may struggle mightily with being at the mercy of these seismic shifts in hormone levels.

To summarize the hormone section, profound imbalances are not typical, but if they exist, they can look exactly like a psychological issue. I recommend a thorough medical workup through the child's pediatrician, either before we explore psychological issues or concurrent with that exploration.

From here, we transition to speaking directly about the different psychiatric or psychological diagnoses that you may see crossing your desks or being bandied about by colleagues, professionals, administrators, or moms and dads. When a child has a psychological disorder, even if he or she hasn't received an official diagnosis, you will probably see the symptoms playing themselves out in their natural habitat.

Chapter 4
Diagnoses Crossing Your Radar Screen

Chapter 4a

Diagnosis of Interest I:
Learning Disabilities, ADD/ADHD, and Oppositional Defiant Disorder

Aha! I Know That Kid!

Chapter 3 covered some normal variations in behavior and then moved to touching on physiological issues that may contribute to poor behavior. We transition now to talking a little more technically about some of the different diagnoses that you may encounter during the time you spend with badly behaving kids. I go over the symptoms required for a particular diagnosis, speak a little about different medications that are used to treat these issues, address the etiology of what typically leads to said diagnoses, and begin the discussion of how to handle some of these kids.

Before embarking, let me say this: I provide information on some of the medical interventions I have seen administered to my private practice clients by their physicians and/or nurse practitioners. I will say, however, that I am not a physician; I am a *psychologist*, so I absolutely encourage everyone to speak to a psychiatrist, pediatrician, general practitioner, or nurse practitioner if you have follow-up questions or concerns about medical issues brought up in the ensuing text.

Here, I use the pronoun *he* in a generic sense. Because many of the disorders I discuss occur more in boys than girls, the male pronoun seems appropriate. I do, however, shift pronouns in sections where the disorder discussed predominantly affects girls.

Learning Disabilities

It may seem strange to include LDs in a book about behavior problems and interventions, but remember one of the themes from the gender section of Chapter 3; frustration can lead to all sorts of creative bad behavior. Children with LDs—particularly those that go undiagnosed—feel tremendous frustration. Believe me, the only thing worse than feeling like you "don't get it" is knowing that everyone around you *does*. These kids experience this frustration on a daily basis and need to come up with coping mechanisms to deflect the resulting feeling of shame. Eventually, they may learn to punt on second down: They believe that school will always be a disaster, so why bother?

At this point, many kids come to an important crossroad; "Am I going to be known as the 'bad kid' or the 'retarded kid?'"

And yes, I know that all of you understand the important difference between an LD and mental retardation. Mental retardation is global, affecting all aspects of cognition and learning. LDs are specific to a single task of learning. Thus, we have several different categories of LD: We have disabilities specific to reading, writing, mathematics, receptive language, expressive language, and a few others that affect less common functions.

But what *you* know to be true is not the issue—the issue is what the student *believes* to be true. Even though this sixth grader only has trouble with reading, he essentially *feels* retarded. And believe this: Other kids are calling him a "retard" out on the playground. For this boy, his trouble with reading will begin to generalize to *all* aspects of school, because he has to find a way to cope with that awful feeling of, "I'm the only one who can't do this … and it will never get better."

This brings us back to that important crossroad. When faced with a choice of being bad or looking shamefully inept in front of his classmates, the student will often choose to be the *bad kid*. There is more dignity in being the bad kid. Plus, this label carries the added bonus of being able to get the student kicked out of the classroom if he acts out, thus deflecting the spotlight from falling directly onto his deficit to falling on his newfound identity. You never have to read out loud in front of the classroom if you are in the principal's office!

The challenge for teachers and parents is to recognize some of the warning signs for LDs. Over time, teachers gain a sense of what is the "normal" range for their grade level. For example, a second grade teacher knows that some of the kids in the class are a little slower on the uptake and some, a little quicker, but there is a range of normal. If a particular student is struggling (suffering?) outside of that normal range, the teacher gets Mom and Dad involved and makes sure an evaluation is underway. By fourth or fifth grade, if the LD has not been caught, the kid will begin to cover his tracks and make it more and more difficult to differentiate the LD from the bad behavior.

Furthermore, once the child with an LD reaches middle school or high school, the horse has left the barn. It is hard to get these students back because they have made up their minds about the success potential they *don't* have. The earlier we catch them, the better the prognosis.

Catching a problem early makes sense in so many arenas. Thinking specifically about LDs, if a child has an LD in reading, can he still learn to read? Of course! What he probably *cannot* do is learn to read the way everyone else does or at the same pace. But that's why we have reading specialists: They figure out how the student's brain works and design a program to teach him to read in a way that will stick.

Here's something else for you to think about: We are getting better at spotting and evaluating students who have processing deficits. "Processing deficit" has become somewhat of a catch-all category to mean a sign that there is a slower processor chip for a specific, task-oriented part if the brain in these students (Disability Online, 2004). Again, this is light years away from mental retardation but still has classroom implications. These kids are able to take in all of the information but cannot process through it at the same clip as students who have a Pentium chip. The students with the deficit have an old 486 processor rather than a Pentium!

Let me explain, using the example of a receptive LD. These kids can actually *hear* every word the teacher is saying at the front of the classroom, but the part of the brain that processes incoming language (located behind the left ear) is spinning at a slower rate. The "waiting room" of information begins to fill to capacity and then overflows. Some of the information gets restless and may walk out or get pushed out before it gets registered.

Thus, the *meaning* of what the teacher (or perhaps, the parent) is saying starts dropping out because that student understands what is being said at a pace that leaves him about three or four sentences behind. Over time, frustration develops, takes over, and can lead that student to either drift off or engage in bad behavior.

These are students who constantly feel pressure because they can be prone to panic when called on to perform. Rather than feel like they have caught up to the flow of instruction, they feel bombarded by a barrage of words that gets jumbled and tossed out of their mind.

The adult's ability to recognize these deficits in kids will help tremendously to stem the tide of bad behavior. At school, the teacher can create a classroom environment that takes into account the differences in processing.

ADD/ADHD

Symptoms common to both ADD and ADHD (APA, 2002) include the following:

- Is easily distracted, frustrated, and forgetful
- Has difficulty with attention (focus), listening, organization, and follow through

Symptoms common to ADHD (APA, 2002) include:

- Fidgets, squirms, or leaves seat often
- Has difficulty engaging in quiet activities
- Runs or climbs excessively when inappropriate
- Is often "on the go" or acts as if driven by a motor
- Often blurts out answers or vocalizations
- Has difficulty awaiting turn
- Interrupts others

As somebody who probably spends a lot of time around kiddos with symptoms such as these, what words spring to your mind when you hear *ADD* or *ADHD* uttered? Do you think about hyper kids—those in constant motion with impulsivity? Kids who drive you absolutely insane—the kind of insane that makes you actually *pick up* an application to work at Home Depot® to carry around with you in the car *just in case?*

Let's get down to the nitty-gritty. You are being polite because you are thinking to yourself, "Dr. Steve is a psychologist and may get offended if he knew *The Truth* about what comes to mind when I hear these terms." Do you, during moments of weakness, think one of these words or phrases to yourself: "Over-diagnosed," "a crutch," "a shield for parents or students to hide behind," etc.?

Of course you do! ADD/ADHD has historically had a somewhat tenuous co-existence with our homes and schools since it exploded onto the scene in the early '90s. Some of you

51

have been around long enough to recall that point in time. There was a fellow in Massachusetts named Russ Barkley who wrote a hugely popular book on ADHD (Barkley, 1997), and low and behold, suddenly, every kid with a behavior problem magically became ADHD overnight. Well, that's a problem, but we haven't even come to the most problematic part of the equation. First, we have to make a few points about the *treatment* of ADD/ADHD.

Try to think about all of the ADD/ADHD medications you can remember. A few of the most popular ones are Ritalin, Concerta, Cylert, Focalin, Adderall, and Metadate, and there are a few other less common ones you may have encountered. Most of these medications fall under the broad umbrella of the popular generic drug *methylphenidate*. To ease the burden on your eyes as you read on, I'll just refer to Ritalin when writing about ADD/ADHD medications, because that's the one that most all of us think of.

The tension around ADD/ADHD for professionals started because of a couple aspects of Ritalin. First, methylphenidate (and all of its name-brand derivatives) is a stimulant. In fact, it's a pretty strong stimulant. Certainly more than the cup of coffee some of you are enjoying as you read this.

As a quick aside, there is a name brand medication called "Desoxyn," which is listed as a potential treatment for ADHD. With no exaggeration, it is the legal branding of the generic drug (hang onto your hats) *methamphetamine*! I swear I am not making this up—the FDA has approved the medication for two purposes: treating ADHD and treating obesity (rxlist. com; Logan, 2002). The point is, and I am not trying to come across as cynical, the stimulant medications are to be handled with caution. We do not want to be cavalier or haphazard in prescribing them. Ritalin and all of its relatives are listed as controlled substances by the DEA because of the potential for abuse. I'll say more about that in a moment.

Now, to the uninitiated, the concept of *stimulant* medication for ADHD seems to be totally ludicrous. I can hear a few of you thinking to yourselves, "Geez Dr. Steve, these kids are like ferrets on Red Bull. Why the *heck* would we want to stimulate them?"

Great question; the answer lies in the nature of ADD/ADHD as a neurochemical problem. In the brain of the child or adult with ADD/ADHD, there is an underproduction of the neurotransmitter *dopamine* (Barkley, 1997; Geller, 2003). Dopamine is a chemical that acts as a carrier pigeon in the brain: It takes messages from one brain cell to another, thus allowing the cells to talk to each other. If we do not have enough of these carrier pigeons, our cells have a hard time communicating with each other. They cannot huddle up and form a game plan, or line up a cogent train of thought. Nobody knows what the others are doing up there, and we have a difficult time staying on track because all the brain cells are doing their own thing.

Ritalin kick starts the brain into manufacturing more dopamine, which delivers more messages. More messages being delivered means the brain cells become aware of what their neighbors are doing. This allows for relevant trains of thought and sustained concentration. The cells all talk to each other, and a plan is formed.

I said I would address the issue of Ritalin abuse. To be fair, the pharmaceutical companies have been taking steps to curb the issue as best they can. To wit, they developed a medication with lower abuse potential called "Vyvanse." It was first approved in the United States in April, 2008, under the generic name lisdexamfetamine.

When you look at the generic name, the first thing that jumps out at you is that the word *amphetamine* is spelled with an *f* instead of a *ph*. That is no typo: It is spelled differently to indicate that the stimulant is different in this medication. In order for the medicine to work, it has to pass through the stomach, because it relies on all of those good ol' gastrointestinal juices to release the stimulant effects (Mattingly, 2010). In other words, unlike with Ritalin and its relatives, if you were to crush the pills up and snort them or shoot them, you would not get *any* effect. This won't completely stop all potential abuse, but it does slow down the introduction of the buzz and potentially frustrates the abuser.

Two other medications developed to minimize stimulant abuse are Daytrana ("the patch") and Strattera (atomoxetine). Daytrana is methylphenidate but is administered transdermally (i.e., through the skin) through an adhesive patch. It looks sort of like a large bandage and was designed primarily for kids and adults for whom compliance might be an issue. So, for kids who are prone to forgetting a pill (and perhaps with parents who aren't good at reminding), the patch can be a useful and effective solution, plus, it cuts down on abuse potential.

Lastly, Strattera and the newer Intuniv (generic name, guanfacine, also marketed under the brand name Tenex) are options with low abuse potential because they are not amphetamine-based stimulants. Instead of targeting dopamine, Strattera and Intuniv target norepinepherine. Lots of big words, I know! Note that the effects are not felt by everyone: Some respond to Strattera or Intuniv, others do not. And I should also mention that medicines that affect norepinepherine *do* speed you up a little bit but not nearly to the extent of the amphetamines.

I just threw a lot of information at you, and for that I apologize. Take a moment to synthesize …

In this section I really want to encourage all of you to not throw the baby out with the bathwater. There are some kids (adults, too) who truly have a neurochemical disorder called ADD or ADHD. For them, the medication more than likely will work and will work well. I will never forget the words of a mom whose son had gone undiagnosed (and therefore untreated) until high school. When we finally began proper treatment, she said to me, "Dr. Steve, that pill is from God's hand to his tongue. The medication saved my son's academic career." Correctly diagnosed kids are not the ones who give teachers and parents grey hair. The problems involve kids who are *mis*diagnosed.

Let's say now that we have a kiddo who does *not* have ADHD but rather is angry. He is defiant, stubborn, and acting out all over the place. If we hang an ADHD diagnosis on that kid, we would more than likely start a regimen of stimulant medication. Now think this through: What happens to a kid who is angry, acting out, and now on a rather strong stimulant? You got it—*disaster!* Particularly with boys, the stimulants lead to increases in aggression.

For the misdiagnosed kids, the treatment actually makes a bad situation worse. But there's more.

Even for the kids who truly have ADHD, Ritalin has another aspect that makes it somewhat problematic: Back in the day, Ritalin was only a 4-hour medication. As with many stimulants, Ritalin is pretty water soluble, metabolizing and passing quickly through the urine. So, a kid would take his medicine with breakfast, then peak out around 9:30 or 10:00 in the morning and begin to backslide into lunch. He would then go to the nurse's office for another dose, peak out around 1:30 or 2:00 in the afternoon and then slide backwards on the bus ride home. Thus, kids taking Ritalin were still having ups and downs during the day as the medication cycled between being more and less effective (or, between the build and the detox). You had the kids with ADHD going up and down and the angry kids misdiagnosed with ADHD being stimulated and teachers shouting, *"Enough already!"* The treatment became more problematic than the problem itself!

In the past few years, we have worked out a number of the kinks with the medication side of the equation. First, we have more options than ever before. As I mentioned, there are different derivatives of the base drugs we can try if one is not effective. Plus, we have *sustained-release* (SR) and *long-acting* (LA) medications to help smooth out the up-slope and detox (withdrawal) cycle. The child will take his dose with breakfast, and it will sustain until he is home in the afternoon. Be aware that some of the kids you see in your office or classroom may still be on the 4-hour medication if their insurance dictates a specific course of treatment.

The only side effect of the stimulant medication we cannot get rid of is tied to the nature of stimulants in general—they kill the appetite. This makes sense when you consider that diet pills are all stimulants in some form. With reduced appetite, some kids will slow down on the growth curve. This is particularly salient for kids who are younger, smaller in stature, or on higher doses of the medicine. We tell parents of such kids a couple of things: First, be sure to watch what your child eats. He may not feel hungry as often, so you may need to be more directive when it comes to snacks and mealtimes. Plus, unless you have a kid who is extremely impulsive and may hurt another child, run out into the street, or do serious damage to property or himself, you can give him a vacation from the medicine on weekends or holidays. "How is this possible?" you may ask. Good question.

We are able to give these vacations because of another nice aspect of many of the stimulant medications: They don't build up in the bloodstream like antidepressants. If you are on Prozac or Lexapro or Zoloft or any of the serotonin-reuptake medications for depression, you will have to take them for 2 or 3 weeks before they build up to a therapeutic level in the bloodstream. In other words, you don't take your happy pill on Monday and then start singing *Zip-a-Dee-Doo-Da* on Tuesday … they take a while to work. Likewise, you cannot just stop cold turkey with these medications. Rather, you wean off of them. There is a residue (or build up) in the body that must be taken into account.

Ritalin works in a different way. Therefore, when the child is not required to sit still or pay attention, you may be able to keep him off the medication. If you want to allow your child to be a nutty 8-year-old in the backyard on weekends or holidays, more power to you. As always; ***CHECK WITH YOUR PHYSICIAN BEFORE MESSING WITH THE MEDICATIONS, DOSAGES, OR DIRECTIONS AT ALL!*** But this information is offered as an option to discuss with the physician to give the child's appetite an opportunity to rebound and to prevent a dramatic slow down in growth.

There are a number of parents who do not wish to put their children on medication. I have two children myself, and so I totally understand that point of view. We feel responsible for protecting and maintaining the innocence of youth; launching them prematurely into the adult world of medication seems to violate that primitive imperative. Sometimes, parents don't want to try medication for their child because they are scared. They have read some horrific tidbit about possible side effects on the Internet or caught the tail end of a doom-and-gloom report on television or talked to someone at the mall who had *her* kid on medications and chaos ensued. There is certainly a lot of overstated and/or erroneous info out there. At least if the parents make an *informed* choice, they can choose from the options with data in hand.

And listen, I always let parents know that the medicine does not "cure" the ADHD. Rather, it will help the behavioral interventions take root more quickly. If the kid is able to pay attention and integrate the educational and behavioral aspects of his day, change for the better (i.e., self-management) progresses a whole lot faster.

So now to the big question: "If the child is not taking medicine to help with the problem, what do I do?" First, take to heart the behavioral interventions discussed in Chapters 13 through 16. Always stick to the basic premise: "Make it better to be good than to not be good." Reinforce the positive and tend to the tenants of positive behavioral supports. In addition, try to teach *self-regulation* to these students.

A good way to do this is to begin emphasizing how *you* are experiencing his or her behavior. To set this into motion, as you give the child a warning and before the consequence is initiated, ask aloud, "What am I about to say?" Or maybe, "What am I thinking?" Help him begin to anticipate the way *you* are seeing his behavior. Ultimately, you would like to have his brain give birth to a little virtual version of *you* that will give him the warning to pull back on the behavior before the real you has to. The more you repeat this exercise, the better able the kids will be able to know in a moment or with a mere look what you are thinking and what you are about to say. Over time, your goal is to have that self-regulatory mechanism be automatic and not involve your intervention at all.

Another idea is to place a wedge of time between the thought and the action. With many impulsive kids, the light bulb will flash on, and they immediately go into motion. A brief pause to allow the filter to do its job can be remarkable. In these situations, I also suggest having the kids count, "One, two …" to themselves before engaging in any action. It would, if spoken aloud (which many younger kids will do!) sound something like this: "One, two … pick up my book. One, two … turn to page 37. One, two … sit down and read."

The resulting cadence will sound somewhat rhythmic to younger kids, but again, the goal here is to wedge a beat between the thought and the action. This exercise adds an extra step to the thought process, or adds some weight to it, in order to slow the cogs in the mental wheel. The more you reinforce this self-management, the more entrenched the pattern of thinking and acting will become. It will not be evident 100% of the time, but the more it becomes a part of the kiddo's routine, the better the behavior will become.

Before leaving the ADD/ADHD segment of this chapter, I need to clean up a few points.

A student with ADHD in your classroom or in your home is relatively easy to spot. He is the one who is not terribly unlike Hammy (the squirrel) in the movie *Over the Hedge*. The parallel is especially evident in the famous final scene, where Vern gives Hammy a can of high-caffeine energy drink.

The "H" in ADHD literally stands for *hyperactive*. This is not the kid I want to draw your attention to … because he is already doing a bang-up job of commanding your attention! Rather, I want to give you a heads up about the student with ADD (i.e., *without the "H"*). What does this kid look like in your classroom or home? The word I hear used most often is *daydreamer*.

This is not a bad kid, for sure—not a child who is doing something awful with a sharpened pencil to the kid in front of him. Certainly this is not the kid who is out of his chair 19 times before lunch. This kid is not on your "Behavior Problem" radar screen. Rather, he has what I like to call "The Drift."

He is the one whose attention meanders out the window for extended periods of time, or he becomes intensely interested in his thumb for a spell. Or, he can't seem to tear himself away from the shoelace he seemingly forgot to tie for the 675th day in a row. Or, this is the child who magically loses a math worksheet somewhere between his desk and teacher's—and that sucker is *gone forever!* This is the student whose desk or locker looks as if a family of badgers has been living in it for 2 years.

Here's the point: This is a kid who can quite possibly slip through the cracks because he does not have a behavior problem, per se. But make no mistake: He is struggling because (to repeat) those neurons upstairs are having a hard time talking to each other due to a shortage of carrier pigeons.

I refer back to the "misdiagnosis" discussion of putting kids and teens on the wrong medication and the bad situations that can result. The main problem we have in the mental health field is properly diagnosing *children*. Once kids pass all the way through the treacherous doorway of puberty, the cement in their heads begins to dry, and they look and act (from a neurochemical standpoint) more and more like grown-ups. Unfortunately, prior to that point being reached, most of the psychiatric/psychological diagnoses we assign actually *resemble ADHD!*

When kids get stressed, depressed, traumatized, or angry, they will spike on any instrument that measures impulsivity and hyperactivity. That is just the nature of the beast, really.

Think about that, and ask, "How do most kids go through the diagnostic process for determining a mental health issue?"

First, Mom has had enough. She has heard from the teachers, from the babysitters, from her mother, and from a slew of other folks who are trying to offer parenting advice, "Geez, you may want to get your child evaluated." So, she does what most parents do—she takes him to the pediatrician. The pediatrician, who does not have the time to get deep into the family history or observe the kid outside of the office, does the next best thing: She gives Mom a couple of questionnaires to be filled out by those who have thorough knowledge of the child and/or the family (i.e., the mom fills one out, and the teacher fills out the other).

A pediatrician does this *not* because s/he is incompetent, uncaring, or in a hurry to move on to the next patient. In general, I like pediatricians more than any other type of physician out there. They tend to be *more* caring, thorough, and helpful than any other type of doctor with whom we lowly mental health folks deal on a daily basis. Unfortunately, they just do not have a lot of time to devote to a psychological diagnosis. Hence, the symptom checklists (questionnaires).

Okay, so the teacher fills out one questionnaire, Mom fills one out, the pediatrician scores them, and—go figure! There is probably a spike in the columns labeled "Hyperactivity" and "Impulsivity." So, what comes next? We try medication.

One problem that can occur is that many parents stick with a bad situation. In other words, even if the medication is not correct, parents, for whatever reason, tend to be reluctant to bring this to the attention of health professionals. They may just keep plowing ahead with the original plan.

Because so many psychological problems show up as hyperactivity and impulsivity, ADHD tends to be the diagnosis that gets used most often. Digging into family history, observing the kids at home and at school, talking to teachers, and ruling out other possibilities are all necessary when diagnosing kids. In fact, the professionals who are (truly) in the best position to diagnose kids, short of hospital staff in the case of more serious conditions, are either a) those in private practice who can put in the time or b) the school psychologist. Hopefully, the pediatrician will make the referral, but sadly, many parents are reluctant to follow through.

Before moving onto the next diagnosis, let me say one more thing: Mental health professionals rely on hard data to generate treatment plans, but we also rely a lot on our gut reactions to the clients in front of us. For the most part, the gut reaction of adults in the life of an ADHD kiddo is something like this: "Great kid—bright, creative, but *whew!* He wears me *out!*" And kids with ADHD will make you +—the kind of tired that may require a bubble bath with lit candles at the end of the day just to help you recharge you batteries so you are able to deal with him the next day.

Have you ever had one of those kids? Thought so!

Oppositional Defiant Disorder

The symptoms for oppositional defiant disorder (ODD) are as follows (APA, 2002):

- Often loses temper
- Argues with adults
- Deliberately annoys others
- Is touchy or easily annoyed
- Is angry, resentful, spiteful, or vindictive
- Blames others for his or her misbehaviors
- Often actively defies or refuses to comply with rules or requests

As a rule, these are kids who come from some sort of breakdown in the authority system at home, and they are angry because of it (American Academy of Child and Adolescent Psychiatry, 1999). There may be an exception to the rule somewhere in the world, but I have not met him yet.

The breakdown in the home does not have to be abuse, alcoholism, abandonment, or any other bad word that starts with an 'a' ... but it *could* be. On the other hand, it may also be that the kid has a single parent who is working two jobs and is either too tired or working too many hours to be present physically and emotionally in the home to provide the structure kids need. Or, we could have the same single parent who is feeling overwhelmed and depressed, which is preventing her from being responsive to the children.

Or, it might be two parents who love their child, but hate each other, so there is constant tension or bickering in the home. Many kids positively *freak out* if their parents constantly quarrel.

Or, it might be two parents who love their children but go overboard and end up creating narcissistic tendencies in the kids by setting the expectation that life will always give them what they want when they want it. These are parents who dote to the point of not doing the hard part of parenting. In our private practice office, we have been seeing more and more cases like this. I think one reason is a new form of "keeping up with the Joneses," where parents battle other parents to see whose kids can have the most stuff. Maybe they are trying to deal with their own feelings of inadequacy through their kids. Who knows?

Another reason some parents have a hard time with the authority system is the "age of information" in which we live. Ordinarily, I advocate for an informed consumer, an informed voter, an informed parent, etc. But too much information available to parents can have some adverse effects. Parents get their brains tied in knots trying to figure out what is the "right" thing to do. For example, "parenting information" is readily available from all sorts of people, usually with different advice to give. You have the old stand-bys of your parents, who relish the thought of karmic payback (now YOU have a misbehaving child!), and then you've got everyone you come into contact with who has children of their own and therefore feels qualified to disseminate the "wisdom" they have garnered over the years.

Add to that the fact that we now have numerous parenting magazines, Internet sites, parenting classes, and support groups at local churches. Parents are inundated with advice, so when a conflict arises at home, they can be so overwhelmed, they opt to do nothing. Or, they go to the extreme. They do something for a while, then give up and try something else before giving the first program adequate time to work; and now they're into the second program which frustrates them; and they go on to a third with remnants of the first and second still present; and so they get more frustrated, so they find a fourth and a fifth and on and on and on and on.

Listen, giving in to your kids and letting them have something they want is the easy part of parenting. We all love to see their faces light up when they are overjoyed. Even better is when WE are the reason they feel so good! Attending to limits, discipline, rules, and boundaries is the hard part—*but absolutely necessary in the social development of children.*

When some sort of breakdown is occurring in the home, kids start to get very anxious (Lahey & Lober, 1994). Children, be they little or big, need to feel like a grown-up is driving the bus. When that doesn't happen, the kids feel compelled to jump into the driver's seat and they start to spin out. Kids are not emotionally equipped to handle heavy life situations (think about why we preach to teens to *not* get pregnant!). That anxiety can be even more pronounced and devastating when abuse or addiction exists in the household and will ultimately lead to resentment; particularly toward grown-ups, whether they are the child's caretakers or other authority figures.

So remember, when you are in the presence of one of these little buggers, their anger isn't about you specifically. Rather, it is rage against the figure you represent to the kid. The world has dealt him a bad hand, and he is taking it out on the people in his life who step into the role of those who have wronged him. You ever met a kid who hates you after knowing you for only 8 seconds? Is that even possible? No—because again, it's not about you but rather what you represent. You step into the role and its game on!

The anger demonstrated by these kids can be vicious at times. Remember when I said ADHD kids will make you feel tired? The gut reaction of adults to a student with ODD is usually *anger.* Kids with ODD will go out of their way to make you angry—and sometimes within those first 8 seconds of knowing you. This will be especially true of the ODD kids with abusive or addicted parents. While this may seem like a bizarre irony (i.e., why on earth would a child with an abusive parent become skilled at making people angry?), your reactive anger serves two very important functions for them: First, if you are angry, that kid can predict how you are going to act and treat them. In other words, you are now on his or her playing field, and they know the rules of the game. And as an added bonus, once you are angry, they are in control of you—and remember the bus-driving example. When a kid comes from a home where there is chaos, he fights for control wherever and whenever he can get it. If you are angry, that kid is now yanking your chain and is in control of you emotionally.

The second purpose is a little more complex and has to do with intimacy. These students want you angry because if you are angry with them, you cannot like them. And believe me, they do *not* want you to like them. Because if you like *them,* they may like you, and that puts you in a powerful position—you can now hurt them badly.

Let me explain. Think back in your life. Have you ever been dumped or cheated on by somebody you really loved? That hurt, didn't it! But now think back again; have you ever been dumped by someone you really didn't care about in the first place? And the only thing you could think to yourself was, "Oh thank *goodness!* That saves me an email!" That probably didn't hurt so badly. When we get close to somebody emotionally, they have power to hurt us. That is the choice we make when we give our love and trust to somebody. In fact, when I see couples for therapy, be they premarital couples, married spouses, or life partners, I give them the same speech about developing trust and emotional intimacy in the relationship: The only way you can build trust in a relationship, the *only way* that emotional intimacy can develop, is when you begin to give your partner a chance to hurt you … and they don't. Trust and emotional intimacy can only evolve if your partner acknowledges, honors, and protects your secrets and vulnerabilities.

Now draw your attention to the angry kids again. They have been hurt badly by the people who are supposed to love, honor, and protect them above all others: their caretakers. When that breakdown occurs, these kids learn that not only is real trust with grown-ups not happening, but it is probably *impossible*.

And hearken back in your own life again: When we are little children, our parents do not seem like mere humans to us; they are like *gods*. They are big and strong, they seem to know everything, and they fix things and make them better. If ever those gods die in our eyes, we are left with cynicism, confusion, and anger. And there you have one destiny of the child with ODD.

Kids with ADHD are born, but kids with ODD are *created*; which makes treatment a little different. There is not a magic pill for ODD. These kids have been molded into the *little bundles of joy* you are now experiencing and now need to be re-taught. But I'm not blind to the difficulty in pulling this off. These kids are like freight trains going the wrong way—especially the ones who are in middle school or high school and have been living the tough life for a while. These are kids who might be 15 years old chronologically but seem like grizzled, battlefield nurses from Vietnam. They have lived three or four lifetimes in their 15 years and are not afraid to take that out on you.

With a runaway freight train, we can't just stop that sucker on a dime and get it motoring the other way immediately. We have to coast it to a stop over a long stretch of track and then slowly build momentum in the opposite direction. Patience is crucial here, but so is perseverance. During the time you are in the life of this kid, the best you may be able to do is to poke a little pinhole of sunlight in the black shroud he is metaphorically wearing over his head. The road you begin to pave may get picked up by other adults in the future, so he or she can continue to get that freight train slowed, stopped, or going the other direction. These kids were not built in a day, and the ODD isn't going to change overnight, either!

When dealing with these kiddos (as with all kids), work the reinforcement of good and punishment of bad as detailed in Chapters 13 through 16 of this book. (This will be a recurring theme as we trudge through these diagnoses.) One additional step is going to be necessary to forge long-term change. Some of these kids have the capability to be really cool people but have such a chip on their shoulder that they get in their own way when the goodness inside tries to pop out and say hi. Adults other than the parents are often in a unique position in the lives of these kids: You might very well be the healthiest grown-up in that kid's life! Pretty heavy, eh? I know!

Here's another fact for you male teachers, social workers, coaches, and employers out there reading these words: You may not only be the healthiest grown-up in that kid's life, but you may very well be the *only adult male* in that kid's life! Men have the added responsibility of putting a good, decent male role model in front of these children. And kids *need* healthy males in their lives, girls as well as boys. The presence of healthy adult males is correlated with self-esteem and confidence. It allows boys to have a role model, and it teaches girls how to appropriately interact with males.

With some of the angry students, teachers may never be able to teach them algebra, but the relationship they begin to form may keep that boy from putting a knife into some poor person at an ATM when he's 19. Forming a good relationship with a girl may keep her from becoming a stripper when she is 17. We may never know the change we initiate in the life of those kids because we might only set in motion the beginning of that change. Their new trajectory may lead them down a very different path in life.

It may sound pie-in-the-sky, and I know many of these tough kids won't be reached. But, the few successes we can affect change the lives of the people around these kids and will carry onward to their children and the choices the next generations make.

How do we forge these relationships? For starters, my advice is always to abide by the three rules of dealing with youngsters with ODD: a) go slow, b) go slow, and c) go slow.

One of the biggest mistakes adults make when they try to strike up a relationship with a truly angry kid is to come on too strong. As adults, we can see the potential a kid like this may have, and we want to tell him just how "wonderful" we know he can be. But remember the basic modus operandi of a kid with ODD: *He doesn't want you to like him!* In a nutshell, he is already geared to have a hard time taking a compliment. Further, if you let the floodgates open and tell him how great he is and how he can become president someday, you are going to lose him forever. Almost invariably, one thing is going to happen: He is going to mock you—either out loud or internally—for being so astonishingly dense that you fail to see how rough he is, or how tough and angry he is, or how bad his life or environment is. You basically lose your credibility.

Compliments have to go easy. It may be somewhat insulting to think about these children or teens with the following metaphor, but I will risk offending you and proceed to illustrate my point. If a dog has been beaten his whole life, you don't waltz up and grab it around the neck to shower it with petting and nuzzling. That dog has not learned to trust, and furthermore, has learned to defend itself against such advances—they have ended badly in the past, with him getting hurt. Instead, you go slow. You put food down to let the dog come to you on his terms and in his time. You let him know that the door is open, but you don't "force" your good intentions. That dog may never be 100% over his past (probably won't, actually), but he will learn to trust—slowly and over time. I'll give you a couple of other pointers to help you in building relationships with students with ODD in the final chapter.

Chapter 4b

Diagnosis of Interest II: Conduct Disorder, Bipolar Disorder, and Autism

Aha! I Know That Kid, Too!

We have spent an entire chapter covering three of the diagnoses you will encounter and have spent some time discussing etiology, manifestations, and possible medical interventions and have begun putting together a plan of action to deal with these issues. Let's continue in that vein and use this chapter to cover three more diagnoses: conduct disorder, bipolar disorder, and autism spectrum disorders.

Conduct Disorder

The symptoms of conduct disorder are as follow (APA, 2002):

- Aggression toward people and/or animals
- Destruction of property
- Deceitfulness or theft
- Serious violation of rules

Kids with ADHD will make you tired; kids with ODD will make you angry, and kids with conduct disorder will make you *scared*. These are the kids who make your spine tingle, as they generally give you the feeling that, should they make a threat they *will* follow through with it. These are not kids who blow a lot of smoke.

I often refer to conduct disorder as "ODD on steroids," but there is more to it than that. Conduct disorder is a far more serious diagnosis to give a kid, so we really try to not assign that diagnosis if at all possible. In fact, it almost implies that change is going to be next to impossible for these children. It is so heavy a diagnosis that we as practitioners cannot (by definition of the disorder) assign the diagnosis until the child is a teenager.

The reason for such a gloomy prognosis is that folks with conduct disorder lack an element of the human condition that makes change more likely: *empathy*. Without empathy, they do not develop a conscience. To follow this to its logical conclusion, without a conscience, they have no remorse, and lack of remorse is mainly what makes these folks scary (on a primitive level) to deal with.

There's no good little angel sitting on their shoulder. Kids with conduct disorder typically are created from the coming together of a few forces: 1) neurologically, they are compromised in the part of the brain that processes an empathetic response, the anterior cingulated cortex (mentioned earlier); 2) socially speaking, some sort of pretty horrid abuse or neglect probably happened in childhood, which creates a sense of rage, and 3) they had a total lack of bonding with any attachment figure (i.e., caretaker) during their early years. So, what we have is a very angry child who *really doesn't care* about the people around him. He will take, hurt, and maneuver in any way he sees fit. Further, he will not have the foundational *remorse* that helps keep the rest of us at least somewhat in line.

Again, no empathy means no remorse, and no remorse means that we as therapists have no leverage to affect change, at least in the short term. We have to appeal to their sense of self-centeredness and get very concrete and consequence directed. In fact, these folks would never voluntarily enter into a therapeutic relationship. Almost exclusively, any therapeutic contact we have with them comes at the hands of the justice system, as court-ordered counseling is often a requirement during sentencing. Later in this section I talk about a couple things I have tried.

Underscoring the serious nature of the diagnosis, at 18, the diagnosis changes to the grown-up version, called antisocial personality disorder (APA, 2002; Lahey & Lober, 1994). In the vernacular, most laypeople refer to those with this diagnosis as psychopaths, or sociopaths. Remember, these folks do not have a conscience. The joke (if you will) among therapists is something like this: "The only therapy for someone with antisocial personality disorder is *jail therapy*." To reiterate, change is a very difficult process to enact if the person does not care and really does not want to change.

I don't want to keep beating a dead horse here, but let me expound on one more thing to emphasize how troubled these persons are. The "red flag" we look to as evaluators when we are assessing children for a potential conduct disorder is the first symptom in the checklist earlier in this section: cruelty toward animals. And we're not talking about burning ants with a magnifying glass or ripping off the appendages of a daddy longlegs spider on a camping trip. Rather, we are talking kids who will torture—sometimes in astonishingly sadistic ways—dogs, cats, rabbits, or squirrels. These are kids who cannot even connect with *animals*. And *that's* saying something.

Even the angriest child with ODD or, to take it in another direction, the most severely mentally retarded or autistic kid, usually can connect quite well with an animal. The angry child with ODD may have a dog or a horse he really connects with. When it is just him and the pet, he is fine; it's *people* who drive him nuts. The profoundly retarded or autistic child may not be able to communicate effectively with people but may well love a guinea pig or have a kitty to have and hold. Kids typically find animals easier to connect with than people because animals are non-judgmental—*they love you no matter what.*

If you are a dog person, think how excited your dog is to see you when you return home from work. Yeah, the whole dog wags, not just the tail, right? In reality, it has nothing to do with whether you had a good or a bad morning with the dog; he loves you and is delighted to see you just the same.

For the most part, kids understand this, but kids with conduct disorder can't. They don't have the internal structure in place to form these connections or to understand the feelings of love or bonding. They understand that they want to get their needs met and will use people to this end.

There is another disorder that is tied to problems in early caregiving: *reactive attachment disorder* (RAD) (APA, 2002). Briefly, RAD is a disorder whereby a child has a poor attachment history. Adopted kids or kids raised in orphanages are often studied as examples of people with RAD. The main difference between a child with RAD and one with conduct disorder is the rage that the kids with conduct disorder feel. Kids with RAD typically do not have the history of abuse, so they proceed with life in a less destructive fashion but have trouble forming relationships. They either avoid intimacy altogether, or they are very clingy with any life raft that happens to float by. This can lead to frustration and acting out—some kids with RAD do have rages if they feel encroached on—but you will not experience the fear reaction that kids with conduct disorder will elicit.

So what is the implication of conduct disorder for the adults around kids with this diagnosis? There are a couple of things to note here. First and foremost, *protect yourself.* This sounds a bit trite, as it should be a no-brainer, but you'd be surprised. I remember one teacher in Texas telling me the story of a seventh grader who stole her identity and then (of course) proceeded to wreak havoc for her. He was eventually caught, and when she appeared in court to testify against him, she found out that he had done the *exact same thing* to several other women. And the crown jewel of this experience for her was to see that he had absolutely no remorse for his actions; he would have probably kept on going forever had he not been caught.

So you should ensure that these kids don't have access to your personal information. Again, this sounds obvious, but bear in mind how much personal info you share with the kids with whom you work. They may know things like the name of your spouse, your kids, where you live, or where your spouse works. And while it may not be possible to censor *all* of this information from your daily interactions with your students or clients, be aware of your audience; these are kids who would gladly use that information to their advantage at some point.

The last thing for you to think about with these kids is that the combination of conduct disorder with high IQ is perhaps the most dangerous in children, diagnostically speaking. These will be remarkably manipulative kids who use people up and throw them away like a dirty tissue when they are done. So, protect yourselves, keep boundaries very clear—if you give them an inch, they will take a hundred miles. It's what they do, and no, they won't care.

Now before proceeding, let me talk you down off the ledge here. Whereas conduct disorder is indeed a very serious diagnosis to hang on a kid, it is also pretty rare (1–4% of kids, with higher prevalence in urban environments; Shaffer et al., 1996). It's easy to panic when you think about it, but in actuality, these kids are not running around everywhere we look. In fact, a number of factors are involved in the etiology of conduct disorder that make it more likely (e.g., genetic predisposition) or less likely (e.g., mitigating attachment relationships). Remember that not all children who come from highly abusive or neglectful situations develop conduct disorder. Some are naturally more resilient, and some formed a healthy bond at some time during childhood, which helped propel them away from conduct disorder. Having said that, some of you do work in schools or treatment facilities where you will have a higher concentration than the mainstream, so protect yourself.

Too, if a teacher has ever have interacted with a teen who has conduct disorder, s/he will never forget that kid. That story will become an anecdote you tell forever and ever, amen. He will hold a special place in your history when you recount your "Tales from the Battlefield" around the water cooler or at a family get-together. Yes, these are young adults who leave a lasting impression, but for all the wrong reasons.

We can try to do an "after-market installation" of empathy, especially if we are dealing with younger kids. I know I said previously that you must be a teenager to receive the official diagnosis, but I am also not too dense to know that there are some younger children we see who are on the road to conduct disorder. Interestingly, as I travel around the country and talk to professionals, I hear stories about young kids who fall into this category. One kid who stands out most in my memory was an 8-year-old student a teacher described in this way: "He was dead behind his eyes." I'll also never forget the details of his story. In a nutshell, he was eventually thrown into "The System" for stabbing his mother with a pair of scissors.

I make a light metaphor when I say "after-market installation," but the reality is a bit more challenging. Empathy, it turns out, is a bit like language acquisition; if you don't get it early on, the window of opportunity slams shut, and it is extremely difficult to open again. Studies have shown that kids with no language skills who have been discovered after the age of 7 years (e.g., incidences of extraordinary neglect and even a couple of documented cases of kids *literally* raised by wolves or primates) made only modest gains in language skills in all the time they were treated following their discovery.

As with most problems, the sooner you catch them, the better off you are. Here is what I advise teachers and other professionals with whom I consult who have younger students that may be careening into the conduct disorder tree. When you send them off to time out or to the principal's office or wherever they happen to be sent, have them go through the following exercise, which is an offshoot of what many elementary school teachers are already doing: Have these kids take advantage of the time away from peers to write what they did to earn the time out and what they should have done differently. With these students, I recommend adding a third component to the assignment; have them also write about *how it made the other person feel*. Whether the wronged person was another student, or you, or the whole class—whoever it happened to be—have the kids go through the motions.

One caveat: With boys, the language of emotion may alienate them from the purpose of the assignment. So rather than force them into accepting an emotional paradigm (for which they may not feel adequate in the first place), have them instead write the answer to this question: What would I have *done* if I were the other person? In other words, keep the exercise more action oriented to facilitate their internal language.

Another approach with these clients with which I have experienced limited success (and sometimes success has to be measured in millimeters rather than yards) is a way to help older kids work through this same process. Rather than having the teens write down the three components, I recommend that facilities create a "Peace Table," where the two actors in "the incident" (i.e., whatever the outburst or transgression happened to be) sit down and then re-create the dialogue of the incident, *but from the other person's point of view.* It works sort of like a "role reversal" made popular in marital therapy portrayed in some '70s sitcoms. The purpose is to force the teen into thinking and talking through the incident precisely from the other person's point of view. This is not a bad plan to implement with all students (not just those with conduct disorder), because it is a good exercise for teaching kids how to understand others. It is especially helpful for students with conduct disorder to walk them through the motions of empathy.

In institutions, the reluctant students (!) are encouraged to participate in the process because it is tied directly into their tier system (or whatever the behavior modification plan happens to be). And for the most part, they abhor participation and conspire with the other teen to just feed the supervisors the lines they are required to generate. That is exactly what it will be at first— the first 75 times the student participates in the "after-market installation" strategy, he only goes through the motions. He does the assignment in a mechanical way because he wants to get out of whatever punishment is being given. Over time, however, your goal is to eventually wear a groove into the gear in his head that helps him make decisions. In other words, through repetition, "How does the other person feel?" will become a part of his decision-making process rather than *incidental*—or *absolutely irrelevant*—to it.

Heck, you can build empathy in a similar (but less consequence-based) manner with any client or student or even with your own children. One exercise I often use is that I show kids magazine photos, pictures on their cell phones, or real-life situations in which we may observe other people. I then challenge them to tell me a story about what happened *just before* the picture was taken or the person entered our field of vision. This way, they are forced to interpret a mood state as not merely a static affair, but rather as occurring within a broader context. Helping a child to understand that emotion and reaction happen in *context* can build empathy and connection.

Even with one of these strategies in place, kids with conduct disorder are going to be tough nuts to crack. Remember, you may only have them for a few hours each day if you're lucky. Then they have to go back and survive in whatever circumstance may have created the problem in the first place. But this is really the only shot we have as professionals to effect long-term change. From a short-term perspective, work the behavior management plan as always, and make some inroads to build the relationship. Above all, keep your boundaries firm and stay safe.

Bipolar Disorder

The symptoms of bipolar disorder in children compared with the symptoms in adults are as follows:

- Moods cycle faster than in adults
- There is a high degree of irritability
- Mania and depression are expressed in ways that are similar to each other

I am going to discuss bipolar disorder not because there is a specific course of action to follow when you deal with these kids, but rather because this is the diagnosis I get the most questions about in the seminars. I understand why: Bipolar disorder is, in my humble opinion, the new ADHD. I say that because we have seen a dramatic increase in the number of children being diagnosed with this disorder, despite it being a relatively new diagnostic category for children. Of course, the disorder is not new—bipolar in one form or another has been around forever—but the number of kids and teens being assigned this diagnosis has been spiking for the past few years. Historically, pediatric psychiatrists have been extremely cautious about assigning this diagnosis instead of a few others. Around the country, most folks with whom I consult generally agree that they are seeing more kids and teens with this particular diagnosis. There are some pockets of America where childhood bipolar disorder remains relatively rare, but the trend seems to be moving in the other direction. Later on, I give my opinions about why that is happening.

Let me make sure everyone knows what I am talking about here. Bipolar disorder is more commonly known in the vernacular as "manic depression." This tends to be a term people relate to more readily, as the words seem self-explanatory and less like *Doctor Speak*.

I'll talk about adults separately from children, as the disorder is far easier to spot in grown-ups. In adults, as the name would imply, "manic depression" is characterized by extreme mood swings, from high to low and vice versa. As an aside, there are actually three different types of bipolar disorders, but for now, I'll stick to the full-bore bipolar I (versus bipolar II or cyclothymia) for the sake of simplicity.

These mood swings are not just having a good day or a bad day. Rather, the adult with bipolar disorder will swing from *dizzying* highs to *devastating* lows, with very little time spent in the middle on "normal" ground. When an adult is in the throes of a manic episode, he or she is like a person shot up on an eight ball of cocaine. The person may not sleep for 3 or 4 days; he or she will be out detailing the car with a toothbrush; he or she will be remodeling the house at 3 a.m.; there may be wild spending sprees, or the person might gamble his or her life savings away or go out and have a string of sexual conquests. He or she will be flying, flying, flying, Flying, *FLYING* until ***BAM!*** He or she swings to the other end of the spectrum.

On this end, the person will not be able to get out of bed for 3 or 4 days. He or she will move slow, think slow, and feel that hope has been blackened by the dark ink of despair. Depression will grip the individual like a ball and chain.

Some adults with bipolar move through this cycle several times per year ("rapid cycling"). For others, it may take a couple of years to go through this cycle. Some adults with bipolar never hit the depression part of the cycle, instead having just the manic or hypomanic (less severe mania) episodes.

As I mentioned previously, there is another type of bipolarity called cyclothymia (APA, 2002), in which the person will have chronic mood swings, just not to the extremes of full-blown bipolar I. These folks will still be driven nuts by their highs and lows but will be more functional in life. They are still at the mercy of their shifting neurochemistry, but they will generally be able to hold down a job, relationships, etc.

Just so you know, the faster a person cycles, the more resistant to treatment the bipolarity tends to be. Its scary stuff, as this is another disorder that is neurochemically driven. While most of us find it difficult to change our moods, we have some conscious awareness and control, whereas the person with bipolar disorder has very little conscious control over the mood swings. Thus, for these people, medication with therapy is going to be a remarkably helpful solution.

On the other hand, children with bipolar disorder do not act exactly like grown-ups with bipolarity (NIMH, 2000). This has the effect of making the diagnosis, with a few exceptions for kids on the extreme ends of the spectrum, a very difficult process. In fact, let me go one step further and say that the National Institutes of Mental Health are still working hard to make the diagnostic criteria for children more clear. Even in their attempts to cordon off a particular cluster of symptoms to differentiate childhood bipolarity from the proposed DSM-5 diagnosis of temper dysregulation disorder with dysphoria (American Psychiatric Association, 2010), the issue presents a set of unique challenges. This being such a popular diagnosis is still new, and while there have been tremendous advances in our recognition of the disorder (and the medications to treat it), we still need to crawl before we walk.

For now, the symptoms we look for in children and teens have to do with extreme irritability. These kids just seem like they have an electric current running through them. They may explode into a temper tantrum of biblical proportions and then in the blink of an eye, be fine, maybe even remorseful or frightened by the fury they had just demonstrated. These are kids who are acting normally one minute and are over-the-top impulsive the next.

As was mentioned at the opening of this section in the symptom checklist, children express mania and depression in much the same manner: It all seems like hyperactivity and impulsivity! These kids tend to have a little more "juice" in their acting out, though. They have more energy or more inertia. They will also cycle faster than adults, making their behavior seem less predictable and more problematic. They may literally blow one minute and then be fine the next, leading the adult to wonder, "What just happened?"

And the tantrum, or explosion, or event, can wear different faces as the kids grow older. Really young kids may have knock-down, drag-out tantrums while kicking and screaming. Older kids may tear stuff off the walls or rip their room apart. Teens may launch into ferocious verbal tirades and shred everyone around them.

Think about Old Faithful (the geyser in Yellowstone) as an adequate metaphor. When Old Faithful blows, it is a spectacular event, right? It is riveting to watch the wonder of nature's focused fury. But when it is done, it is *done*. The water falls back to Earth, and calm is restored. And yet, even during the quiet periods, you know that tension and pressure are building beneath the surface and that another explosion is imminent.

When a child or teen is in the throes of an event, both the emotional *and* the cognitive parts of the brain are involved. Many an adult has realized that verbal engagement during the event is all but impossible, as is cognitive redirection or distraction. These kiddos may (literally) not remember the event because they are mentally checked out while it is happening. Furthermore, when they emerge from the event, they may be a bit stony for a few minutes, as if they are coming out of a seizure. It may take them a moment to get their legs underneath themselves to feel connected again. Or, with younger kids, they may *fall asleep* in the aftermath because of the amount of energy burned during the event.

Along with the criteria we use when making a diagnosis of bipolar in children, family history is relevant. There will typically be some evidence of a family history of bipolarity or anxiety disorders. Uncovering that history may require a bit of digging and clarification, as often, emotional disturbances are either considered dirty secrets about which nobody dares speaks or are known by less clinical names. "Nervous breakdown" tends to be one of these semi-clinical terms that can have different meanings. An emotional disturbance can be masked by alcoholism or other substance abuse, too. Drugs have a funny way of covering up symptoms or creating new ones. Other times, the child's parent may not know whether the adults in the family tree were on medication, or if they do know, they may not know specifically what the medications were.

And speaking of medications, here is where we start bumping into the problem again, especially with prepubertal children. In grown-ups, the old standby for treating bipolar disorder medically has been lithium carbonate (or, most folks just refer to it as lithium). Lithium has always been used because *it works!* Lithium snips off the ends of your moods—it has a dampening effect on the highs and lows. The "worse" your bipolarity, the higher the dose you are on, and the more restricted your range of emotional expression tends to be. It becomes more "truncated." Some people don't like the fact that lithium makes them feel emotions less intensely, but it does help even out the extreme mood swings.

That's the good news. The bad news is that lithium tends to be a pretty harsh drug on the body and actually tears up the kidneys pretty badly. People taking lithium have to see a physician at regular intervals to get blood drawn. Physicians have to do a balancing act to ensure good quality of life in the present while also minimizing damage in the future.

We do have other options that have been developed over the past few years, although these are not without their concerns. Current drugs fall into one of two families: mood stabilizers/ anticonvulsants, and atypical antipsychotics. I click through some examples of each, mention their effects, and address some concerns.

While lithium is still considered the granddaddy of mood stabilizing medications, there are several "new kids on the block" in this category, each also serving as an anticonvulsant (i.e., if there is a seizure disorder present—remember Old Faithful?). Depakote, Lamictal, Tegretol, and, to a lesser extent, Topamax, are all prescribed to help with stabilizing the bipolar events in children and adults. As you can imagine, these medicines have a dampening effect on mood and are being prescribed to children and teens with some caution because no long-term data exist on their potential cumulative effects. As kids as young as 4 years are being diagnosed with bipolar disorder, you can see how they might accumulate a track record of (potentially) 14 years of taking a medicine before they turn 18! More research is definitely on the horizon for this family of medications.

One word of caution: There is a rare side effect that can be fatal when taking a mood stabilizer/anticonvulsant. It is called Stevens-Johnson Syndrome, and it is a nasty one. If you are working with caregivers of a child on these meds, be sure to have them be on the lookout for any sign of a rash on the kiddo. If they find one, have them take the child to the Emergency Room right away; a Dermatologist will be called in immediately to consult if the attending physician feels this syndrome may be active. Again, it is a rather rare possibility, but keep your caregivers alert.

The other family is the atypical antipsychotics and includes brand names such as Seroquel, Abilify, Clozaril, Zyprexa, Geodon, and Risperdal. As a point of reference, these are called "atypical" because they are the second generation of anti-psychotics, developed to address and curb tardive dyskenesia (TD), a common long-term effect of the first wave of anti-psychotics (like Haldol and Thorazine, for example). Unfortunately, we are finding that these medicines do not completely eliminate the potential for TD, which is somewhat akin to a medically induced Parkinson's disease, complete with loss of control of fine motor muscles. The issue with TD is not just the inconvenience of a tremor, but, more importantly, that it tends to be irreversible.

Anecdotal evidence suggests that if a child or teen begins to demonstrate early symptoms of TD, often manifesting in odd tongue thrusts or motions, then the medication can be withdrawn and the symptoms corrected. Still, this can serve as another cautionary tale of side effects when prescribing for children. Plus, there has been some research that links atypical antipsychotic use to type II diabetes (Sernyak, Leslie, Alarcon, Losonczy, & Rosenheck, 2002) although further research will need to be conducted to firm up that relationship. In the end, a physician or psychiatric nurse practitioner has the unenviable job of determining the balance between cost and benefit with these medications before giving a prescription.

So yes, these are some pretty heavy-duty drugs we've got here. So much so that pediatricians won't generally touch a diagnosis of bipolar in kids. This right has been reserved primarily for pediatric psychiatrists and psychiatric nurse practitioners who have more specialized training in understanding the impact of the medications on developing bodies.

The other thing about the mood stabilizing medications is that regardless of the level of severity of the disorder, *they will work.* We can give a high enough dose that the medicine will knock you down a peg. You can think about their effect as being like throwing a wet towel over the brain. It will dampen emotional expression. So until we really nail down a hard-and-fast method of diagnosis, we are in danger of falling into the same trap that was sprung on ADHD in the '90s. The question is: "Are we merely masking symptoms with these medications, or are we actually treating the neurochemical imbalance in this kid?"

I'll close by reiterating that there is not a specific, unique course of action to take when dealing with kids and teens who have bipolar aside from moving toward self-management. In fact, and in remaining true to the Old Faithful metaphor, the point of intervention has to occur *before* the event begins. Look for any "tell" that may let you know an event is coming. Most parents will mention "a look she gets on her face" or say, "his knee starts to shake a certain way before he explodes." Once the "tell" is identified, we can deflect, distract, or redirect while the plane is still on the runway, and before the kiddo takes off into the open skies of the event. Once they launch, you may have to ride the storm out and try again next time. You may not eliminate the events entirely—probably won't, in fact—but if you can reduce their frequency or intensity, then you have achieved an important goal.

If it truly is a neurochemical issue, self-management becomes difficult. This difficulty will be evident in adults with this disorder. Now take that and up it two or three notches for children and teenagers, who may have some difficulty with self-monitoring in the first place! Just think about how difficult it may have been for you in the past to monitor and/or control your behavior if your chemistry was compromised by, for example, drugs, alcohol, or hormones. Whatever the case, when you tickle the delicate balance upstairs, perception, reality, and even awareness can become skewed.

Encourage parents to get a thorough diagnosis so we know what we are dealing with. Reinforce self-control whenever possible with these kids. Parts of the acting out will not be under their control, but some parts are, and we must teach these kids how to handle them. Kids need opportunities to practice self-control, or cooling down, every chance they get.

Autism

Symptoms of autism include the following (APA, 2002):

- Marked impairment in use of nonverbal behaviors
- Failure to develop peer relationships
- Lack of seeking to share positives with other people
- Lack of social or emotional reciprocity
- Communication impairments
- Repetitive, stereotyped patterns of behavior

Because most everyone who is currently reading this book has a basic familiarity with popular movies, I think it is safe to say we all think of a certain character when we hear the word *autism*: That character is Raymond in the movie *Rain Man*. Dustin Hoffman as "Rain Man" had a significant impact on the world's understanding of autism. He put a face to a disorder that was often misunderstood and brought autism onto the front burner of our awareness. Hoffman's character, and real-life folks like him, tend to make people uncomfortable because of their odd behaviors, but *Rain Man* helped many folks have an "aha!" moment and get a better grasp on what was up with someone they knew from home, work, or while growing up.

Think about some of the wild behaviors that made Hoffman transform into the character of Rain Man. I can picture many of you beginning to smile to yourselves as you remember some of the quirky idiosyncrasies that made Rain Man a delightful, if not frustrating and enigmatic figure. I'll run down a few.

When I ask my seminar groups to list Rain Man's characteristics, the most frequent first answer shouted out is something about his uncanny ability to calculate numbers or count cards or flash to the number of toothpicks on the floor. The ability Rain Man had, essentially making him into a human calculator, is called *savantism*. Rain Man was indeed an "autistic savant." But here's the catch—not all autistic folks are savants. In fact, it is a very low percentage.

Still, the fact that there are savants serves as testimony to how incredible the machinery of the human brain truly is. In fact, medical science still does not know exactly what causes some autistic folks to become savants (Treffert & Christensen, 2005). But as science fiction–like as Rain Man's ability seemed to those unfamiliar with the disorder, there really are folks like him out there. Once in a while you'll see a blurb on Dateline NBC, or 20/20, or the CBS Evening News about a very special, yet profoundly autistic, fellow who cannot communicate effectively with the people around him but can play Rachmaninoff on the piano.

It's amazing how parts of the brain can be shut down entirely, but a spotlight of angelic grace can shine on another. So again, while savantism is what caught most of your attention when it came to Rain Man, it is a rarity of autism. We'll turn now to the most salient symptoms.

First, and perhaps foremost, Rain Man had a very difficult time connecting with other people, right? Relationships became strained almost immediately, and despite some witty banter between him and his brother, he could never connect on an emotional level.

The reason for this lies once again in the neurology and chemistry of the brain. Without going into too detailed an explanation, suffice it to say that the emotional centers of the brain do not work the same in a person on the autism spectrum as they do in you and me. Emotions are neither felt nor understood on the same level and thereby are rendered as rather puzzling to the autistic person. In effect, emotions become a sort of interpersonal Rubik's Cube for them to spin and try to solve. The stress caused by trying to "figure out" what other people are feeling or needing leads autistic folks to avoid the discomfort and therefore avoid interaction.

Rain Man took this avoidance as far as he could, as he would not even make eye contact with those around him. In fact, if you recall, he even walked with a bit of a slouch because he looked toward the floor all the time.

Eye contact is avoided by folks with autism spectrum disorders, by the way, for two primary reasons. I will hit the second in a moment, but in terms of emotion, think about eye contact as being a simple and reasonably quick communication between two people but also something that can be extremely emotionally intense. And if you don't believe that, seek out your spouse, partner, or other loved one and try to stare into his or her eyes for 60 seconds. You won't be able to do it! You'll invariably start to giggle or may even burst out laughing. The discomfort you feel after 60 seconds is felt by Rain Man after a half of a second, so he avoids the contact.

Taking the emotional issue to its logical conclusion, connect some dots. Without a basic concept of emotion, subtle social "rules of engagement" will also be lost on the person on the autistic spectrum. Without understanding the unwritten rules of interaction (that the rest of us take for granted and do not even think about on a conscious level anymore), interpersonal comfort becomes nearly impossible.

Before leaving the subject of eye contact entirely, one of the most basic interventions for folks on the autism spectrum is to work through a number of common facial expressions with them. There are formal card sets designed for this (they have over 100 photos of real people showing subtle variations of facial expressions), and you can also use emoticons or do a quick Internet search for photographs. The goal is to help the kiddo understand a couple things: (a) What is the person in the photo feeling/thinking? (b) What might be a good thing to do when you see somebody who looks like this?

It sounds like a silly and simple intervention, but research has shown us that folks on the autism spectrum tend to view faces from the nose down rather than from the nose up. As a result, they are not nearly as in tune with the emotional state of the person with whom they are interacting (Roth, 2010). Allowing them the freedom to observe clear facial expressions without fear of reproach can create improvements in social functioning and reductions in social anxiety.

As an example of the "rules of engagement," think about how you shake someone's hand. When two people shake hands, they incorporate seven or eight rules that were learned about 100 years ago and never thought about anymore. How far apart do you stand? Who holds out their hand first? How hard do you squeeze? What do you say? What tone of voice do you use? At what volume do you speak? How long to you hold it before you let go? All of these things seem pretty easy to us but are troubling to an autistic person.

The second main symptom Hoffman displayed as Rain Man involves a trait that resembles obsessive-compulsive disorder. Folks with autistic spectrum require a high degree of structure and routine in their lives. Everything has to be how it has to be how it has to be. For example, where is the correct place one goes to purchase underpants for Rain Man? K-Mart[SM], I hope is your response. Furthermore, what did Rain Man have to do at 4:00 p.m. every day? Yup … he *had* to watch Wapner. If he did not get to watch *The People's Court*, what was the outcome? Bad times, I would say. Rain Man required that structure in his life, much to the chagrin of his busybody brother. In fact, that was the tension in the movie: Tom Cruise's character wanted Rain Man to live with him but kept running headlong into autism! Alas, Rain Man needed the tight structure of his institution and had to return. In the final scene of the movie, Rain Man boards a bus for home.

Back to symptoms … Rain Man had a "go-to thing" he would launch into whenever he would begin to feel anxious. He would recite Abbot and Costello's "Who's on First" routine. Rain Man would begin to feel stress, so he would separate himself from it by (metaphorically speaking) pulling his head into his shell and soothing himself with a good round of "Who's on First." That mechanism both removed him physically and also provided tight structure to soothe him during the anxious moment.

A "go-to thing" serves as a coping mechanism when emotional arousal gets too high in nearly every child with autism spectrum. If that arousal passes a certain point, a meltdown will ensue. Perhaps the most common reason for this overload is related to sensory input. And here is where we bring back that image of Rain Man keeping his eyes cast downward. Keeping eyes down limited the amount of sensory input buzzing around in Rain Man's head.

For this brief discussion, we turn again to the brain of the person with autism spectrum. The "filter" mechanism we have on our brain allows us to screen out most of the superfluous sensory information that bombards us every moment of every day. As I sit here writing this, I am wearing headphones (with Bon Jovi's *Bounce* album playing loudly), I am sitting in a rather uncomfortable chair, I can hear the droning buzz of the ladies playing cards at the next table, I am a little too warm, I have a full belly after a turkey sandwich and small bag of chips, and to top it all off, my fingertips are getting beat to heck by pounding their keystrokes on my laptop. For the most part, I am blocking these stimuli out and focusing on the words that are flowing out of my muddled brain and onto the screen. I imagine that you, too, are dealing with a number of inputs that you are filtering out so you can concentrate on the words you are reading.

Folks with autism spectrum have a difficult time weeding out what is important from the background noise. Therefore, sensory input comes in at a far more intense pace than it would for us. Sights, sounds, and even touch can be overwhelming for an autistic person. Remember the few times Tom Cruise tried to touch or hug Rain Man? That was difficult for him. Remember the scene toward the end of the movie when the smoke alarm went off in Cruise's apartment? Rain Man *totally freaked out.*

As an aside, ironically, while a slight touch will make an autistic kid wince, *overstimulation* of touch can actually trigger a calm-down reaction. I once had a teacher tell me about a student whom she could not tap on the shoulder without eliciting a harsh reaction. But that same student would at times come up to her and give her a "whole leg hug," where he would—almost literally—wrap himself around her leg. This caused him to calm significantly. I address this phenomenon in a later chapter when I talk about interventions discovered by "the cow lady," Temple Grandin.

Unless you deal exclusively with kids on the autism spectrum, you will most likely never see a little version of Rain Man—especially in the school system. Think about how such a child would handle a middle school or high school hallway between classes—kids yelling to one another, lockers slamming without rhythm, elbows ramming randomly into him, figures darting back and forth through his field of vision—in a word, *disaster!*

Let's spin the time machine backward a bit. What is the typical kindergarten classroom like? I would venture to say that the typical kindergarten classroom is best described as *barely controlled chaos!* Kids laughing and playing; paper airplanes craftily avoiding the instructions from the flight deck; colorful, fluffy stuff hanging on the windows and from the lights; *A Very Snoopy Christmas* belting from the CD player on the teacher's desk ... Rain Man would be over in the corner hugging himself and rocking. He would not be able to handle the hysteria.

So, as a bridge to the next chapter, keep in mind that most of you will not see a student who is as seriously autistic as Rain Man. Nowadays however, we are thinking of autism in a different way. Rather than seeing it is a discreet diagnostic category (i.e., like pregnancy—either you are or you are not pregnant), we see it more as lying on a continuum. On one end are folks with the more serious version of the disorder (Rain Man would be an example of this), and at the other end are those with milder versions.

The metaphor I use to explain this phenomenon is this: Picture the old, 1970s stereo rack systems that had a slider bar for a volume control. If the bar is slid to the right, we have Rain Man ... if we slide it back toward the left, we have folks who display all of the symptoms that Rain Man had but to a much lesser extent. So, what you *will* see in your classroom with some relative frequency is that stepped-down, slider-bar-to-the-left version called *Asperger's syndrome*. I discuss this disorder in Chapter 5.

Chapter 5

A Few Other Possibilities for Acting-Out Behavior

Hmmm ... I Never Thought About That

Break time is over! I would blow a loud whistle or hit the "POP" button on the air horn I purchased specifically to keep on hand while writing this book, but I know it's getting late in the day. So, I'll keep it quiet.

Picking up where we left off, let me repeat the bridge so as to acclimate you to the direction we are heading. You will probably never see nor treat Rain Man if you do not work in an institution, but you will likely at some point see a child with a scaled-down version of autism, called Asperger's syndrome.

Asperger's Syndrome

The symptoms of Asperger's syndrome include the following (APA, 2002):

- Qualitative impairment in social functioning
- The presence of restricted, repetitive, or stereotyped behaviors and interests
- No significant delay in language
- No significant delay in cognitive development

Kids with Asperger's really do have exactly the same symptoms as Rain Man but not nearly as extreme. Thus, these kiddos are able to survive school or home life with far more ease than Rain Man would have. Keep in mind, however, like anyone on the autism spectrum, kids with Asperger's will show some variability depending on their location on that slider bar. Some kids with Asperger's slide more toward Rain Man's end (or, have more severe symptoms), and some slide away from Rain Man. But for those who are more toward the lower end of the spectrum, school in particular can be a place where they excel. In fact, these students may actually be the brightest kids in the classroom!

The reason such a child may perform at high levels has to do with how his or her brain works. Think about a computer as a good analogy. For folks on the autism spectrum, their mind works similar to a computer. It is logical, sequential, linear, data-driven, and tends to mimic a flowchart. I say more on that in a few pages. Suffice it to say that kids and teens with Asperger's can have laser-sharp focus on topics in which they are interested. And boiling the pieces and parts down to their bare essence, without the background noise of emotions and social convention to distract them, these kids can be sharp as a tack, particularly in the areas of mathematics and science.

And I'll go one step further. The main goal on which we set our sights when we treat kids at the Asperger's end of the spectrum is to just help them *survive the social aspects of childhood!* For many of these clients, if we can just help them limp through the dangerous waters of the elementary school, middle school, and high school social strata, they will end up fine. Once they get out of high school and go to work or get to college, if they choose to pursue higher education, they will be fine. They will become comfortably isolative and excel in mechanics or engineering or in a lab doing research in math, chemistry, or computers. Whatever the case, they will arrange their life to minimize interactions with other people. In other words, they will attack with their strengths and have a high probability of success.

To further illustrate what I am saying, the world right now is actually run, pretty much, by a fellow who seems from afar to have many of the symptoms of Asperger's syndrome. Who, you may ask? Well, think about the person who has more power than, perhaps, anyone on earth. He is a person who has his hands in nearly everyone's cookie jar and can make changes to how we live our lives at the stroke of a hand.

That man is Bill Gates. Don't believe me? Think about it: How many times per day, hour, or minute do you see Donald Trump's mug on television? Probably too many! But how often do you even catch a *glimpse* of Bill Gates on TV? Next to never, I would imagine! That's because as undeniably brilliant as Bill Gates is when working with computers, he is remarkably uncomfortable in social settings. It takes him out of "his game." Bill Gates has extraordinary power and strengths despite his (apparent) social limitations. And although being the richest and most powerful man on earth probably has its perks, I would imagine that high school was difficult for him. I recommend the *Bill Gates A&E Biography* (2006) for more info on his incredible life.

So finding a way to help kids with Asperger's syndrome understand themselves better and weave their way through the landmines of being in school can pay off in the long run. Still, due to the nature of the autism spectrum disorders, these kids will still bring a couple challenges to the home and the classroom that should be treated a little differently than you would with your other kids.

There are really two issues that will be particularly unique to the student with Asperger's. For starters, recall some of the outrageous social faux pas that Rain Man made. Relationships were impossible not only because he avoided them, but also because he had a hard time "fitting in." The things he would do and the expressions he would give were immediate beacons to the world around that he wasn't like the "rest of us."

Now, take that same concept and step it down a notch. Kids with Asperger's may or may not have a desire to mingle with peers, but if they do, these social interactions are going to be fraught with problems and ultimately lead to acting out behavior as the kiddo with Asperger's becomes more and more frustrated.

To illustrate, I'll talk about one of my favorite Asperger's clients of all time, Andy (whose name and a few of his characteristics have been modified slightly to protect his identity).

Andy first came to me a few years ago when he was a fifth grader at a local elementary school. His parents were fairly well off and tried to become very knowledgeable in the area of Asperger's because of Andy. For this reason, I would act more as a "collaborator" with his folks, as I had an educated and cooperative ally in his treatment (a novelty for most therapy clients). Still, at times, they would reach an impasse with Andy and would need my help to come up with a creative solution because they were a bit too close to the situation.

I talk more about one of these examples when I cover the second issue kids with Asperger's bring to the home and classroom. For now, let's stick with Andy's social problems.

Because Andy had Asperger's, he had a hard time establishing connections with the kids around him. Still, he was far enough away from Rain Man on the continuum that he knew he *wanted* to have a few buddies.

Before I complete this anecdote, you need to know one more thing about Andy, I use him as an example specifically because he is my favorite client with these issues and he has a couple quirks that are very similar to those of Rain Man, thus making it easy to use him to demonstrate a point.

All folks on the autism spectrum have a "go-to thing" they use to calm themselves under stress. Rain Man recited "Who's on First," if you recall; some kids are more physiological and wave or rub or flap their hands. Some rock their upper torso slower or faster; some may have a blanket or stuffed animal or article of clothing that they will stroke or clutch for tactile comfort. Andy, like Rain Man, had a recitation as his "go-to thing."

While it was no "Who's on First," Andy had an entire episode of *SpongeBob SquarePants* memorized ... and it would even include commercials! For my money, there is no better form of entertainment than hearing Andy hammer that baby home! I found this quality of his to be absolutely delightful, but on the other hand, I am not a 10-year-old classmate, so perhaps my perspective is a bit skewed.

But it's not that nobody liked Andy in his class. He was a bit of a know-it-all and not afraid to point out the faults of others, but for the most part, he was harmless. The one word that I most often hear from classmates to describe Asperger's students is, "weird." Andy was no different in his classroom or his neighborhood. His peers don't hate him, but he's perceived as quite odd, and, therefore someone to be cautious around. Plus, his oddities make the kids around him feel uncomfortable, so they end up avoiding interaction with him. In the end, nobody tends to play with the "weird kid."

Let's get back to Andy's social struggles, specifically. Here is (metaphorically) what would happen repeatedly in Andy's life: He would begin to approach a group of other fifth grade boys on the playground, which would immediately put them on high alert. They may have held their ground for a few beats, but they certainly began to get their hackles up internally. *"Oh geez ... here comes Andy. We're* supposed *to play with him"* may have been whispered among them.

Andy, who was already in uncharted waters with his initial approach, now really began to feel anxious. So, he launched into the only thing he's got: *SpongeBob SquarePants*, Episode 712 (or whichever one it was)—all the dialogue, none of the emotion.

Now, what do you suppose happened to that group of fifth grade boys? Yes, sadly, they would usually bolt. A little wisp of smoke was all that was left where they had been standing. Andy would be left rejected and frustrated. And that was one of the issues that brought him into therapy: He would have bad tantrums as he fought to contain some of the frustration spilling over.

So here is one intervention you can initiate. If you pull your "Andy" aside on a somewhat regular basis and give him or her some social skills training, you can have an impact. I understand, of course, that you do not have the same luxury of time or structure that we have in our therapy office. We run social skills groups where the kids can practice with each other and go through the repetition they need for the changes to begin to stick.

There are two things to bear in mind with this suggestion: First, as I alluded to previously, these kids will need a *lot* of repetition. They do not learn through observing others like you and I do. We can pick up pointers not only through direct experience but also through watching others succeed or fail. Thus, the amount of exposure it takes for a lesson to be learned by us is sharply reduced. Kids with Asperger's are not as quick on the uptake in this area.

Second, bear in mind that these kiddos will need to be nudged in directions that you and I take for granted. Simple, subtle social "rules of engagement" need to be taught. Remember the handshake example? Or how about this one: How far away do you stand from a person to whom you are speaking? For most of us, this is a no-brainer. For a kid with Asperger's, personal space may be a rule that is totally lost on him. So, we coach: "When someone you are speaking to backs up a step, you don't keep moving forward. They are trying to establish a little extra space while they are speaking to you."

Social skills training is the first issue kids with Asperger's bring to the classroom or the home and the first point of intervention you have to truly make a long-term difference. The second issue has to do with that computer analogy again.

A computer basically works as a series of flowcharts. You've all seen flow charts, right? They list a series of "if, then" statements and "yes/no" questions, and as long as the decision boxes never hit a wall (or a "no" as the answer), the chart keeps right on flowing. The brain of a kid with Asperger's works in much the same way. It is data driven, and the chart needs to keep flowing.

If ever the kid hits a wall and the flowchart comes to an end, he is forced to either adjust—to move in a different direction and start up a new series of if/then and yes/no—or drop that series entirely and go to a different flowchart. Here is the rub: If a person with Asperger's reaches that wall, he can make a decision that is terribly far from where you need him to be.

I mentioned a bit earlier in this chapter that Andy and his folks would occasionally get to an impasse, during which his folks would get extremely frustrated, and they would need me to help them see their way clear of the wall. One of the issues that created an impasse with Andy's folks (and his teacher) was when Andy decided he was not going to do a rather significant English assignment.

I, being the astute and resourceful clinician that I am, asked a provocative and insightful question of Andy: "Why the heck aren't you doing your English assignment?" Brilliant! His answer was very telling, however, and taught me a good lesson about the legendary sense of stubbornness that kids with Asperger's can have. He said, "Because when I'm 35 years old, nobody will care if I have done this assignment."

I was flabbergasted for a second as I tried to come up with a witty retort to his proclamation. But in the end, his logic was watertight; when we are grown-ups, nobody actually *does* care if we have completed the English assignment for Mrs. Drayna's sixth grade class. So, we cannot use pure "logic" to work our way around that flowchart wall.

And with Andy, as with many kids with Asperger's, his unwillingness to do the assignment was a purely data-driven decision. It was not about defiance or anger or any of the "traditional" reasons for our lovely children to not do what they are supposed to do. When I talked to his dad about this later, I called Andy "a mule sitting on the freeway." He would sit there, quite content, with traffic flying around him at 80 miles per hour … and that was okay with him. He was sitting there because that was what he decided to do. Sitting there made the most sense. Cut and dry, that was it.

So, we need to help nudge these students toward adjusting their flowchart by using a technique that forms an umbrella over simple logic: We *build a broader structure.*

Let me explain.

Andy is not old enough or experienced enough to understand the "big picture" of any grade school assignment. It feels completely random, or arbitrary. To him, there does not seem to be a long-term upside to doing the assignment, so he isn't going to do it. For right now, it seems to Andy that the teacher gave it to him just because she gets paid to make his life miserable. To you and me, we see that this assignment is not an isolated event; rather, it is a piece to a puzzle that will eventually lead to a payoff.

Here's how I conveyed that to Andy. One of the walls in my office is a whiteboard. I walked Andy over and did something pretty simple but effective in the long run: I drew two islands on the board. On one island, I drew Andy at 10 years old, sitting here today in my office looking at me like I'm strange for having drawn him as a crude stick figure. On the other island, I drew him at age 35 (still a stick figure, but a little larger). Between them, I drew a bunch of circles that represented stepping stones.

I asked him what he wanted to be when he grew up, and he answered (in his 10-year-old voice), "a biogeneticist." As it turned out, he wanted to clone himself and eventually rule the earth. I gave him that one and started to move backwards, on the stepping stones, from age 35 toward the present. I started by noting that, to become a biogeneticist, he probably would have to go to college. He reluctantly agreed, so I wrote "college" on the stone nearest to his 35-year-old island. Next back, I predicted that in order to go to college, one probably has to get through high school. Again, he agreed. We kept working our way backwards until we found that doggone English assignment resting on one of the stepping stones nearer the present-tense island.

Now for you and me, that exercise seems to be too simplistic to actually work. With Andy, however, it had a *freeing* effect. I could almost hear the wheels turning in his head as he took in the whiteboard. Now, that English assignment fit into a whole different flow chart—one that led directly to his long-term goals. For him, that assignment was no longer "random" or "arbitrary" but a rung on a ladder. In other words, it fit into a "broader structure" for Andy. This freed up the flowchart, and he was able to again move ahead.

Make it make sense, and remember to think like a computer. And to "make sense" means that it has to appeal to the mindset of the child or teen with whom you are working. Each of them has a unique perspective on the world, and unless you try on their glasses for at least a little while, you will not be able to reach them in a meaningful way.

There is actually a third issue that an Asperger's kiddo may bring to the home or classroom setting, and it is a little like stubbornness. With this one though, neurochemistry makes a return to our discussion.

In the brain of any person on the autism spectrum, and kids with Asperger's are no exception, there is almost invariably a chemical imbalance. This imbalance particularly involves a neurotransmitter called *serotonin*, which makes these folks lean naturally toward anxiety (McPartland, J. & Klin, A., 2006). Some kids have higher levels of anxiety than others, but anxiety will be an issue with which each will have to learn to cope. In fact, in the family history of these kids, you can trace an almost direct path of relatives who have likewise struggled with symptoms of anxiety—even if they were not on the autism spectrum.

With kids who have high levels of anxiety, you may see them occasionally go into "vapor lock," whereby they seem to be "stuck" and cannot move ahead with their task at hand. For example, a teacher with whom we had consulted asked about a client of ours whom she had in her classroom. This student was taking a midterm exam in Geometry class and had 80 minutes to complete the task. Question number one led with an instruction for the students to draw a triangle and then to perform some operations with it. The student in question took the entire 80 minutes to draw and re-draw his triangle—he couldn't *not* draw it perfectly. He spent his time obsessing (literally) over being perfect in his rendering.

That "loop" in which he was caught was a function of neurochemistry, and must be treated medically. We have to adjust his chemistry to allow him to unlock and move forward. And it is not all or none—brain chemistry has fluctuations, and when these kids hit a high or low tide, it can have serious implications. There is not much a kid can do to break out of that loop once it has begun.

Because of this symptom, some kids with Asperger's, particularly those who lean more toward the Rain Man end of the slider bar, are at times mistakenly diagnosed with *obsessive compulsive disorder*. And do you remember how Rain Man *had* to have everything in perfect order? Kids with Asperger's may have a touch of that trait as well.

Before moving from autism spectrum, there are a couple of other autism diagnoses you may bump into. They are exceedingly rare, so I only mention them in passing. They are *Rett's syndrome* (girls) and *childhood disintegrative disorder* (boys) (APA, 2002). These are the male and female versions of roughly the same issue: These are children who develop normally until they are 2, 3, or 4 years old and then backslide into an irreversible state of autism. If you work with kids older than this age range, this disorder will have run its course, and the kids will appear autistic (with a couple exceptions that are unique to each of these disorders). Tuck these names into the back of your mind, as you may hear them from time to time. In my travels, it appears that more professionals have bumped into Rett's than childhood disintegrative.

That is all I have to say about autism spectrum disorders. Anything more would be beyond the scope of a book like this one. For now, I briefly hit on a few other issues that may create some behavioral issues.

Childhood Depression

I want to make a couple of points about childhood depression (APA, 2002). I think I have made reference to it a few times over the course of these first five chapters, so I don't want to belabor the point. To reacquaint though, remember that childhood depression is one of the array of disorders that can *look like* ADHD, in that when kids get depressed, they tend to accelerate rather than slow down.

When a grown-up gets depressed, he or she moves in the opposite direction, the exception being masculine depression, which tends to express itself as irritability, anger, or hostility. Think what a depressed grown-up looks like. He or she tends to look ... well ... *depressed.* The person gets lethargic and droopy, moves slowly, thinks slowly, and feels a sense of hopelessness.

Kids, however, tend to spin out when they are depressed. A depressed kid has all of the natural energy of an 8-year-old, coupled with a big ball of "yuck" in his belly; and that combination leads to more energy. Hyperactivity and impulsivity are hallmarks of childhood depression.

Even for adults though, many of the symptoms of depression can mirror ADD. Many of us have been depressed at one point or another in our adult lives—maybe not a major depression, but the doldrums, nonetheless. If you can recall that time, you probably had difficulty concentrating, you became more impulsive and more emotional, and you could not pay attention to one thing because your thoughts would wander back to the thing driving your depression—all symptoms of ADD, right?

101

Sprinkle in a little energetic nuttiness that most kids naturally have, and *wham-o*, you've got an ADHD look-alike!

However, that is not to say that a depressed child can*not* resemble a depressed grown-up. It would take a lot to suck the life out of a 7-year-old, but it can be done. We have had (I am not making this up) kids in single-digit ages who have come to our office with suicidal thoughts. And some are indeed quite intent on following through with this ideation. If a depressed child looks like a depressed adult, it is a profound depression and needs immediate attention. When we see a droopy, depressed child, we take it *extremely* seriously.

Plus, with prepubertal kids in particular, medication for depression is not an exact science. Nor is it with adults, truth be known. However, the traditional antidepressants don't work in as linear of a fashion with kids' brain chemistry, so professionals with pediatric experience are required here.

Angry kids, hyper kids, and nutty kids are going to afford us the luxury of *time* to deal with their issues. Serious depression is another animal entirely. It brings with it a sense of urgency that the other conditions may not.

Eating Disorders

Traditionally, there have been two eating disorders we have studied and treated: anorexia nervosa, and bulimia nervosa (APA, 2002). Along the way, we added binge eating disorder (APA, 2002). When it comes to discussing the role that eating disorders may play in bad behavior, I narrow our focus to only the first two.

As another point of clarification, I break from the structure I set up in Chapter 2 and actually use the pronoun "she" to refer to those who suffer from an eating disorder. Although I totally understand that there are boys with eating disorders (it is actually a growing population), these are still, overwhelmingly, disorders that affect girls and women (Kotler, Cohen, et al., 2001). In fact, the typical demographic for eating disorders remains white females 14 to 21 years of age. High school and college represent open windows of opportunity for the development of eating disorders, but we have seen younger and younger girls who are referred to us for evaluation of eating disorders. To date, I don't believe we have seen a girl in single digits, but it is no longer unheard of to treat 10- or 11-year-old girls for symptoms resembling eating disorders.

Anorexia Nervosa: Anorexia is a disorder whereby the sufferer does not eat—or at least not much. I do not say too much about anorexia in this book because, frankly, it is reasonably rare. Plus, it is not too hard to spot as a layperson. If you were to have an anorexic girl in your presence, you would probably see it in a second. She would most likely look like a girl who (for lack of a better term) *looks like she doesn't eat.* There are some exceptions in early stages of the disorder, of course, but usually an anorexic girl looks emaciated, gaunt, withered. They do not see themselves in that way, but that's all part of the disorder. (Big word alert: The phenomenon of not seeing themselves as others do is called body dysmorphia.)

Although anorexia is typically easy to spot, it is *remarkably difficult* to treat. Anorexic girls tend to be proud of their "control" (i.e., not eating) and therefore have no motivation to change. Estimates say that about 25% of anorexics will die from the disorder (Herzog, Greenwood et al., 2000), usually from some sort of heart failure due to low or unregulated electrolytes. Anorexia may appear horrific from the outside, but many of these gals choose to go down with the ship rather than change.

Bulimia Nervosa: Because this is a diagnosis that tends to get a lot of press, it is more likely to be misunderstood than anorexia. Therefore, I open this segment with a definition. Bulimia is the eating disorder whereby the girl binges and purges. While not all bulimics purge in the ways we imagine (e.g., vomiting or laxatives; some use overexercise or fasting), there is a common denominator in the binge.

Binging, of course, is eating, and eating *a lot.* A binge is not just going and having an extra cheeseburger at McDonalds.

Rather, it would be like eating an entire cheesecake or a half of a turkey, or a box of cereal and a half-gallon of milk, or a loaf of bread at a single sitting. A binge can be legendary in proportion.

Following the binge comes the purge, and this is where it really heats up. This is where the girl will "absolve" herself of the binge. A purge means to get rid of the food.

Vomiting is the most common form of the purge, as it is relatively easy to complete and arguably the most efficient means of removing the food. Some girls who are "good at" making themselves vomit can initiate a gag reflex simply by thinking about it—they no longer need to mechanically manipulate their throat with a finger or other object. The trigger that controls the gag reflex can become very loose and cease to need physical stimulation.

But, as mentioned previously, vomiting is not the only method we have seen come through our office over the years. Some prefer laxatives (we have had clients who have eaten Ex-Lax by the bar each day), some will abuse or overuse diuretics, and some will utilize a method we have seen picking up some steam in our corner of the world: compulsive exercise.

Exercising is not only socially acceptable, but it is actually socially *reinforced*. In order to understand how exercise can play a purge role in bulimia, you have to understand one other thing about the disorder. Bulimia is sort of like the coming together of *addiction* and *obsessive compulsive disorder*.

The "addiction" piece of bulimia comes from the reason the disorder exists in the first place: Girls use the binging and purging to manage and contain bad feelings—similar to any addiction. Bulimic behavior becomes the dam that holds back the swell of anxiety or other demons lurking in the background. If you are not bulimic, this doesn't seem to make sense, but that's the deal.

The "obsessive compulsive" aspect comes into play when we discuss the binge and purge, in that they typically involve some sort of ritual and are nearly cast in stone. When a bulimic girl gets onto the treadmill, she will probably have calculated *to the calorie* exactly what she "needs" to burn. And she is *not* getting off the treadmill until she hits that magic number. Other binge and purge routines will, similarly, have "rules" surrounding them.

Now here is where the eating disorder can play a role in acting out behavior. If, for whatever reason, the girl is not allowed to complete the ritual, she will begin to spin out. The dam she uses to contain and manage bad feelings begins to crumble, and the result is spillover of *yuck*. Maybe she was kicked off the treadmill after a certain number of minutes, maybe someone walked into the bathroom when she was about to vomit, maybe somebody unexpectedly invited themselves to lunch with her, maybe she was around other folks and could not binge like she needed to ... something happened to interrupt that routine. Now, she will have all the anxiety of not being allowed to finish off her OCD routine coupled with all of the negative feelings she has been trying to squeeze down via the binge-and-purge cycle; that combination will spike her anxiety to the point that she may not be able to control it.

Hence, bad behavior may ensue. She may need to get kicked out of her classroom or sent to her bedroom so she can purge (for example, she can hit the bathroom on the way to the principal's office), or she may just start acting out because she is feeling burdened with mounting pressure.

The problematic feature of bulimia from the standpoint of a parent or teacher is that it is a lot harder to spot these girls. What does a bulimic look like? She looks like everyone else—these are normal-looking girls who seem to be just living their lives, but they are living in desperation. From my perspective, bulimia is far nicer than anorexia in that it is easier to treat. Bulimic girls *hate* being bulimic—they feel comorbid depression and shame almost every single time they binge or purge (Walsh, Roose, Glassman, Gladis & Sadik, 1985). Shame is a wonderful motivator, and we therapists take advantage of it as leverage to help pull these kids out of the mess they are feeling inside.

Because of the shame, the bulimic girl is reluctant to let anyone in on her "dirty little secret." In fact, if anyone knows, it is her best friend who has already been sworn to secrecy—or who may be engaging in the exact same behaviors. Therefore, any acting out behaviors may seem like they are straight out of left field to you. Girls who had been just fine and firing on all eight cylinders prior to these episodes may start acting in ways contrary to what you expect and without explanation. In fact, these kids may have been models of civility prior to the new incidents, because bulimics tend to naturally lean a little toward the compulsive side.

Let me talk about one more thing before leaving this section entirely. A final undercurrent that can lead to behaviors that will puzzle you is *aggression*.

Aggression

Are girls mean to each other the same way as boys are mean to each other? I think we can all agree that the weapon of choice for our boys to act out anger is often a good old-fashioned knuckle sandwich. In a nutshell, it seems pretty clear that boys are not too subtle when it comes to conflict resolution, right?

But then there are our girls. The weapon of choice for girls tends to be *words*. "Bullying" in a more masculine manner is on the rise among girls, but social isolation and emotional torture are still mainstays and very much in order when girls go at it. In the eye of the hurricane tends to be a ringleader—a *mean girl*. The problem is that the mean girl is probably sweet as an angel when grownups are around, but sinister and heinous when she is around her peers.

Here is my point in this section: Most of the time (and, yes, there are exceptions), if a boy is being picked on, he learns fast that he has to bloody somebody's nose or else he is going to be picked on for the rest of his life. Boys will act out, and once again, be reasonably easy to spot.

Girls, however, tend to turn victimization inward. They will develop anxiety and/or depression and may start to act in ways you could not anticipate or explain. The girl who was *never* a problem in the past may start to miss homework assignments or have her grades drop or act out against "safer" peers. The culture of aggression between girls remains hidden and thus is harder to identify.

So my advice: Keep your ear to the ground with your girls. There may be an undercurrent of hostility being played out behind the syrupy cover of niceties. There is a great book called *Odd Girl Out* (Simmons, 2002) that details this phenomenon in a user-friendly and readable way. That book should be read by anyone raising or working with girls and particularly the adult males (who may be shocked to find out how girls do these things to each other!), as they will need to understand how this process works. Most women know *exactly* the score of the game because they lived it in their own childhood.

Chapter 6
The Ten Commandments for Initiating Behavior Changes
Basic Guidelines for Maintaining Control

I use these "commandments" as a connector to build a bridge between the two foundations of a strong behavioral management plan. The first part of this book discussed the kids and you. What is the relationship potential that can grow between you? The remainder of the book is dedicated to the positive reinforcement aspects of PBS.

Let's discuss the ten commandments for initiating behavior change!

1. All behavior has meaning.

I'm sure you have heard the suggestion to "distinguish between the child and the behavior" before, right? In technical terms, we refer to this concept as "symptom estrangement" (Redl, 1972).

When it comes to dealing with a troubled or troublesome child, ask yourself the question, "Is this a bad kid, or is it bad behavior?" The way you answer that question is extremely vital to your dealing with the kid, as it speaks directly to *prognosis*. Let me explain what I mean.

If your answer is that this is a "bad kid," you pretty much kill much of the motivation you may have to initiate change, because you have very little hope for him or her to ever get better. Let's use a shirt as a metaphor. If it is a "bad kid," it is almost like the problem is woven right into the fabric of the shirt—not much chance of getting that out, right?

Now, let's say you answer that important question by noting that the kiddo is demonstrating "bad behavior." Continuing with the shirt metaphor, it's as if the problem is like a ketchup stain on a shirt. You rub a little Spray 'n Wash® or go ahead and Shout® it out, and the problem is resolved. There exists *hope*, because bad behavior can be unlearned and more appropriate behaviors learned instead.

Behavior—good or bad—does not randomly happen. It all contains meaning for the person performing the behavior. This meaning may not be at a conscious level for the child or teen, but it does motivate (or, push) the behavior. To you, however, it may *feel* like the behavior does happen at random because as adults, we are not always in a position to see what may have led to it. All we see is the acting out, and we are forced to deal with the consequences. The better you position yourself to understand the *why* of a behavior problem, the better off you'll be to redirect the energy.

2. Change bad behavior before it happens.

At risk of going to the well with this advice once too often, I present it for the sake of posterity one more time: If you nip the bad behavior on the runway, it never has a chance to take off into the majestic open skies of your eventual insanity!

It is easier to diffuse a bomb than it is to clean up the room after the explosion. Whatever the consequence happens to be (hurt feelings, a bloody nose, negative attention seeking), collateral damage will not materialize if you control the context and never let acting out occur in the first place.

This is especially hard to do in a classroom, because if you are a teacher, you are trying to wrangle the other 23 students in the room. But continue to train yourself to ask what happened just before the behavior. Is there some way you can structure the experience of this particular kiddo to keep the bomb from going off? Work it as best as you can—everyone around the kid will benefit from not having to deal with the behavior problem.

3. Remain physically engaged: Make eye contact, use physical proximity, and say the child's name.

You get people's attention when you are physically engaged! More importantly, though, you *keep* attention when you *remain* engaged. Use your physical proximity as a tool in maintaining order. If a child begins acting out, move toward him or her to put the child on notice. Even placing a hand on a shoulder or tapping lightly with a forefinger on the child's desktop can be an unobtrusive means of sending the same message without calling him or her out.

Plus, remember that as you begin your behavioral planning, you must not forget the relationship-building process. Using eye contact, using the names of your kids, and using touch or proximity are all signs of *respect*.

I know a lot of you have a concrete set of rules with your kids. Come to think of it, I hope that *all* of you have rules for your kids. My guess is that one of those rules pertains either directly or indirectly to respecting others, respecting you, respecting property, etc. Kids will have an easier time knowing how to behaviorally manifest respect if you model respectful behavior, and the three means of engagement listed in the title (eye contact, physical proximity, and using student's name) are all good examples.

I don't mind when teachers or parents use nicknames of students when addressing them, but overall, I tend to like using formal names best. When addressing older kids (perhaps middle school and high school for certain), a more proper "Mr." or "Ms." when talking to kids may set a good precedent. It imparts some status on them while also reflecting the manner in which you expect to be addressed.

You can even balance respect with familiarity if you use the title (Mr. or Ms.) with the child's first name rather than his or her last. The result will be less formal and may have a bit more bounce to it. In the end, an exchange will sound something like, "Mr. Jason, please bring me that rubber band," or "Ms. Amber, might I see the note you were about to pass to Ms. Tiffany?"

4. Give kids an opportunity for positive interaction.

This one may be another that falls into the "Yeah, no kidding— really?" category. But, we tend to forget when we get frustrated that we actually become surrogate parents to some of the difficult kids in our classes or therapeutic settings. As I am sure you have surmised by this point, some children do not come from households that have a lot of room for nurturing or guidance. So, you step into an important—dare I say, *critical*— role for these kids and have an opportunity to begin changing the rules.

Think about friends or even authority figures in your life. In fact, step that down a notch and think about some clerk you just met at Sears®. Aren't you far more motivated to engage and deal with a person who seems to care about you? I'll never forget some of the truly wonderful people I have met over the years. By the same token, I can recount a number of horror stories about schlumps I have met who have actually made living my life more difficult *just by being a part of it.*

Let me expand upon the preceding example. When I walk into my local Sears® store, I can usually size up in about 6 seconds which employees are the ones who have been hired just to fill space. They tend to be obvious, even though they probably think they are stellar workers. On the other side of the coin, I feel really good when I meet the employees whom a boss wishes he or she had ten more of. Good employees are hard to come by and harder to keep, but hopefully good role models for kids are more common.

Most everyone is motivated to please those who make us feel good. The guiding philosophy is that you are more motivated to make a person happy if they make you happy. Children react the same way. A solid relationship provides firm footing for that positive spiral to begin spinning.

5. Watch your words! Kids may have heard and internalized negative messages from adults before you.

On the surface, this one seems like a reiteration of a rule most of us carry with us anyway. We never set out to treat a child badly or dress him down. Still, there are a couple subtleties to bear in mind that may come across as negative or unkind, thereby leading to a greatly diminished motivation on the part of kids.

First, I hearken back to our discussion of sarcasm a few pages earlier. For those of you who use sarcasm to interact with your kids, remember the two crucial elements of a sarcastic remark. To be successful, sarcasm relies on *tone* and *timing*. In fact, sarcasm by definition is rather cutting in nature (e.g., "Hey kid … *nice shoes!*" or "Is this handwriting, or did a chicken with blue feet walk across the paper?"). If you have a good rapport with your kids and are in control of tone and timing, you can get away with a sarcastic comment as leaning toward playfulness or jocularity.

But if you are having a stressful day or are in one of those grouchy places we all go to once in awhile, you are not as in control of your tone or your timing as you think you are. In fact, what may sound funny and endearing while it is rattling around in your head, but may actually come out of your mouth with a sharp edge. You may hurt a kiddo without even meaning to.

Even if you are having a good day, your child may be having a bad one, thereby rendering him or her vulnerable to misinterpreting your attempt at levity. He or she may not be able to weed through the subtle quality of your sarcasm and may be more prone to taking it literally. Younger children who are still concrete in their thinking may be totally unaware of the double-edged nature of sarcasm and thereby not get it at all.

So if you are feeling "off" on any given day, I advise you to pull back on the sarcasm. Save it for when you know you will be able to use it as a relationship builder! I'm sure I am preaching to the choir with this one, but your tone can say a lot of unintended things to your kids. This brings me to my second point.

Recall that the "bad kids" are given that label early in life, and adults can inadvertently be quick to reinforce that label, not only in tone but also with something as subtle as facial expression. When you are tired, frustrated, and sick of dealing with a kiddo or two, your tone and expression may be off-putting even when the kids are not acting badly.

Yes, this is easy for me to say because I am not down in the trenches with you. Remember to pay attention to the way you communicate with the kids, even on a nonverbal level. The "bad kids" will pick up on your distaste and will begin to exploit it— they are darn good at being "bad kids."

6. Balance work with play.

I'm sure most of you do special stuff for and with your kids. Play is the fun part of life and gives the kids a chance to unwind with you and/or their siblings or buddies. Special things are important in the context of this book because they hit both ends of PBS—they build the relationship *and* they are positively reinforcing.

Play can run the gamut from big events to smaller, special interactions with a parent (i.e., pizza parties, fun days, renting a special movie, playing H-O-R-S-E in the driveway). The point is that forms of play are important to incorporate. Kids need to feel that glow of acceptance or being special.

7. All behavioral plans need consistency to gain traction and be successful.

I know you've heard thousands of times that you have to be consistent, right? Sure you have. It's sort of a trap we like to set so we can look smart. Here is how the trap works.

We tell you that 100% consistency is the only way that a good behavioral plan can flourish. So, you go out and try it and, of course, fail miserably at being consistent 100% of the time. Then, when you call us to find out what may have gone wrong, we can always tell you that it is because you were not consistent 100% of the time. We end up having a built-in good reason to tell you why it didn't work without really having to do any work ourselves.

But here's the reality of the situation: *Nobody is consistent 100% of the time!* What a lot of adults end up doing, though, is falling into a different sort of trap. That's the one where they *think* they are consistent but are actually giving one warning after another without any follow through. Another problem is to have kids perform well over and over without the agreed-on re-enforcers being introduced. Kids learn that game quickly and will exploit it and you.

I close this one out with a word about keeping promises. I am sure all of us have made a promise that we just kind of forgot about after a couple weeks. Here's the deal: Do your kids ever forget? No! They live to trip you up on a deal you struck with them in an unguarded moment then hoped would slide .between the cracks!

Promises can create some levity when the kids catch you in a moment of "Oops!" But on a deeper level, following through with promises serves a more profound function for some kids.

Again, I am speaking of the tougher kids in your life. Kids can approach life, relationships, school, etc. with a cynicism that is born of harsh reality. For them, the relationship you forge with them *must* be based on trust—trust that comes from following through on what you say you will do. Walk the walk, not just talk the talk—you know what I mean? Tough kids have learned that grown-ups are not to be trusted—that if a promise is made, it almost invariably will fall apart in the end, usually when that kid needed it the most.

With many of our kids, opportunities for building trust are like buses; if you miss one, another will come along soon enough. But for the kids who have been pulled through the keyhole of life, the next bus is a long way off. If you do mess up and drop the ball, it may be worthwhile to back the truck up, apologize, and process what happened. Then you can work together to forge a plan to make it right. Parents, teachers, and therapists are human, too, right?

Be the change you wish to see in your tougher kids and teens. Make and keep promises so that level of trust can develop. And if you break your word and there is not some follow-up to make it right in the kid's mind, you may lose that kid forever because now you are "just like everyone else."

8. For teachers and parents: Recognize possible learning problems—help the frustrated child.

Not being an educator by trade, this is the one area I am least versed in and thus the least able to give concrete advice. You can check out David A. Kolb and his Learning Styles Inventory for a more thorough discussion (Kolb & Fry, 1975). What I do know, however, is that kids come to the table with different strengths and weaknesses when it comes to the *how* of learning. What's more, the boys are more likely to act out the frustration they feel if their learning style is not matched by your teaching style.

Learning takes place in several parts of the brain, and accessing those parts requires various media. Using speech (i.e., lectures), hands-on experiential exercises, music, art or visual media, repetition, or even some of the ridiculous mnemonic devices we learned as kids (e.g., "H-O-M-E-S" for the names of the five Great Lakes) can dramatically improve a kiddo's retention.

Remember your most favorite teacher of all time? It was almost like the knowledge just fell out of his or her head and into yours. Somehow, that teacher was in complete sync with how you absorbed information. It was osmosis at work in that classroom.

Now, think of the worst teachers you have ever had. Whatever they may have known might just as well have been locked in a vault somewhere in a bunker in the middle of nowhere. There was no way those morsels were ever going to be devoured by hungry students. And by the way, over time, that hunger for knowledge was eventually sated by the complex carbohydrates of anger and disgust.

It isn't just about communication or the ability to be an effective communicator. It is also related to recognizing when your students "get it" and when they gaze at you with those puzzled expressions. You know those expressions; it's kind of like how my kids tend to look at me when I ask them who fed a strawberry Pop-Tart® to the goldfish!

The ability to adjust your game plan to maximize the potential to reach your kids will reduce the frustration and allow them an opportunity to have a positive experience in school. The less awful their experience becomes, the less the likelihood of bad behavior on their part. And, as an added bonus, if you become that most favorite teacher, you may actually be spared some bad behavior!

P.S. Did you all remember the names of the five Great Lakes once I resurrected that mnemonic device? Thought so! And for those of you who didn't cheat and look it up, they are (in order) Huron, Ontario, Michigan, Erie, and Superior—HOMES.

9. Stay realistic with expectations—remain positive and encouraging.

I refer you back to the section on not accepting underachievement. Keep the bar raised for your kids, but be aware that if it is *too high for too long*, they will learn that they can never hit the mark and will give up before they even try. When kids feel trapped on that wheel, they will punish you for putting them on it.

I also want to remind you that with some kids and teens with truly awful behavior problems, success may have to be measured on a different scale. To illustrate this, I always remember the movie *The Miracle Worker* (1962).

The movie was about Helen Keller and her tutor/mentor Annie Sullivan, who took what was basically a feral child and turned her into a well-behaved little girl who eventually learned to communicate through the written word and, later, the spoken word. What makes this even more amazing is that Helen had to overcome the double-whammy hurdle of not being able to see or hear.

I bring that up as a case study because had Annie entered the relationship expecting Helen to immediately stand up and utter, "So nice to welcome you, Mumsy. When is tea?" she would have felt like a failure. Indeed, she would have actually failed. Instead, Annie set goals that Helen could achieve, allowing both Annie and Helen to begin to feel success rather than failure—small increments, like just *holding* a fork in her hand. Helen didn't even have to eat with it right away, for that would have been too distant of a goal. Rather, successive approximations were reinforced and small victories rewarded. Success can be addictive, but only if you have experienced it.

10. Get excited—become passionate. Realize the unique position you have to "change the rules" for kids.

Have you ever been around someone who just simply *digs* what they do? You all know somebody like that, don't you? I'm talking about somebody who carries themselves with a quiet confidence, somebody who just enjoys doing whatever it is they do. That energy—sometimes called a "good vibe"—becomes contagious. It lights up and energizes everyone close by.

On the other side of the equation, have you ever been around someone who is just like a human version of Eeyore? They're the kind of person who sucks joy and laughter out of a situation. They are the type to notice that, when they enter a conversation, suddenly everyone else gets really quiet and starts looking awkwardly down at their shoes. I always think of them as a little ray of darkness in a sun-filled room.

Kids will reflect your level and type of energy. The more surly and Eeyore-ish you become, the more the kids will act that out and send this energy hurling back in your direction. If you don't want to be there, the kids certainly will not want to be there. Granted, not every positive, upbeat, optimistic adult will be met with thunderous applause and fanfare from some of the angry, oppositional darlings. But, the more positive you are, the more the door swings open for good behavior.

Part II

Proactive Strategies Laying the Groundwork

Chapter 7
Determining the Re-enforcers
What Lies Beneath the Surface

Before launching into the behavioral portion of the book, let me take a moment and throw a few concepts out there for you to chew on and apply as we proceed. Bear in mind that the re-enforcers we try to determine in our planning can be as simple as SweetTarts® or more complicated, such as power and control. I address this issue in a moment but begin with the A-B-C model, exemplifying the two basic points of intervention we have at our disposal whenever initiating a behavioral program.

The A-B-C Model

I like the A-B-C model, not only because it very simply illustrates a point, but also because I have very little difficulty remembering how to spell it. Again, this model demonstrates the two windows of intervention that open for us when we think about initiating a behavior plan.

As you have undoubtedly surmised, A-B-C is an acronym, and the letters all stand for something.

"A" Antecedent. Antecedent means *context*.

The first window of intervention we have opens before the behavior even happens. In a nutshell, this point forces you to think about the situational or environmental variables that set the table for the bountiful feast of bad behavior in which we are about to indulge.

If you diffuse the bomb, you don't have to clean up the room after it goes off. From here forward, this is referred to as *intervening at the "A."* Here is an example:

A few years ago, a seventh grader was referred to me. He (we'll call him Jacob) came into my office, accompanied by his rather angry-looking mother, because he had started to act out against classmates. He was being disruptive, aggressive, and defiant. Some of this behavior had spilled onto teachers as well but it seemed to be mostly limited to other students. In fact, the crown jewel of Jacob's bad behavior, the *piece de resistance* that had earned him a 3-day vacation at the hands of the principal, was something to behold. His mom took the reigns and told me about this one.

His best friend in the world, James, had injured himself at home about a week prior to the incident and had his ankle wrapped. Nothing too serious, but he got around with a notable hobble. Jacob went over to his best friend and proceeded to kick him, hard—*on the affected ankle!*

When I heard this, I immediately raised an eyebrow and tried to catch Jacob's eye. He kept his gaze turned downward, more a move of embarrassment than defiance. His mom's glare was pretty pointed, as she had *no* problem maintaining eye contact with me, although her glare vacillated between me and the reddening side of Jacob's face.

The other piece of information that is relevant to this example is that Jacob had literally *never* had a behavior problem in the past—quite the contrary until now. I do want to throw in that the ankle-kicking had caught my attention because of the extreme nature of the offense. Jacob was clearly trying to say *something*, but the grown-ups involved (teachers, administrators, and parents) were all busy being angry and didn't bother to try to piece together what was happening in Jacob's mind. Not that I can blame them; it is their job to try to steer Jacob right, and frustration mounts when confusion and defensiveness come together.

What was happening, it turned out, had slid under the radar because Jacob, at age 12, was in middle school. Therefore, he did not have any one teacher for more than 52 minutes at a stretch during his day. Add that to the fact that he had an irregular schedule: It turned out that he did not have gym class on a predictably regular rotation.

Okay, you've got it now: Jacob was having problems in gym class. It didn't take Columbo to solve the mystery, but because the evidence tended to be scattered throughout his week, nobody had been able to piece together the pattern that eventually emerged. Oh, and Jacob, being a 12-year-old boy, wasn't talking. He would rather have taken a sharp stick to the eye than talk to anyone about the trouble he had been having in gym. He wasn't very close to his mom, and his dad was a pretty masculine man, thus making it difficult for Jacob to approach anyone about this topic.

I eventually earned enough trust for him to discuss with me what had been going on. This came at a cost, as I had to agree to not tell his parents. (He eventually did, with me there to smooth things over.) We worked with the school to get him out of the offending gym class, and things in Jacob's world started to get better almost immediately.

Teens and preteens (especially boys) may have a hard time talking to adults about matters of the heart, but they have no trouble figuring out ways to get kicked out of gym class.

I recognize that this has been a pretty clear-cut example of how to spot contextual variables that lead to bad behavior. I also realize that many of the situations with which you will be dealing may be more multifaceted. Jacob came from a good family and had a singular issue driving him crazy. Still, this example shows that we can prevent bad behavior from happening if we are able to control key environmental components.

So, yes, in case you are wondering, after we were able to make an adjustment to Jacob's schedule, the problems began to resolve themselves almost immediately. He had some amends to make with his buddy, James, and we began to cover some different ways to handle conflict, but in the end, things worked out for Jacob.

Sometimes, even a rudimentary tool for helping kids to monitor their own behavior at the "A" can be quite useful. With individual kiddos or in group settings, providing a common language by which kids can define and express complex and ambiguous psychological states (like "anger" or "nervousness") can be a powerful intervention. When we create a common measuring stick, we can clearly delineate current emotional states, therapeutic progress, or personal regression.

For example, use a thermometer to describe/define anger. We can call "0" totally calm and "10" a violent rampage. Then, we define the degrees in the middle, and every kid in that group understands what each is talking about when they report feeling a 6.5 after going home for a weekend visit. What's more, a client or student can proudly report that he used to feel 5.3 when his dad came home drunk but last night he only felt a 5.1! You can congratulate and reinforce this self-monitoring and improvement.

Another metaphor I use for anger in particular is the length of the fuse on a bomb. I tell kids that when they are with me, their fuse is a couple of feet long. I have built enough trust that I can mess with them a little and they are still okay with me. But at school, the fuse may only be 1 foot long. At home, it may be 2 inches long. Our goal in therapy is to increase the length of the fuse so that the kid does not "go off" and damage his health, reputation, or freedom.

Moving right along …

"B" Behavior. With the "B," we don't have a lot of control. This is not necessarily a point of intervention, as the bad behavior is already appearing before your eyes. You may at this position attempt to intervene, but once that horse has left the barn, our only true option is to wait for the …

"C" Consequences. The "C" is the second point of intervention at which you can elect to hit with a behavioral plan. This is the point where you control the re-enforcers and punishers following a behavior (good or bad). Another way this concept has been presented in the past has been to call it a "reactive style of discipline." While this position may not be as powerful as intervening at the "A," it may be your only option while you train yourself to look for the context. And don't fret about being reactive at times—this may be all you've got to work with, especially early on in a management program.

Plus, good behavior should always be reinforced, thus, by definition, requiring an intervention at the "C." Bad behavior should be clipped off at the knee before it even gets off the bench, but good behavior should be reinforced after it has been practiced by the kid.

There are about 11 bazillion examples of consequences or re-enforcers after the fact. For punishers, we have time-outs (or, sending a kid for "quiet time"); detention (in school or out); write-offs/punishments (e.g., write, "I will not make potion out of glue and magic markers" 100 times—this example was my personal all-time favorite); and the ubiquitous "You're grounded!" For re-enforcers, we have treats; parental attention (like shooting hoops with your child or taking one of the siblings along to the hardware store with you); extra time on the computer, video game system, or TV; and homework passes. I address token economies in an in-depth manner later in the book, but let me give parents a quick means to begin stabilizing behavior in the home in a way that emphasizes intervening at the "C," the listening jar.

To use the listening jar, parents need to begin by finding a very small container, roughly the size of a shot glass. Then, gather some sort of "currency" that can fill the jar (kidney beans, marbles, jelly beans, etc). The child's objective is to fill the jar with the currency, and the way they earn the beans is by practicing good behavior. (This can be dovetailed with a warning system, described later.)

Let's say the parent instructs the kiddo to pick up her shoes and put them away. If she does this on the first request, she is rewarded with two beans. If the parent has to issue a warning before asking a second time, the girl earns one bean for completing the task. If a third request is issued, the girl has to still pick up the shoes and put them away, but now she earns zero beans AND she is sent to serve some time away from whatever situation is keeping her from attending to the parent's request.

Success has to be relatively immediate to ensure that the child get the gist of the game and also realizes that she is *capable* of "winning." Kids who get in trouble a lot feel that they can never win, so I instruct parents to MAKE SURE the child wins *that night*. I even tell them to make up stuff for the child to do just so that he or she can earn enough beans to fill the listening jar.

Each successive jar is a little bigger than the one before it, and each reward becomes bigger, too. And that does NOT mean that the parent spends more money—only that the rewards move up the chain toward the "big ticket" items on a child's list. These can include time with you, time with friends, time on the computer, special dinners, etc. You are only limited by your creativity and the child's.

Of course, the last jar is the size of a rain barrel, and the child walks away with a Ferrari when it gets filled!

Whenever we talk about behaviorism, even in generalities, I am reminded that most of us have a rudimentary understanding of the basic courses on behavior theory. When we work with real kids, though—or even *our own* kids—the needs they are meeting and the re-enforcers they seek or require can be far more complicated than a simple food pellet in a Skinner box. If only 15 year olds (or spouses), were as simplistic as pigeons!

For example, we could easily teach a dog to roll over on command, right? Likewise, we could probably just as easily teach a 1- or 2-year-old child the same trick for roughly the same level of re-enforcement. But think about this: Would it be *equally as easy* to get a high school senior to roll over? How about a fifth grader or a first grader? How about your spouse?

The issue I am getting at is that once cognition becomes a variable in the conditioning process, or perhaps once socialization kicks off those good old Freudian unconscious drive systems, the re-enforcers with the most punch become more complicated—both to analyze and to dole out. Providing a food pellet, doggie bone, or piece of candy is pretty easy; however, providing for needs such as attention-seeking, power and control, revenge, and displays of inadequacy is not quite so easy!

Because of this, I have spent a good deal of our time and space in this book describing some of the issues that difficult kids bring to the table. Understanding such children is the best way to equip you to reformulate the relationship in a way that allows for their needs to be met and for sanity to be restored to your life.

I spend the remainder of this chapter discussing some of those more complicated needs that are to be met for many of the acting-out kiddos we help every day ... just before we head out to the parking lot to make sure we have an updated resumé in the same file folder with that completed Home Depot® application.

Goals of Acting-Out Behavior
(adapted from Johnson, 2006)

1. Attention

We start with the easy one: attention. Everyone loves attention! The "good kids," the "bad kids," we grown-ups kids ... all of us want—dare I say, *need*—attention. In fact, if I were to poll the adults across the country and ask the

Family Feud–type question, "Name a reason for acting-out behavior," the number one answer on the board would be "negative attention-seeking!"

Incidentally, I think "to make one's father nuts" would be a close second.

When it comes to attention, don't just consider the kids from bad homes; also consider the kids with two loving parents—they still jockey for position with two or three brothers and sisters to gain the focus of their folks.

In fact, I remember reading when I was in college that, on average, working parents spend less than 30 minutes of quality time per night with their kids on work nights. I recall being somewhat mystified by that statistic. But then I grew up and had kids of my own, and I now realize that many of us are truly in danger of having that be true.

Kids can do the math: What is the quickest, most efficient way to get the attention of an adult when you really, really want it? Acting out/bad behavior, of course! For example, if you want to get Mom's attention—right *now*—and she is busy making dinner, chatting with her sister on the phone, trying to watch the evening news, and take care of your baby brother, what do you do? You do something awful ... to the cat ... with a fork. Now *that* will get Mom to table all of her other activities for a moment and get down to business.

Kids learn that little trick early on and then bring their knowledge of it into every arena of life—particularly in school, where they don't have two or three brothers and sisters with whom to compete but have 23. And in school, they don't have a mom and a dad; they have a single, solitary teacher. So it's GO TIME for the students, and they will find a way to get the teacher's attention when they really want it. The "bad kids" will have more options with regard to the behaviors they have at their disposal.

So kids can turn to behaviors like interrupting, forgetting, or clowning to get attention. And let's not forget that it's not necessarily *your* attention that can feed that need. The other students in the room, other kids in the neighborhood, or other siblings in the home can fulfill that need. In school, behaviors for the benefit of other students can even take on a more subtle nature: It's not always Arnold Horshack (from the TV show *Welcome Back, Kotter*) pulling the infamous "Ooh, Ooh, Ooh!" in the back of the room that can grab the floor. Behaviors like dropping stuff constantly, catching the eye of a classmate, passing notes or drawings, or giving a well-timed chuckle or snort can also draw in the room and re-route students away from whatever the teacher is trying to accomplish.

Remember, even though a good scolding is a negative repercussion, when you are "locked in" with that kid, you have just established a very intense one-on-one interaction in which the rest of the world may no longer exist. What you see as a punisher may actually be a re-enforcer when you intervene at the "C."

One possibly effective intervention for acting-out behavior is to initiate a "planned ignoring" (sometimes called "tactical ignoring") program, during which you essentially cut off the reinforcement (i.e., attention). This is an intervention that is almost always taught at behavior management in-services and seminars but rarely comes with the necessary caution labels. For now, suffice it to say that the targeted behavior must meet certain criteria in order for the planned ignore to even be relevant.

First, it must be behavior that is only *solely* designed to grab attention; it cannot be meeting other needs that may still be fulfilled even if the attention is removed. Second, the behavior must not be one that *has to* be dealt with in a more immediate sense. Behaviors that may be harmful or dangerous or are maximally disruptive are those that cannot be put off for the amount of time required for a planned ignore to take root.

While a planned ignore will work over time, there are a couple of issues inherent to the model that make it very difficult to successfully pull off. Let me just tease you with these for now and hope you keep reading through Chapter 13 when I discuss the pitfalls in more detail.

The other thing I want to bring up in this section is to channel Jay Haley and write about dealing with class clowns in school. Clowning around is a fantastic means of usurping focus in the room and can work to derail both the teacher and the rest of the class. The neat thing about clowning is that it almost doesn't matter who the attention comes from—*anyone* can fill that void. So, it could be the teacher, it could be the kid's buddies (and class clowns are almost exclusively the domain of the boys), it could be the jocks or the girls or the others students in the hallway—it really doesn't matter.

We have all probably had a little class clown in our room at one time or another, right? But you've got to admit, some of them can be pretty talented! Have you ever had a class clown say something so funny but so doggone inappropriate that you literally had to turn your back so the kid didn't see you laughing? The thing that class clowns have going for them that can really be a strength (if only they would use it for good instead of evil!) is that they can probably think pretty fast. A sense of humor requires a Pentium chip upstairs. If a student has an old 486 up there, he wouldn't be able to make the connections or turn the phrase lightning fast to be truly funny.

So, one thing we recommend for class clowns—and really for almost all poorly behaving kids—is to teach them to control and contain their bad impulses and then channel them in a more appropriate direction. If all we try to do is squash the energy these acting-out students bring into our classrooms, eventually it will start to leak out from between our fingers. What I am about to describe can allow them the freedom to express themselves and that energy, while also giving them a skill that they can carry with them outside of the school setting.

So, for class clowns, here is something to consider. It is usually reserved for older students (i.e., middle or high school) whose sense of humor lends itself to this intervention, and secondly, this intervention will only be effective if the student is mature enough emotionally to handle it: You can try to "prescribe the symptom" (Haley, 1993).

Here is what I mean. Let's say you (the teacher) have a class clown who gets too disruptive with his "gift." You sit him down one day and say to him, "Listen, next Thursday when we are all filing in from recess (or changing classes, or whatever), I'll give you 2 minutes of open microphone time. Save up, get some of your best material together, organize it, and let's see what you've got. I don't want to hear it during the class period. Really—get it together for your floor time."

Your goal in doing this maneuver, by the way, is not to hope that he fails. Quite the contrary—you want him to succeed. You want him to impress and entertain the jocks, the girls, his buddies, or you so that now you have a vital tool—*leverage*. Now you can tell him that if he's good next week, you will give him 2 minutes on Tuesday as well. If he acts badly, he is down to 1 minute next Thursday.

And most teachers have 2 minutes somewhere in their schedule to plug the kid in. Whenever we change rooms or situations, it usually takes the kids a couple of minutes to settle in. Take advantage of this! And if the student hands you the line, "Two minutes, that isn't very much" remind him that it *really is!* Have you ever tried to get in front of a group of your peers and be entertaining for 2 minutes? Or worse yet, have you tried to be funny only to find that your joke died a horrific death in front of the group, when a minute can seem like a virtual weekend?

Prescribing the symptom allows the need to be met in a manner that is more appropriate, provides the student a good outlet for the energy, and affords the kid a chance to practice mastery of control and contain. I say more in a little bit.

2. Power

Ah, here is the driving force of many of our angry kids, those delightful children and teens with ODD we have grown to love so much! Those aggressive, defiant, stubborn, oppositional kids!

Actually, my metaphor for these kids is that they are like good hunting dogs. Now, bear in mind that I am from a small town in Wisconsin, where the school absentee rate among students on the first day of deer season can approach 40 or 50%. But deer aside, when you hunt fowl, you have to take a good hunting dog with you.

Let me spare you the hunting lesson and get straight to the point. When you are out shopping for a good hunting dog, you need a test to figure out if a puppy is going to work out or not. So here is what you do: You grab the puppy under the belly and flip him over onto his back. If he jumps right up and looks you in the eye and says, "*Hey!* Knock it off!" you have the makings of a good hunting dog.

What you don't want is a dog that stays on his back, acquiescing to you. You don't want a wimpy dog; you want one with a little bit of *chutzpah* … one that will be appropriately assertive when he needs to be.

Kids with ODD are like those good hunting dogs: They will not back down or back off. If you rise up, they will meet you stride for stride. As you escalate, they will match you in kind. So, to deal with these kids, we have to look at yet another dog metaphor.

For those of you with dogs: Have you ever played with a tug toy with your pooch? Either a tug toy specifically designed to be such, or maybe a piece of rope, or a sock, or whatever? Most of us have. As you try to pull on that thing, what does your dog do? My guess is, the dog clenches his or her jaws, haunches back, and digs all 20 toenails in to the Harvest Gold shag carpeting, right? The harder you pull, the harder the dog adjusts and pulls back. A weird sort of equilibrium is met.

So, how do you get the tug toy away from the dog? Simple: You stop pulling and (*most importantly*) give a little slack. You wait for the dog to relax a bit. Then, as humans are seemingly programmed to do, we yank that sucker away, fake the throw, and feel superior to our canine companions.

But the point is this: If you don't unseat your dog's feet, the dog will never give up the tug toy. You have to get those nails out of the shag carpet. Kids with ODD operate in almost the same way. If you try to push, they dig in. If you try to pull, they dig in. The only way to move them is to unseat their feet by allowing them a little slack.

Here's how we bring that metaphor into your office or classroom. It has to do with giving *options*. Options are important because they offer at least an illusion of power and control. Even options that are really still on *your* terms can give the child just enough room to "save face" in front of his buddies or, at the very least, feel like he is now in control of the pace and/or the direction of the next move.

For a concrete example, let me go back to a school setting. Say you have a student who has been acting out and now has to go to the principal's office. As the teacher pushes, the kid rises up to challenge him or her a little. In actuality, if the teacher continues to push, he or she *will* win the battle—after all, the teacher is the grown-up. In the same manner, you could always rip the tug toy out of your dog's mouth because you are bigger. But what are you doing if you "force" the kid into something and make him feel strong-armed into it? You win the battle but eventually lose the war because you are creating anger and damaging your relationship with him.

A better solution lies in using a bit of finesse. Rather than force the student, offer a choice: "You can go down to Mr. Johnson's office right now, or you can take a few seconds to breathe, and we'll go in a moment."

While this statement still keeps your needs on the front burner, it simultaneously allows Little Johnny some room to look like he was a part of the bidding process. Thus, it can free him up enough to get him moving in the right direction while still maintaining some protection for the relationship between you two.

Oh—and keep the number of options down to two, *maybe* three on special occasions. Too many options can be overwhelming to kids. Worse yet, too many choices can also work to shift the power base to the kid's camp, thereby rendering you powerless. You give a choice, but you are still in charge.

3. Revenge—Bring on the Bullies!

Does this sound like a nightmare you have had at one time or another? It certainly is a recurring one for the frail kids everywhere. Most of us have had some dealings with a bully—either as kids or as grown-ups in our schools, parks, and neighborhoods—heck, even in some homes. Whenever your exposure to a bully happened, it was probably not a pleasant experience. Bullies kind of have that "gift."

Now, I could write a whole book on dealing with bullying behavior, but instead, let me throw out a couple of suggestions to give you something to think about if you are scratching your head and wondering what you may be able to do.

Bullies, almost without variation, are the products of the coming together of two distinct factors: First, they have experienced some sort of abuse at home—physical, verbal, or emotional. Whichever it happens to be, the abuse serves two purposes: (a) It creates anger in the heart of the bully, and (b) it robs him of his self-worth.

The other factor is typically that the bully has some size. Bullies have the genetic influences that allow them to bring the law of the jungle to the playground: "Might makes right, and I am far mightier than thee; thus, I am going to impose my will upon you."

As another aside, I am using the pronoun *he* again in this section. We have been seeing a rise in the number of girls who are bullying like the boys typically do, but by and large, bullying in a physical way still seems predominantly male. Girls, for the most part, bully with words and social exclusion more often than with fisticuffs.

Let's look at the bully's point of view. From a psychological perspective, the bullying behavior is doing a couple of things. First, it is re-creating the trauma the bully has felt in his life— only now, he is putting himself in the power position and putting the victim in the position in which he has been at home. Let's face it: Does the bully usually pick on the linebacker of the football team? Heck no! The bully isn't stupid! He wants to live to bully another day! So, he singles out weaker members of the herd who are more easily dominated, thereby making them exactly like he is compared with his own abuser.

The other thing bullying behavior is doing is giving the bully a sense of being respected by the children he dominates. He fuses and *con*fuses fear with respect. After all, because his self-worth was stolen from him years ago by the grown-ups in his life, he (at some level) does not feel as though he has anything to offer other than his size and strength. In other words, in the mind of the bully, other kids have no other reason to respect him, because he really has nothing else of value to offer (Batsche & Knoff, 1994). If you were to ask him to earn respect any other way, he would feel as though he had nothing to give.

I can imagine you might get fed up with the explanation, "A bully is just a misunderstood kid with low self-esteem." You still have to deal with the fact that he is either creaming or intimidating everyone around him! So, to treat the bullies, we have to approach and deal with them on two separate fronts, each addressing a different aspect of the bullying.

First, and as is the case with all kids with behavior problems, pay attention to the rewards and consequences of the bully's behavior plan. Make it better to be good than to not be good. This will work toward curbing the behaviors on a short-term basis. For longer-term change, we work on the second front.

We can effect tremendous longer-term change in the life of the bully if we can instill some self-worth or value in the kid's sense of identity. This may sound a bit "pop-psych" when I phrase it this way, but there is some legitimacy to this approach.

If (for example) we can make school seem like less of a disaster to the bully and if we can begin to affect the underlying energy that is pushing his bad behavior, we can change the rules of how he approaches the world—and remember that this world includes *you!* To accomplish this task, we have a couple options

To work toward creating a sense of accomplishment rather than an atmosphere of failure in school, we go back to Gardner and his different intelligences. Do you all remember Gardner? He was the fellow who took a look at standardization in intelligence testing and asked the philosophical question, "What the heck *is* intelligence, anyway?"

Back in my day, there was only one kind of intelligence. It was called "*g*" and it was measured quite succinctly on a Weschler Intelligence Test (a WPPSI, WISC, or WAIS). The scores were normalized with a mean of 100 and a standard deviation of 15, and if you didn't fall within two standard deviations of the mean, there was something either very wrong or very right with you.

Along ambled Howard Gardner, and he turned the whole theory of intelligence on its ear. He started to think and write about how people could be smart in a variety of ways—some of which may not even show up on a Weschler test (Gardner, 1983)!

Blasphemy! Clearly Gardner was not a founding member of the Flat Earth Society. But think about it for a moment. Think about some of the smartest people you have known. For me, I think I mentioned before that I grew up in a small town in Wisconsin. My town had its fair share of farmers. The farmers around me, many of whom were either neighbors or the fathers of my friends, would probably not have performed well on a Weschler test. Quite a few did not even finish high school, in fact. But I'll tell you this: If my car broke down, who do you think I called to help me out? Or when the water heater blew in our basement, to whom do think we were grateful to live near? Yeah, the farmers! They were extraordinary when it came to fixing stuff and knowing how to problem-solve. They could figure things out in a way that I still admire to this day!

So ... were they intelligent? Of course! And, that was Gardner's point. So, he came up with a number of intelligences in which a person can be proficient (and the number grows every few years—we're up to 9 or 10, depending on whether you include or exclude "Existential Intelligence"). Some folks are very smart when it comes to music, or art, or sports, or reading other people. Let's bring this back to bullying.

Are the bullies in school typically among the smartest students? Maybe, but maybe not. Look, it is quite possible that these kids may never sit on the Supreme Court. But, they may be really good at tearing down a lawnmower engine, building things, being artistic or athletic, or at other things that they won't admit to because they're "too cool" to engage in them.

Although it often doesn't, the system can work toward building self-worth by creating success in a setting the bully has grown to hate—school. Find activities where he can succeed and allow him to meet a challenge. Perhaps you can create a group project where each participant can contribute based on their unique strengths rather than forcing them to feel the pang of individual deficits.

For example, let's think about English or Literature class. If you create a group project that has students put together a book, you could create a situation whereby the students contribute from a position of strength. So, those who are creative may come up with the concept; the ones who draw well can do the illustrations; those who write well can do the text; those who are more mechanically inclined may physically put the thing together from a gum wrapper, a Fruit Loops box, six inches of reflective duct tape, and a 26-inch shoelace. You get the picture. However you conceive of the project, allowing the students to choose their own piece of the pie can set them up for success.

There is another option, but it is only going to work in certain circumstances. It involves building self-worth by allowing the bully a chance to have others look to him as having something of value to offer besides his strength.

To pull this off, you really have to get the bully out of his current environment (e.g., classroom, neighborhood, group). This is because if the bully remains in his current context and changes begin to happen, with the bully starting to move—even slightly—off of his position as the bully, the rest of the group will work hard to yank him right back into that role. They do this because the only way they are comfortable is to understand him as being the bully.

This may sound like I have ripped a page form the *Bizarro World Daily News*, but hear me out. I'll give an example to which you may be able to relate on a more personal level. Have you ever gone "home" for Thanksgiving? Your parents, aunts and uncles, grandparents, etc. all gather together at this festive occasion. And when you go into this atmosphere, do you feel like you're 12 years old all over again? If your answer is yes, it's because the family system (and all of its members) have a hard time seeing you as a grown-up. They grew really used to seeing you as a kid and now don't see you quite often enough to grant you the dignity of being a grown-up. They will pull you back into that role because the family system is stronger than your ability to resist!

Here's another one: For those of you who may have been rebellious teens, do you feel a little of that rebellion begin to stir whenever you go back into your parents' house? The same principal applies.

In group situations, even if *you* start to treat the bully differently, the rest of the kids will be adjusting at a far slower pace. They will still be avoiding eye contact with him, they will shrink away from him in the hallway if he gets too close, and nobody will hang with him socially. In essence, their fear and loathing will suck him right smack back into being the bully, and order will be restored in the universe.

To effect long-term change, we need to get him out of an environment whereby everyone knows him as "the bully." To ensure success, a few variables need to be in place. First, this option has to be available to you in your particular setting.

Second, the bully has to be emotionally ready to handle it, and this typically works better with bullies who are a little older.

In school, a viable plan might be to take him down to the kindergarteners or first graders and have him read to them, help them with some task or assignment, or coach them at gym class. The point is that you set up a situation where other people can look to him as having something of value to offer other than his ability to beat them up.

Further, this plan works best when the bully is helping little kids, because, for the most part, bullies have an unwritten limit as to how small their victims can be. Once a bully reaches a certain age, he won't pick on the really small kids anymore. Thus, the kindergarteners or first graders may not even know that he is a bully —he is just another big kid coming to mentor or teach them.

Community service projects can also provide a good opportunity for the bully to shine. One situation I have seen work rather well is to arrange to have a bully help work on a Habitat for Humanity house. He will be taught a life skill, see the result of his work (i.e., feel satisfaction and accomplishment), and be mentored by folks with talent and passion. But again, use whatever means you have available to you.

4. Display of Inadequacy

I throw kids with this issue into the mix because they are also demonstrating a lack of self-worth in a different way than bullies. These are kids who do not feel adequate or worthy but do not have the level of internal anger or the physical size of bullies.

In the interest of clarity, I'll be a little more specific as to who these students are. These tend to be the kids who, as matter of course, punt on second down. They are the ones who refuse to try because there is more safety in defiance or self-handicapping than there is in trying your best and failing. That vulnerability (or their belief that they cannot possibly succeed in the first place) is too frightening a force, so they avoid by chopping their own legs out from under themselves.

Another way that this feeling of inadequacy can play itself out behaviorally is in kids' speech patterns. For example, you may know a kid—or maybe even a grown-up—who falls into the category of folks who I call "The Disclaimer People." These are folks who preface every personalized statement (i.e., statements they make about themselves) with a disclaimer, such as, "I know this is going to be wrong, but ..." or "I know you're going to hate me, but ..." or "This is really going to sound stupid, but ..."

Even without a clear-cut disclaimer, anyone can have a speech pattern that indicates an underlying depression or lack of self-worth. These can be kids who are *angrily* brutal when tearing into themselves. They will say things like, "I'm so *stupid*," or, "I can't get anything right" or the all-encompassing, *"I hate myself!"*

As a general rule of thumb, the way we talk belies the way we think. Depressed and anxious people actually think and talk differently than non-depressed, non-anxious people. When you hear speech patterns like these, what the person is effectively doing is opening a little window into his or her mind and allowing you to hear the soundtrack that they constantly hear playing in the background.

When a kid gives you one of his patented disclaimers, what he is hearing in his head is, "You are *always* wrong" or "*Everyone* will/should hate you" or "You *always* sound stupid." Believe it or not, the words that actually make it out of these kids' mouths tend to be a watered down version of what they are saying to themselves. Hey, do you recognize any of the following cognitive distortions your kids may be carrying?

Typical cognitive distortions of troubled kids:

- "Nothing is fair."
- "Everything sucks."
- "Nobody should tell me what to do."
- "I know better than you."
- "Nobody cares."
- "It's your fault."

For these kids, you can make a powerful intervention without a lot of work. Just start to nudge them cognitively and change the way they talk.

Obviously, I don't mean that you should pull the kid in front of a mirror and have him do his best Stewart Smalley imitation, whereby he is forced to recite, "I'm good enough … and I'm smart enough … and doggone it, *people like me!*" That technique would have little effect because it is trying to force a mindset onto the kid that to him feels a million miles off base.

Instead, try a gentler touch. With the kid who uses disclaimers, for example, merely snip off the disclaimer. At first, this requires a firmer hand and a bit more directness in your instruction. Obviously, your goal over time is to have the kid catch himself before the disclaimer slips out.

For kids who are more straightforward or harsher in tearing at themselves, you may have to be completely overt and direct—to the point of having them stop, back up, and restate whatever they were saying from the beginning *without* the self-deprecating remark. If what they say seems too far off, start out by having them repeat (word for word) the slam in a milder or matter-of-fact manner. It sounds a whole lot different when they are forced to pause and actually hear the words coming out of their mouth! Over time, you can push them to eliminate it all together.

Another approach is to begin attacking that demonic musical soundtrack directly. So, provide for the child or teen a mantra to detoxify the negative self-talk. I always start them off with something neutral, such as having them begin a loop of saying, "I'm okay," or perhaps, "I'm good enough," or "I'll get through this" over and over. Use whatever feels right for them: These statements or self-affirmations can reduce the potency of the negative self-impressions driven home by the adults in their life.

If you change the way they talk, you will change the way they think. Over time, this will change the way they feel and the way they behave. This type of technique is called a *cognitive intervention* (Beck, 1987). For you, it can be the difference between a kiddo moving forward with a sense of confirmation of all his or her worst fears or moving ahead with a renewed sense of value.

Before fast-forwarding, I remind you that all of the kids we examined in this chapter still have to go home at night. Whatever environment has set them up to either aggressively seek attention, grab power like a dog with a tug toy, bully other children, or self-handicap, still exists out there in the "real world." Whoever created the mindset in that kid may still be in the home and may be a far-from-helpful element in the daily grind of your client or student. So, the strides you make during the time you have them may be systematically torn down and torn apart while he or she tries to manage at home each night.

Have some patience and remember the oil tanker or the freight train analogy: Some days it may feel like two steps forward, one step backward—and this may be true! The parental/ caregiver forces are usually going to be more powerful than any force you can generate as a therapist, mentor, or teacher— particularly for the younger children. But don't underestimate *your* level of importance in the child's life. Your goal should not be to have a Hollywood ending to your relationship—an ending where you and the kid march hand-in-hand into the setting sun with some Whitney Houston tune playing in the background and everyone is happy, all is well, with dog people and cat people living together in perfect harmony. Rather, you are inching and nudging his trajectory toward a brighter destination.

Chapter 8

Behavior Plan Common Denominators

Finding the Common Ground

Let's get down to business and talk about some of the common denominators of any good behavioral plan (adapted from Johnson, 2006). I also place these under the general heading of, "Regardless of which plan you use, this stuff has to be in place."

Bearing in mind that I discuss several ideas for managing behaviors in upcoming chapters, know that it doesn't matter which you choose: Each of you has a different personality and will feel more comfortable with one plan or another. By the same token, each of the plans is adaptable to your specific situation. All of the plans, though, need to have an umbrella of "behavioral common sense" to protect them from failing miserably! Let's look at that umbrella.

Specific Instructions

1. Make Sure Everyone Knows the Rules

Perhaps the most important rule of all is to have the rules clearly understood by all who play the game. I'm sure you all have rules in your home, therapy office, or classroom. Incidentally, whenever I ask what the rules are in a teacher's classroom, I get examples such as "keep your hands to yourself," "raise your hand before you speak," "come to class prepared," and "respect others' property and person."

I actually chose to include "respect" last on purpose. This is because that concept seems to be the overarching rule that governs all others. In fact, if you could boil all "life" rules down to their bare essence, you would have something like a residue of "respect" left at the bottom of the pot. It is the guidepost for all good behavior, and in fact is the foundation of the Golden Rule ("do unto others …").

I would like to take a moment to remind all of you to break "respect" down into concrete behavioral terms for your kids. An ambiguous term such as *respect* can either be confusing for the younger kids or can begin to morph into all different directions for bigger kids (i.e., how many faces does "respect" wear in any given high school?). So for the sake of clarity, be sure to set aside a couple of minutes at the beginning of your relationship to outline very specifically what *you* mean when you say "respect."

Think about it this way: How do you show another person respect? Usually, there are specific signs such as making eye contact, respecting his or her property by not wrecking or stealing it, not interrupting when he or she is talking, using the other person's name when talking to him or her or referring to that person, and using positive language or words when discussing the person.

I'm sure most of you are doing these things already, but reinforcing them to know you are doing a good job can feel good.

Make sure everyone knows the rules. And furthermore, it is important to let the kids feel like they all have a hand in creating the rules. (I'll explain why in a minute.) In schools, for example, on the first day of class, go through the shell game of making the kids feel like they are moving through the process of developing rules for the classroom with you as the guide.

And I use the phrase "shell game" because it is a bit of a parlor trick to actually create the rules with the students (or with any kids, for that matter!). Some "smoke and mirrors" techniques have to be applied because, as I am sure you already know, you adults tend to have a *pretty good idea* of what the rules are going to look like before you even ask the kids for input. This way, if one kiddo throws out the suggestion that everyone should keep their hands and feet to themselves, and another kid in the back row insists that they need a water fountain that shoots chocolate milk, you can highlight the hands and feet rule and nudge things in that direction.

Having kids feel some responsibility for the "rules of the castle" combines with item #2 to create a base of power for you.

2. Have the Rules Graphically Displayed

This rule is pretty straightforward—have the rules clearly posted on the wall. Now, let me bring in the concepts from item #1 and tell you what I mean when I talk about establishing your power base.

If the kids know the rules, feel a sense of responsibility for the rules, and can see the rules clearly on the wall, it frees you up if there is ever conflict. You do not have to get sucked into the fray because a scenario has been set up where it is no longer the child versus you. Rather, it is the child versus the rules on the wall. You are now free to be above the chaos, and instead of thinking up the rules on the fly, you are firmly in a position to circle around the fray and merely be the *enforcer* of the rules. From a power point of view, this is a superior position.

I know that may have sounded a bit confusing, but here is an example to (hopefully) clarify my position on this one. Let's use another school example: Say you (as the teacher) have a student who is acting out and you are forced to initiate a consequence. Rather than getting sucked into an argument with the kid, which typically starts with him saying something to the effect of, "You're just picking on me," you can back out of the chaos, point to the rules, and say, "No, it's number 6 up there on the wall." You can even throw in for good measure, "... and furthermore, you helped come up with number 6! So don't tell me I'm picking on you!"

Now, the student is against the wall (metaphorically), and the wall becomes an external force that no longer involves or requires your subjectivity. The class has agreed on the rules and can see them whenever they choose. You are freed up and above the din!

I tell parents something similar if they employ time-outs at home. I instruct moms and dads *not* to keep the time if they send their kids to time-out. Rather, they should set an egg timer or the microwave timer to keep track of the time spent. This way, parents can avoid the power play of kids who try to pull this one: "Can I come out now? Can I come out now? Can I come out now ...?

If a kid pulls that out of his bag of tricks, you do not have to descend into battle. Rather, you remain outside of the fray and are able to point out that you have not heard the timer go off, so clearly the time is not over. Instead of your child against *you*, it is him against *the clock*. And from a power perspective, this is, again, a superior position in which to be.

So utilize items 1 and 2 to bring yourself out of the war zone of whichever battle happens to be raging. You are not engaging the kids in battle; you are only monitoring their engagement with the rules on the wall.

3. Have Positive Expectations

I bring this one up for a couple of reasons, and each has to do with maintaining sanity! First, let me open with a brief anecdote that drives home the point that distressed parents often use history to guide their negative expectations—even if they are trying really hard not to. I have changed some of the information in the following example, but hope that the poignancy still shines through.

A while back, I was working with a nutty 6-year-old boy and his single mother. For you therapist-types, you know that often, sessions with parents and kids tend to open with the tales of what went wrong over the past week. This situation was no different, as the mom opened by asking me several questions about serial killers and sociopaths. Of course, I couldn't stop myself from asking what the heck had happened, at which point she gestured angrily toward her son and said, "He killed our fish!"

As it turns out, all four of the family's fish were lined up on the counter, dead as doornails, making it look like a mafia-style hit had happened in the kitchen.

The boy looked like he wanted to disappear into the couch, so I asked what turned out to be a novel question: "Why were the fish on the counter?"

This was novel because Mom, in her fury, had never bothered to ask *why* it happened; history had torqued her to the point of only seeing *what* had happened. When the boy answered my question, it hit Mom like a ton of bricks.

I discovered that the boy had decided the fishbowl was too small, so he wanted to give the fish a bigger place to live. His problem was not devious intent (obviously, there was none) but rather, his order of operations. He had taken the fish out of the tank, lined them up neatly across the counter, and set off to find a bigger fishbowl.

Now, this kiddo has pretty serious ADHD and got into about 14 things in the other room that distracted him from the task at hand. The fish perished in the meantime, and Mom was sent into orbit. Had she taken 30 seconds and reset her compass toward a more positive direction, she may have learned that her son was doing something wildly caring for the fish instead of sociopathic.

Back to the point …

Think about how you begin each morning at home or each class period in school. Do you start the kids off on a positive note? Giving some sort of affirmation, or on a very basic level, saying something like, "Good morning!" can help begin the arduous process of moving some of the troubled kids out of their axis.

I am not Pollyanna-ish to the point of believing that this can shake a bad mood out of a teenager who has had a really tough morning or bus ride or transition in the hallway. No, some kids are really going to struggle within a pretty bleak bubble of space. But, I do believe that your best shot at creating an atmosphere conducive to positive behavior begins with the pace and tone you set at the onset of your time together. Make it a ritual to leave the kids' baggage at the door. Remember, if you don't want the kids there, they certainly won't want to be there, so do your best to create a positive space.

For teachers, I *know* you each get a good feel for how the class is going to be when your kids are strolling in. If you sense a dark cloud over a head or two, do your best to move those kids in a different direction.

And on a related note, do any of you start the day or the class period with a recitation, starting with the Pledge of Allegiance or a prayer or a school slogan or a more formal affirmation? Remember effective leadership: You want to create a special, boundaried space for the tougher kids. When you start the class with a recitation—and it really does not matter *what you are actually saying*—you are encouraging a collective consciousness and getting all the students marching in stride and at the same time. In other words, you are setting the remainder of your time together apart by creating a boundary.

You can use something other than a recitation, and this sort of boundary-setting is not limited to the classroom. Some adults begin each interaction with a kudo or a stroke to engage the child. Maybe they "hit the rock" (knock fists) or high five or smile broadly when the kiddo comes into view. Here is the second reason for starting the day on a positive note: It creates a better chance for your own self-fulfilling prophecy to come true.

By this I mean that your internal expectations have an impact on how you approach a student or a situation. Remember my client with the fish! If you truly believe that today is going to be awful or that one or a few of the kids are going to have you banging your head against the wall, your behavior will be influenced by that line of thinking, and it may not be overt!

A positive table-setting allows you the best opportunity to approach the day fresh and behave in a manner that will maximize the potential for good behavior.

4. Utilize a Warning System When Behavior Escalates

I trust that each of you has a warning system whereby you afford the kids an opportunity to lasso the horse and drag it back into the barn without consequence. I don't mean issuing a smaller consequence before hitting them with a bigger one; rather, I mean truly giving them a chance to practice control and containment before they get the penalty.

By the way, *everyone* knows this rule, but it is among the first to go out the window when parents are pushed to the wall or teachers are confronted with the constant nag of the troublesome student. A quick pep talk may be in order, as well a primer regarding the reason for all of the hubbub.

The more common warning systems I hear about involve either a direct verbal warning ("Justin, this is your first warning") or some progressive steps (such as parents counting to three; teachers writing the name of the offending kid on the board; moving clothespins from green to yellow; holding up one finger, then two, then three).

I particularly enjoy hearing about those teachers who simply stop talking! They grow silent in an effort to stir the pot and get the students to notice. Bear in mind, the humor for me lies in the fact that this system relies on the do-gooders in the front row to hurriedly turn around and issue the more auditory, "Shhh! Shhhhhh!" to their slower-on-the-uptake classmates in the back of the room!

151

As an aside, I always remember the light-flippers in my academic history. You know those teachers—the ones who flip the lights on and off if the classroom as a whole starts to get out of hand. Ah, the good old days.

Warnings are an extremely important part of any behavioral plan, because the opportunity we can give the kids to work on self-control and behavioral containment is a vital developmental concept.

Think about some of the environments from which the kids may be coming as they make their way through the world each day. These kids experience all sorts of parenting styles at home, and for some, the knowledge that they even have the *capability* to reign in their behavior (i.e., control and containment) is indeed a novel thought! For them, control is always externalized. Here's what I mean: Think about kids who come from a home where they have a very punitive, intrusive, and/or overcontrolling parent. Whenever these kids begin to act out, their parent is immediately on top of them, crushing them and their behavior. The end result is that these kids never learn that *they* can be in control—they never have to or get an opportunity to. Over time, they will learn to rely solely on external forces to provide that control for them.

In a classroom or therapy office, these kids tend to be easy to spot because they are the ones who will keep prodding and poking and figuring out how to push your buttons until finally you snap and force control on them. It may feel to you as if they *refuse* to bring themselves down. In actuality, they don't know how to or even that they are able to.

So, giving all kids a chance to practice control and containment without immediate punishment can not only develop a skill, but will also help build a relationship with you because trust will begin to develop in an area in which the kid may not expect it. And by the way, what is the right number of warnings to give before hitting a kid with the consequence? One? Two? Three?

The answer is that there is no magic number. The situation will depend on the kid's age, emotional maturity, and other factors. All of these elements will influence the number of warnings you need to issue, but always bear in mind that it is better to err on the side of low rather than high.

What happens if you start to issue seven or eight warnings before you slap a kid with the consequence? If you give too many warnings, the kids will blow through your yellow lights, because there is never a cop on the other side giving tickets.

Another problem, something I see quite often, is when adults who know not to give a lot of formal warnings will *inadvertently* issue quite a few informal ones. I call this scenario "the mom trap." In the mom trap, many a good, hardworking parent or professional may catch himself or herself staggering warnings throughout a time period. These are warnings that are not labeled as such but still have the power of teaching the kids your rhythm or cadence; for example, if you catch yourself going through something similar to this: "James, sit down … I said sit down ... I—hey—I mean it—*sit down* and pay attention … JAMES … knock it off … okay, this is your first warning!"

Get the picture? You only issued one direct, formal warning, but you actually fired several warning shots across his bow before you even got to the formal warning stage. This has taught James that he can push you to four or five before he even gets smacked with warning number one—and he will take advantage of this knowledge! Kids do the math quite well and will respond to the structure you impose.

Give them the chance to practice control and containment.

I also employ the same technique of reinforcing the control, not the acting out, when I help parents of kids who have temper tantrums. Nothing will unbalance a household like one or more kids who employ tantrums as a weapon or a means of manipulation! I am sure you have all seen a really, *really* good temper tantrum, right? I mean a tantrum that makes everyone walking out of the store say to each other, "Now *that* was impressive!"

Before moving on, let me say someting to the poor parents who are controlled by their 3 year old. Almost all kids go through a tantrum phase while they are developing. They do not have the means to wall off frustration, so it flies in all directions like stroganoff in a topless blender set to *purée*. When this happens the first or second time, it may catch the parent off guard and he or she will swoop in to fix the problem. Now, as they say, the hook is set. The tantrum has been reinforced to the point that it is sealed in as the "go-to thing" for when that kiddo wants what he wants.

For many kids, a tantrum is used as a tool, similar to any device designed to gain control over a situation. The litmus test I give a lot of moms and dads is to provide them with the following directive: Pay attention to your kid the next time he tantrums and notice if he *scans the room* every once in a while.

I ask this, and parents have an "aha!" moment. I also ask the following: "If your child is throwing tantrums at home, does he have them on the linoleum or on the carpet?" For teachers, I ask the following: "If the kid is flipping out on the playground, is it on the pavement or on the grass?"

These questions usually produce a lot of "ahhaas." The best way to treat tantrums is by using the same conceptual approach I described when I talked about warnings. Once again, we reinforce the control and containment but *not* the tantrum.

To do this, we take advantage of one of the wonderful qualities of every temper tantrum. A tantrum cannot go on for very long before the kid has to pause to catch his breath. Tantrums burn energy, and kids cannot sustain them for very long without a brief break—regardless of how fleeting this respite seems. I know I brought this up in an earlier chapter, but the worse the tantrum happens to be, the more this is true.

Now, the first rule of treating a tantrum is that the kids cannot be allowed to hurt themselves. Once that has been ensured, we move into the treatment phase. For this, I remind parents to remove *all* reinforcement from the environment. For example, if you have to move your child, pick him up sideways like a log instead of in an embrace. Don't make the contact reinforcing. Even remove eye contact. If this will be hard for you, grab a newspaper or magazine to hold your gaze.

Now, as soon as the kid pauses to catch his breath, swoop in and reinforce the heck out of his ability to stop himself. This maneuver will invariably kick off another round of tantrums because now he has the attention, but that's okay—again remove all forms of reinforcement and await the eye of the storm. Then, repeat the treatment phase.

This method of weaning a child from temper tantrums emphasizes an opportunity to feel reinforcement during times of controlling and containing. It parallels your warnings system. With warnings, you give your kids a chance to have their capabilities reinforced, which will begin to turn that oil tanker around by giving them another option when it comes to seeking reinforcement—controlling and containing their behavior.

If you are searching for a warning system that will work well, or perhaps you are ready for a change, I recommend one that may seem a bit medieval on the front end but will have some staying power. Let me explain how to use one in a classroom setting, but this technique can work quite well in the home, too.

To accomplish this warning system, first go down to your local pet supply shop, and get yourself one of those clickers that animal trainers use. (For those of you who were hoping I would instruct you to get a shock collar, *shame on you!*) The clickers are small and easy to use and make a very sharp, distinctive noise when you press the button.

Using a clicker has several advantages: First, is is small enough to fit right into the palm of your hand. Therefore, a teacher can be tooling along with his or her lecture, and if there are a couple of students messing around in the back of the room, he or she can hit the "click" button without missing a step. In fact, some clickers even come with a gizmo that wraps loosely around your wrist, so you can't drop it by accident!

Second, the noise a clicker makes is truly unique, which makes it difficult for kids to *not* hear it. Think about this: If you use your voice for a warning, kids may get very skilled at tuning you out. Think about how easy it is for your own children or your own *spouse* to tune out your voice! You can't tune out the clicker.

By the same token, while the noise is unique, it is not overbearing. Thus, it acts as a more subtle reminder than that bell or whistle you have been thinking about utilizing. You hit the clicker, and your neighbor doesn't poke his or her head in your door to make sure everything is okay!

Lastly (and this one is for teachers in particular), using any auditory warning has a couple advantages over a visual warning. The first is that when you hit the clicker, you put the whole class on notice. For this first warning, you are not "calling anybody out" and either embarrassing them or giving them the attention they may be seeking. You provide for them a chance to pull it together without having the glare of the spotlight hit them between the eyes. And don't worry about the students being confused about what just happened—most kids know the score of the game. They know for whom the warning has been issued. And even if they don't, a hint of ambiguity may make them *all* sit up a little straighter and pull it together for themselves!

Secondly, we have to remember one of the qualities of our boys that I described in an earlier chapter: If you have a couple boys messing around in the back of the room and you do something that is solely visual, they may not have any idea that you are trying to get their attention. However, when you hit the clicker, they will hear and know that they have been duly warned.

You can work out the remaining details to fit your particular setting. Give one warning, or maybe two or three—whatever your system happens to be—and go over the rules of engagement before you begin the program. Then, institute the rules with as much consistency as you are able to manage.

5. When Misbehavior Occurs, Stay Calm and Be Concise

Here's a rule you probably already know: When the world seems to be crashing down around you as if the Four Horsemen of the Apocalypse are galloping at full gait through your classroom, *stay calm!*

I'm sure you have heard this little pearl of wisdom in just about every training and staff development seminar you have attended since you were a college student. As trainers, we love to blow hard about all the "shouldas" and "oughtas" out there. These universal truths are pretty easy for us to articulate but difficult (at best!) to actually pull off in the heat of battle. Heck, remember the fish example. But let's say you begin to recite this mantra while the tectonic plates are mounting tension—what's the point?

The point has to do with *energy*. In most escalating situations, your goal should be to remove energy rather than create or add to it. If you begin to get hyped up, you are actually adding energy to an already out-of-control situation, and that emotion will act as jet fuel and lead to a hotter flare-up.

In fact, we always advise adults to remember a technique connected with the parasympathetic nervous system that was discussed earlier in this book: Control your breathing and model deep breaths (Benson & Klipper, 1975) for kids and teens in a state of distress. This is important for little kids who, when they get amped up, sometimes push themselves past the point at which they are able to even *speak*. You ever get around a younger child who is that upset? He or she will be breathing rapidly (almost hyperventilating), probably with the bottom lip stuck out, and almost invariably with tears streaming! These are kids who are almost wild eyed with emotion. Set them down, make physical contact (e.g., putting your hands on their shoulders), keep good eye contact, and begin to *breathe* while you are addressing them.

The goal here is to have them—even on a subconscious level—recognize the breathing pattern you are modeling and eventually start to reflect or mirror that same pattern. They cannot get themselves calmed without controlling the breathing. To reiterate, you will not be able to accomplish this feat if your stress level is also beginning to escalate.

Shifting over to big kids for a minute, the same principal applies. Let's say you have a couple of high school kids going at it in the hallway like prizefighters. As you step in to break things up, they will invariably be in a state of sympathetic arousal—with adrenaline flowing full bore, open throttle. As you split them up and take one of the offenders over to the penalty box, make a conscious effort to control your own breathing. Model calming down and they will have a better shot at grabbing control.

Some folks call this a form of yoga or meditation; some call it relaxation. Whatever the moniker, your goal is to suck the propane out of the grill rather than open the valve to maximum.

A common way I assist parents and their teenage kids in diffusing household tension is to help them learn to *negotiate*. Understanding how to negotiate is a life skill that is becoming a lost art because of the immediacy built in to our tech-savvy world. So often, simple rules like "curfew" become battlegrounds on which lines of demarcation are drawn.

I won't get into the millions of ways you can negotiate a curfew time, but I totally understand that parents get more rigid when their trust has been betrayed by their children. To build trust in this area specifically, I use technology to our advantage.

First, I tell the kid that he has to figure out why the parent sets the curfew when he or she does. The issues typically revolve around safety, accountability, and trust. We can address these neatly using the teen's cell phone.

Let's say the teen wants to go to Benny's house for a party, and he lets you know that there will be girls there! He knows Benny's mom will be home and swears he will go only to Benny's house and nowhere else—and you know straight out that his dad will never buy this! In this scenario, you might tell your client to work this deal with his dad: Perhaps three or four (it's really up to Dad) times throughout the evening, Dad will shoot a text message to his son. The son has, maybe, 3 minutes to find Benny's mom, stand someplace that shows he really is in Benny's house, and snap a picture of them together. He sends the pic to Dad, and bingo!

The teen cannot fake the time stamp on the photo, so it is concrete proof that he is where he says he is and that Benny's mom really is present. Dad can also purchase a cell phone app that utilizes GPS technology to give an exact location of the son's phone—he looks up the location on the Internet, calls his son, and if the kiddo answers, he is where he says he is. (No accounting for Benny's mom in this scenario, however.)

I also remind my client that he may ask for an extra hour of curfew time, but if Dad only agrees to 20 minutes, TAKE IT! Trust builds slowly with parents, so 20 minutes this time could grow to 60 minutes next time. Demonstrate trustworthiness and Dad will loosen the reigns over time. Also imperative is that the kid had better have that doggone phone with him and on mega-vibrate—he only has one chance to make this work, so he had better not screw it up by missing Dad's text!

The last part of item #5 has to do with being concise. To illustrate what I mean by this point, let's go back to a previous example in this book. Remember the "talkin' lickin'?" (This was where Dad would explain exactly why you were the recipient of said lickin' while he was dishing it out—and that generally didn't go over too well.) In moments of crisis or high emotion, there's really not an opportunity for a teachable moment.

All of us look for those rare opportunities to impart a life lesson in the face of some mini-disaster. We do this because we are trying to give wisdom to our youngsters, an admirable intent. We want to impart on them wisdom that transcends the fundamentals of the daily grind. We try to help teach our kiddos how to *think*, and teachable moments are incredibly powerful opportunities in which to pull this off, because a child will relate best to a situation immediately before him or her than one that has already passed.

The art of delivering a solid teachable moment lies in its timing, however. Think about this example to drive home my point: Have you ever had a real doozy of an argument with your spouse or partner? I'm talking about the kind of argument that doesn't lead to physical acts of violence but still causes the neighbors to pull their kids in off the streets for protection.

Now, let me ask you this: Do you really *hear* what your partner is saying during the heat of battle? My guess is that you probably don't. Resolution in marriage or any intimate relationship usually occurs in moments of calm, not moments of distress. Same for our kids: Teachable moments are moments of quiet, not moments of intensity. Once kids pass a point of emotional arousal, their capacity to process logic takes a back seat to survival mode.

Thus, your best bet to create a teaching moment is to get the kid separated from the herd and out of whatever situation is overstimulating him. Give him a chance to get himself together, and *then* launch your teachable moment. This provides the kid with the best opportunity to hear and retain what you are saying even before you try to say it.

Being calm and concise will accomplish this in the most efficient manner.

6. Empathy

Does everyone know what empathy is? We touched on it during the discussion of conduct disorder in Chapter Four. Empathy is the ability to understand how another person feels— to put yourself in his or her shoes.

I bring up empathy for two reasons. The first is to remind you to be careful with *how* you deliver a consequence. Do your best to deliver a consequence in a manner that builds rather than destroys the relationship you are forging with the child.

For example, let's say you are a teacher and have to send a student off—to time out or the principal's office or wherever.

There is a big difference between something like, "Get out of my room … I'm sick of looking at you" and something like, "Jeremy, you are getting way out of control and need to cool yourself down. Let's go down to Mrs. Mitchell's office to get it back under control."

One way says, "I can't stand you!" and the other says, "I am looking out for you." Remember, the goal is not only the child's behavior, but also the relationship. Parents take heed: Your words have a ton more impact than a teacher's, and the message you may be delivering when using harsh words may come across as, "You are worthless" or "I am sorry to be your parent."

The other issue salient in this section deals with how you react when a kid returns to civilization after serving a consequence. To illustrate this point, let me ask you another question about your past: When you were growing up, did you have a parent who would give you the *silent treatment* if you did something wrong? Or maybe you had a friend or acquaintance whose parent would give them the silent treatment?

The silent treatment creates an almost unmanageable state of anxiety in children because they have a hard time dealing with feeling like Mom doesn't love them anymore because of something they've done. Or, they have difficulty dealing with thinking they have somehow "damaged" their relationship with Dad because of their behavior.

Take this same concept and bring it into the classroom. When you send a student off (again, to time out, the principal's office, sitting out recess or lunch period, or whatever), they serve their punishment. When they return to your classroom (or wherever you happen to be), they bring themselves back into the fold. And it doesn't matter how angry or tough of a kid he is, he will be looking toward the teacher to see what exactly the temperature is now.

In other words, he is feeling tension—wondering if you and he are going to be good now, or if the adult is going to hold a grudge and perhaps take it out on him somewhere down the line. This will be particularly true for kids who come from a home where the silent treatment is employed as a parenting technique by caregivers.

My recommendation is to take a half a second to let that kiddo off the hook when he re-emerges. You don't have to sing *Kumbaya* and hold hands whilst dancing around a campfire, but take a minute to convey a message such as, "You did the crime, and you did the time; now, welcome back. If you're good, we're good." Remove the anxiety he may be feeling by creating an atmosphere in which he can bring it back together without ill will hanging in the air.

7. Make Effective Discipline a Team Approach

I'll be brief in making the last two points of this section, as they do not require a lot of explanation. The first is to problem-solve together, particularly during times when you are feeling extreme frustration. This works especially well with the kids and teenagers who are like the "good hunting dogs" I described earlier, as it gives them a sense that they are not being "forced" in any one direction and that your consequences are not arbitrary in nature.

Let me raise one caution about how to begin a conversation such as this: Be careful to maintain your power position when problem-solving with a youngster. At no point should it seem like you are putting the ball in his court, as that is not his role. Remember that *you* set the bottom line in this equation, not the child.

Here is a good opening to use when speaking privately to a repeat offender. "Listen, Zach, we've been around this tree a hundred times this year, you know? What can we do to better manage this situation?"

He will probably respond with a shrug and a sullen, "I don't know." But, seize the day! Respond with firmness but empathy: "Yeah, it's rough. There's got to be a better way, though. This way is getting pretty ugly, you know?"

In a public setting (e.g., classroom, group home), you can even appeal to the kid's sense of loyalty with something such as, "I hate to keep calling you out in front of your buddies, so what needs to happen here?"

If you continue down this path and he continues to disengage, you will have to wrap up with a bottom line of your own. If, on the other hand, he begins to open up and participate, ask what is going on with him or what his opinion is regarding what you can do going forward. Guide him rather than acquiesce to him. Allow him to feel he has some say without giving him the authority to undermine you.

For teachers, this technique is especially important when dealing with leaders in your classroom. Again, aligning yourself with the leader will require one-on-one conversations at times, and gaining his or her insight may give you a valuable perspective to which you wouldn't otherwise be privy. Plus, you have the added bonus of reinforcing his or her "leader" status in the room.

To better manage the classroom or other group as a whole, you may want to hold a "town hall meeting" once in a while to air some difficulties in the group. Even if this does not evolve into a two-way conversation, you can still bring about the desired effect with a "state of the union address" to the room!

8. Leave the Door Open for Deeper Discussions

This point naturally evolves out of point Number Seven, but it also goes a bit deeper. And before explaining this further, I want to point out that you should not underestimate how important you may be to this child. A kid may never let on that he respects or even *likes* you, but there may be a current beneath the surface (that is heavily protected) of regard for you.

Having said that, tread cautiously but confidently into the inner lives of your kiddos. Beware! You may uncork some pretty heavy issues. Some kids come from a place that is pretty awful. In these cases, just keep in mind that you are not there to save every kid but can give them support and understanding outside of their world.

I would be remiss to not also remind you that legally, we professionals are obligated to report incidences of abuse or neglect—even *perceived* abuse or neglect. If you are trying to build relationships, reporting, too, must be done with finesse. I recommend bringing in another professional to help talk you through the manner by which the reporting is conducted, not only to help you think through the procedure, but perhaps even to "take the heat" so you can maintain and protect the trust in the relationship you have with the child.

Now, let's return to talking about feelings, as even kids from great homes may need help with this. Sometimes, teachers do a great job starting the day or the period by having an "open forum," whereby students are afforded an opportunity to talk about whatever happens to be on their mind. Encouraging an honest exchange and an atmosphere of acceptance can build trust and will give your behavioral plan more power.

If this method is not in line with your personality or not possible given your specific circumstances, I encourage you to, at the very least, identify feelings when they happen in a non-threatening way. For example, you see Jackson embarrass William, so William slugs him. As a result, William has to go to the principal's office. At some point during that journey, you could say something like, "Geez, that had to be embarrassing. Sorry about that." Then, let it drop completely.

The point in doing that is not to further embarrass William. Rather, it is designed to do two things; first, it lets him know that you get it. You understand what is going on for him, and that understanding may be unusual in his world. However, what works best for most of the angry kids is hitting it and then letting it go. Just state your case, then drop it so the kid does not feel pressed into responding in a way that takes him totally out of his protected comfort zone.

The second thing you accomplish by identifying the emotion is that you allow William to understand that he is able to have an emotion *other than* anger. "Bad kids" are good at anger. They are angry a lot and have probably mastered it by now. It is particularly important to help the boys differentiate or identify emotions, as this will give them options in the future. A kid may never act on those options, but at least you are giving him a choice rather than allowing him to keep reacting in the only way he knows how.

Bottom line: Establishing trust, as described throughout the first section of the book, will give more power to the structure you impose via your behavioral plan. Trust will calm some of those hunting dogs, put some slack in the tug toy, give the mean girl some pause, and relax the group as a whole. Building trust allows a behavioral plan to be more effective, because kids are more likely to buy into it if it comes from a grown-up they know has their best interest in mind. Give them a chance to practice control and containment, and be an ally rather than an enemy!

Help kids learn to trust. It is amazing, really, when you think about how often we grown-ups need to place our trust in the hands of fate (and others!). We trust our spouses and lovers to keep the relationship sacred. We trust that the dollar bill in our pocket will still be worth a dollar tomorrow. We trust that other drivers on the highway will not swerve across the center line. We trust that if we close our eyes tight, the world will be the same when we open them. The fabric of civilized society is stitched together with tenuous threads of trust in others!

Chapter 9
Functionalizing Behavior
Making It Easier on You …
How About That!

Let's keep plowing ahead with the behavioral part of the program and talk about another simple concept that sounds more complicated than it is: *functionalizing* behavior. Functionalizing merely means *operationalizing*. Another big word, I know …

Functionalizing (or operationalizing) refers to the idea that in order to attack any targeted behavior with a behavioral plan, the behavior you are going after must be *concrete, observable,* and *measurable* (".com" as the acronym).

The reason we do this is twofold: First, and perhaps most importantly, you use this approach so you are able to achieve success. If you have a more ambiguous goal—one that does not involve a concrete, observable, measurable behavior—it will be very difficult to ascertain whether you have achieved the goal. Following this through to its logical conclusion, such a goal would therefore be impossible to achieve.

For example, if your goal is for little Johnny to "be good," you are set up for failure. He will have good days and bad days. You will have good days and bad days. Pretty soon, you are back to the drawing board and feel as though little Johnny has rolled over you. Unless Johnny suddenly becomes a model child, his improvement will be fleeting—a carrot on a stick that you will never reach.

The second reason we functionalize is because it helps keep us from feeling frustrated and defeated if the results do not cross home plate immediately. I hear this defeat and frustration most often when a parent comes into my office, plops down on my couch, and opens the intake with some form of the following line: "I've tried everything, but nothing works."

You ever hear a mom or a dad say that? You ever hear yourself say that? Sure! By the time a parent gets to my office, he or she has been through the ringer with behavioral stuff. When I hear a parent say, "I've tried everything but nothing works," I realize that, almost without exception, what that this implies (and we'll use Mom as the lead parent in the example) is the following: Mom got some advice about a cool behavioral plan to try at home. She tried using it for a while, but it did not work completely, so she shifted and tried something else. Then, she tried the new plan, but it did not work completely either, so she shifted and tried something else. She tried that one for a while, and then tried something else … and so on.

Believe me, there is no shortage of "Other Things to Try" out there for worried moms and dads. Those of you with kids of your own, think about how many people give you parenting advice. Everyone? Sure—everyone you meet, from your own mom or dad to the friendly (but somewhat meddling) stranger in line ahead of you at the post office is an expert in parenting their own kids, and they are not shy about sharing with you the miraculous behavioral fixes they have effected.

Add to this the number of audacious parenting magazines boasting headlines such as, "Turn Your Child from Devil to Angel in Three Easy Minutes" or "Get Control of Your Wolf-Boy by Using Nothing but a Spatula and a 16-oz. Bottle of Yoo-Hoo" or "Last Week, Our Home was a Bowery: Thoughts From Our New Garden of Tranquil Paradise."

Plus, for good measure, we have about 15 bazillion Internet sites for parents; the professional words of pediatricians, teachers, and seminar speakers; overzealous journalists writing for the local newspapers; and the jabber of popular TV and radio talk show experts. Mix all this advice together in the already overwhelmed brain of a frazzled parent, and you have the recipe for failure.

Why? Because typically, parents are trying to do the best they can and feel that if success is not realized quickly, they must be doing something wrong. So, they grab onto the next life raft that floats by and try using that one for a while until a seemingly better one comes around. See the problem with this pattern?

The behavior programs that parents choose may or may not be good ones, but that is irrelevant because the plans aren't given a chance to gain any traction with the kids. Parents may have the rich loam of intent, but a plan cannot grow roots without the sun and water of time and opportunity. When they feel like there must be a "next something better" out there, they jump on and off of various bandwagons. In the end, their kids aren't able to develop past a certain point.

Teachers and therapists can get caught on the same treadmill, which is why we recommend that all adults *functionalize* behavior. This can keep you from growing frustrated: You won't be caught chasing your tail around the "next great idea" tree. A well-functionalized behavior plan will *change your perspective!* We need an example to make this clearer. Feel free to extrapolate this example to fit your particular set of circumstances. Let me draw from a classroom environment again, but the same rules apply to using this exercise at home.

Let's say you have a child in your room named Martin. Martin does about 74 things that drive you absolutely insane, but pare those down to one or two concrete, observable, and measurable (.com) behaviors to target for intervention. If you try to create a behavior plan to address all 74, you are going to truly go batty because there are not enough hours in the day. Plus, let's face it—you do not have enough energy to keep up.

Pick one or two behaviors over which you can have some semblance of control in a .com sense. For the sake of argument, let's say you choose to modify his "getting out of his seat" behavior.

The initial step in developing any behavior plan is to create a baseline. To pull this off, you must obtain the expensive and hard-to-find tools of 1) a pencil and 2) a pad of sticky notes. For the next 2 or 3 days, let Martin do whatever it is that he does. Allow him to exist unabated in his natural habitat. You do this because you want to know what kind of behaviors (or, more specifically, what kind of *numbers*) you are dealing with.

You set a certain period of time within which you will conduct your data collection. For this example, let's say you are interested in marking the period between opening bell and the first recess. Now, every time Martin jumps up out of his seat during this time frame, you nail the sticky pad with a tally mark. No intervention yet, just observation and recording.

After you collect your data, you find that, on average, Martin gets out of his seat 19 times in the allotted period. Next, you start the treatment phase. Whenever Martin is sitting still in *his own seat* and marginally paying attention, you reinforce the heck out of his behavior. You make it better to be good than to not be good. You make eye contact, you give a verbal "atta boy," you nod, you smile, you give a token, you pull out your wallet and hand him 20 bucks … whatever it is that you decide to do behaviorally.

After 7 or 8 days of the reinforcement, you take another baseline. Now, you find that, on average, Martin is getting out of his seat 14 times during the allotted time period. Is 14 still a lot? You'd better believe it is! But here's the rub: If you're not paying attention, 14 and 19 feel *exactly the same* and feel like "the number of failure." They are both too much—and they both make you wonder if the orange aprons at The Home Depot® will make your hips look slimmer.

However, if you *are* paying attention, we suddenly have a different *perspective* on the number 14: If you weren't paying attention, it would have felt like failure, but now it becomes progress. Martin does not go from 19 to zero without passing through 14. And by the way, Martin may never be a "zero" kid—he may get down to three or four, which is manageable, particularly compared with where he was before.

In this scenario, you renew your resolve because rather than feeling defeated ("I've tried everything, but nothing works"), you now feel effective. After another week or two, Martin may be down to 11 or 9 or 12, but as long as you are moving toward the finish line, you still have forward momentum.

Here's the other secret about Mr. Martin: When you begin to get the one or two behaviors under control, others in the big, gloopy glob of 74 will start to follow suit. Perhaps not all of the behaviors will change, but Martin's oil tanker will start to swing around to point in the right direction.

The reason is that you have now effectively begun to change the rules of engagement with Martin. Too often, teachers (and parents) get caught up in the negative spiral of only paying attention to the kiddo when he or she is behaving badly. Now that you are making an effort to create positive reinforcement and forcing yourself (for lack of a better word) to look for moments of good behavior, Martin and you will have a different playing field.

In other words, you set up a scenario whereby Martin can behave in a manner designed to *achieve positives* rather than to *avoid negatives*. It may seem to be a subtle difference, but that shift in philosophy can be very powerful, and that shift is made possible when you functionalize behavior.

Once the problem has been adequately defined, we shift focus and become as much like a private investigator as we possibly can. By doing this, we train ourselves to pay close attention to context, because the context unlocks the key to understanding and controlling the behavior.

Simply put, we are trying to intervene at the "A" as much as possible so we can diffuse that bomb before we have to clean up the room afterwards. To do this, you will need to answer some key questions about the lead-in to the bad behavior, questions such as:

1. *Who* is present when the behavior tends to occur or does not occur?

2. *What* is going on when the behavior tends to occur or not occur?

3. *When* does the behavior tend to occur or not occur?

4. *Where* does the behavior tend to occur or not occur?

5. *How often* does the behavior occur per hour _____, per day _____, per week _____?

6. *How long* does the behavior occur per episode_____?

This is a simplistic way of looking at it, to be sure. However, once again, adults are not always privy to the lead-in. We hear the explosion and are then forced to react. Although we may feel as though the explosion happened randomly, remember that all kids are trying to get a need met when they act out. Whether they are seeking attention, power, revenge … these are kids who, at their very worst, have been shaped into the bad behavior machines you see before you.

The next step as you continue down this path is to work backwards to figure out more specific details about the "A." Ask yourself questions such as:

1. When did it happen (time, day, date)?

2. What happened before the behavior occurred?

3. Describe the behavior. Include how intense, how long, how often.

4. What happened after the behavior occurred?

Note that, again, the first question deals with the lead-in (i.e., the "A"), but Question 4 moves you beyond the "A" and deals specifically with potential re-enforcers or consequences (i.e., intervening at the "C").

Let me give some easy examples of how context can be understood when you play private investigator. Perhaps the simplest example is a scenario I am sure many of you face when working with groups of kids. You have Richard, who is fantastic one on one, and you also have Kenny, who is great one on one. But, you get the two of them together and look out! You've got vinegar and baking soda—a made-for-TV third-grade science fair volcano! In this example, changing how close Richard and Kenny sit to each other (or how far away from each other!) can have an impact.

I get to more specific behavioral interventions later in the book. For now, here are a couple of additional examples of how context can play a role in behavior. These may not bring any dazzling insight into your life, but they are easy to follow and illustrate how the "A" can wield a certain power.

Some kids have a "time-of-day" issue when it comes to bad behavior, and this can be driven by a couple factors. First, you might have kids who get cranky and start acting out with greater frequency and intensity if they have gone too long without food. In the period leading into lunch or snacktime, these kids' blood sugar may be dropping, and they may get harder to manage (by both you and themselves). If this is the case, offering a quick snack may even them out to help them maintain until the next meal.

Time of day is also the culprit in schools for some students who come from high-stress homes. These kids may start to spin out toward the end of the day as they look ahead to a brutal evening (or maybe a tough walk home if it is through a bad neighborhood). This also wreaks some havoc during the period leading up to vacations and school holidays. As the time of separation draws nearer, these kids feel their internal stress ratcheting up, and they spin out.

Teachers may want to help bridge the gap between today and tomorrow with these students—particularly younger ones— by using a transitional object. A transitional object is a small, concrete representation of you that the student can take with him or her.

To accomplish this, simply grab a knickknack off of your desk, hand it (on the down low) to the student, and say something like, "Listen, I need somebody to look after this tonight. Do you think you can help me out with that?"

If that student likes you, this will be very meaningful, and he or she will probably agree to it. Asking a kid to safeguard a knickknack may seem like a hokey intervention, but you are giving him or her a little piece of you to have close and rely on during times of stress. It is easier for kids to identify with an object than to hold on to abstract memories or thoughts of you.

We use this same concept to teach parents how to help their kids deal with divorce or separation. Usually, when parents split up, it is the dad who leaves the home. Kids have a tremendously difficult time wrapping their brains around losing one of their parents. Surprisingly, things like the sex of the child or the amount of stress in the house prior to the split-up don't seem to matter much. Generally speaking, and there are some truly remarkable exceptions to this rule, kids will put up with a bad situation forever if it means having both parents in the house. In fact, how many times do you see or hear about kids falling on their sword just to try to save an awful union between their folks?

When a parent leaves the home, we recommend that he or she gives the kid(s) a transitional object. If this cannot be a visual representation (i.e., photos, trinkets), go for an olfactory object. For example, a dad might dab a bit of his cologne, deodorant, or shampoo on a stuffed animal, pillowcase, or something else absorbent that the kid has around during quiet times. The scent of the father will hold a position of power in the mind of the child and will work to soothe in the absence of the real person.

Getting back to our discussion of timing and behavior, the end of the school year can be problematic. This is particularly so with kids who have had to deal with caregiver separation due to divorce, death, or abandonment. These kids feel their old wounds being torn open when they look ahead to an impending separation from you. In other words, the feeling of loss will reignite the trauma of past losses. Termination in the therapy process can reopen the same wounds.

With these kids, bridging the gap is also important. Rather than exclusively using you as the bridge, it may also be important for that student to spend some time with next year's teacher so he or she has a more concrete representation of what to expect when he or she returns the following year. That student can leave knowing that there is a real person at the other end of the long summer. You might have the next teacher come into your room and play checkers with the student or engage in some sort of interactive activity to ease the transition.

By the way, here is another reason why therapist and teacher turnover is troubling for youngsters: The kids we are talking about—those who are feeling the pain of missing you before the year has even ended—need to know that even though they will not be in your particular classroom or your particular office, that you are *still going to be there*. That kiddo may fall into stride and never come see you again, but knowing he or she has that option can calm his or her anxieties, and, yes, can curb some bad behavior.

These are just a few examples of how understanding the "A" can help you cut bad behavior off at the pass. A great way to encapsulate this information into a quick-and-easy-to-read format is to put it onto an FBA (Functional Behavior Assessment) form.

Following, I include an example of an FBA form to help you picture what I am talking about. Now, for those of you who work in special education or for therapists who sit through many IEP (Individualized Education Program) meetings, you probably see these things in your sleep. After combing through more than 147,000 of these over the years, you may not be able to close your eyes without seeing one pop up! I put this form in the book more for those of you who teach in a regular education room and only see one every so often. For teachers who work in private schools (and for parents or therapists who do not work within the school system), you may have *never* seen one!

Every individual state or school district has its own version of this form, so check with your district's special education coordinator to see what your school-specific form looks like. If you are interested in perusing examples from around the country, there are literally more than 100 of these forms available on the Internet—just do a quick Google search. The one I found was on the Sevier County School District (Tennessee) web page. I like this one because it is comprehensive, easy to read, and simple to understand. It provides a good example of how one might conceptualize problematic behavior.

Once we have gathered all of the data included on this form, we can launch into the scientific method of putting it into practice. You all remember the scientific method, right? You form a plan, you test the plan, you evaluate the plan, and then you reform the plan consistent with the data you have gathered. Another form that can be used in this process is a BIP (Behavioral Intervention Plan).

As a quick aside, the other reason we use these forms in my private practice office is to help parents prepare for the planning and/or IEP meetings. Let's face it: Parents are usually pretty defensive during those meetings and typically feel outgunned. After all, how many school employees are present in those meetings? Quite a few, is my guess. The vice principal is there and sometimes the principal. Every teacher who touches the student's life is rounded up. If there is testing to interpret, the school psychologist makes an appearance, and the special education coordinator sits in the meeting. Wow! No wonder a parent—especially a single one—can feel overwhelmed! It can feel like sitting on a folding chair at the end of the gymnasium with white-hot spotlights glaring down!

As a therapist, I am often put in the position of defending the student and helping to support the parent(s). Going over the form can also help us formulate a game plan ahead of time. Although some of the concepts on an FBA can be useful to structure a behaviorally oriented game plan in the home, as stated in the previous paragraph, I generally have used these forms to help parents understand what is going to happen in a meeting at school. It helps take some of the "unknown" out of the equation. Helping parents know what to expect alleviates a lot of anxiety. Remember, it is about diffusing energy, right?

A good example of a BIP is found on the State of Illinois website. As with FBAs, there is a gaggle of BIP forms in the public domain to peruse and evaluate. Some are more complicated, and some are less so. I use this one because it is somewhere in the middle, combining ease of use with detail.

Part III

Proven Management Strategies That Any Adult Can Use

Chapter 10

Less-Involved Strategies

Tweaks and Tinkers

I know I've alluded to a number of techniques already, but in this chapter, I discuss in more detail some specific behavioral techniques to use as you manage the little lovelies! First, I describe a few simple interventions that are reasonably easy to employ. Compliance aside, these will be less involved (in terms of time, attention, etc.), and as I mentioned, do not require that you plumb the depths of the child's inner workings.

From there, I move on to some strategies that are a bit more involved. I take this opportunity to help teachers set up behavioral programming for their entire class, or for parents and therapists to bring a sense of order for individual kids and teens. As always, bear in mind that we try to hold to some of the basic rules of making target behaviors be "concrete, observable, and measurable" (again, .com for short). In this portion of the book, I take special note of the token economy/response cost approach and go through a step-by-step method of creating and implementing this program for a variety of developmental levels.

Finally, I take you through a few strategies to help in dealing with the kids who truly are bent on giving you grey hair. These are the ones who will fight you all the way to the finish line, because that seems to be somehow written right into their DNA.

These strategies won't guarantee overnight success, but they will help to get you moving these kids in the right direction.

Oh, and before I begin with the less-involved strategies, I do want to deliver a disclaimer that you are not going to like: In the following sections, *I am not going to give you what you want.*

Here's what I mean; you have picked up this book because you, in some form or fashion, have an "if, then" question or scenario in your mind. Each of you has a specific client, son or daughter, or perhaps a classroom *full* of students who are making you nutty and subsequently motivate you to look for some answers. You want to get to the part of this book where I answer your specific "If this ... then what" question, right?

But here's the deal. If I were to tabulate every single specific scenario or situation my readers are currently experiencing with their kids, I would have to come up with finely differentiated responses to about 2,453,678 questions! In other words, every single one of you is in a unique constellation of students, family dynamics, parents, administration, physical surroundings, region, and even variables in your own personalities. I cannot— nor would I— address each and every one in a book of this size.

What I am offering to you is a general overview of some of the best tried-and-true methods of implementing behavioral strategies. I am not saying these are *The Answer*, nor are they anything that Moses brought down from the mountain and handed directly into my waiting arms. Rather, what follows in the remainder of this book are more like pliable pieces of warm plastic—they have a shape and a form of their own, but they are adaptable across numerous situations; they can expand, contract, be painted, cut up, added to ... or loaded into a cannon and shot toward the sun! In other words, take these ideas and make them your own.

Not all of you have exactly the same personality that your neighbor may have. Not all share the same set of strengths and weaknesses, have identical delivery methods, or use similar management styles. Mold the ideas to fit *yourself.* Take the ones you like, and leave the ones you don't.

1. Planned Ignoring

I have already alluded to "planned ignoring," but simply put, you are intervening at the "C" by removing all re-enforcers for an unwanted attention-seeking behavior. You choke off the fruit by no longer feeding it, thereby allowing it to die on the vine. The proper psychological term for this act is *extinction*, and for the most part, a "planned ignore" will work over the long run (Haley, 1993).

However, as you can imagine, there is a catch. Planned ignoring is extremely difficult to accomplish! Now, that's not to say that the idea should be scrapped entirely. Rather, I would recommend using the planned ignore for situations that are more individualized and lean away from the planned ignore when an entire class or a number of kids (sibling groups, for example) is involved. Let me explain a little further.

A planned ignore is almost impossible to pull off when there is a broader audience for a few good reasons. Believe me, I know that you have been told to use the planned ignore by the authors of behavior modification books and speakers at behavior management seminars. What they don't tend to tell you, though, is that it is a lot harder to do than you may think!

The first pitfall: Bad behavior is extremely difficult to ignore. In psychology, a similar phenomenon is "the cocktail party effect" (Cherry, 1953). Simply put, let's say you are around a large group of people. Everyone is chatting, laughing, and buzzing. If you hear your name mentioned in any of the conversations, you will automatically orient your attention toward those speakers. You do this because attending to your name and hearing it above the din is an overlearned response. The cocktail party effect describes our ability to focus our attention on one voice or conversation, ignoring other conversations and background noise.

The novelty of bad behavior grabs you in a similar manner. If you look out over a sea of heads, and one starts bouncing up and down in the back, it pulls you in. It is the "shiny ball" phenomenon: Novelty forces attention unless you really take a moment and psych yourself up to avoid giving in to the tendency to orient toward the unusual thing. What's more, in the case of bad behavior, that novel thing may also be intense, annoying, and disruptive.

Another caveat: Because of the cocktail party effect, even if *you* withdraw your attention, the rest of the group may feed the fruit by offering the sweet nectar of their own delightful attention. The acting out child, therefore, may shift his or her focus away from you and onto the rest of the folks in the room. After all, attention is attention, right?

The second pitfall: When you use a planned ignore, despite eventual extinction, the bad behavior invariably *will* get worse before it gets better. The reason is fairly obvious: The kiddo figures, "Well, I've had the volume at six, and the adult has been ignoring me. Let's see what she does when I turn it up to eight." And believe me, the volume knob on some kids goes well up into the 70s!

Don't throw planned ignoring onto the scrap heap, but utilize it to extinguish minor nuisance behaviors or behaviors that are demonstrated in a more personalized setting (i.e., when it is just you and the child, or if there are just a few people around).

Home examples are a bit easier to envision because there are generally not more than a few kids around, compared with in a school setting, where the issue compounds. A practical example of success in a school environment would be if the teacher were trying to help one student, and another was trying to horn in on the conversation or trying to snatch your attention from your charge. In this instance, the teacher has most of the external variables covered and will be able to—without eye contact if possible—hold out a hand in a gesture to let the interrupting student know he has been acknowledged but then continue engaging with the first student. If the interrupter persists past the yellow light, maybe placing a hand on his shoulder will give the message. In the end, even if you have to take a beat to let him know that you will be with him in a moment, be sure to debrief and let him know the most appropriate way to approach you in that situation. Provide an alternate behavior in a nonpunitive manner to facilitate learning.

2. Humor

Because I addressed humor when I discussed diffusing a volatile situation, I'm not going to write much about it here. Each of you has to assess how comfortable you are in using humor. Also, it is hard to write about specific humor techniques, because everyone is so different in their style, content, and delivery of humor.

Still, let me provide a few guiding principals:

a) Use humor to deflect tension, to quell the building storm clouds, and to diffuse anxiety. Allow the student an "out" if there is a standoff situation and he or she feels painted into a corner. Humor can de-escalate a situation.

b) Use humor to build relationships. Humor is like the loop ends of Velcro, and the kids' personalities are like the hook ends—with a good sense of humor, you offer them a place (or an opportunity) to connect with you.

c) Any relationship has to have a good balance of humor and seriousness to it. If you overuse humor, you lose respect because the kids (teens in particular) will not trust you to take them or their situations seriously. A jokester is just about the last person on earth you would ever confide in, right? He or she can be a lot of fun to hang out with but not somebody you can get close to. So walk the line and feel out the best way to use the sense of humor you carry.

d) If humor is not your forte then don't try to use it! Nothing is more painful to watch than a person who is totally uncomfortable with humor but insists on awkwardly stumbling through a joke or witticism. In essence, they *become* the punch line! Use what you got, and stick with your strengths.

3. Nonverbals

This section falls a bit under the "self-explanatory" umbrella, as I am sure you all have the "stink-eye" honed to a science. In fact, if you wear glasses (as do I), you can underscore the stink-eye by first snaring the upper corner of your glasses with one hand, then forcefully removing them whilst maintaining stink-eye contact with the kiddo in question! But nonverbals can also take a couple other meaningful forms.

First, you can use physical proximity or contact as either a part of your warning system or even to quell uprisings or misbehavior. To use it as an indicator of a warning, you can stroll casually past a child who may be misbehaving and lay a hand on his shoulder (or maybe give a gentle tap) as a warning. In school, a teacher can tap a forefinger on a student's desk to indicate that he has been "served." Incidentally, using the finger tap is a wonderfully subtle means to issue a warning, as it can be done in an unobtrusive way, thereby not alerting the rest of the class to this student's plight. The finger tap can also redirect, as it can draw the student's attention away from the fascinating bug crawling across the floor and back to the surface of the desk where it belongs.

A teacher can also utilize proximity to be subtle yet strong. If there are students misbehaving in a sector of the classroom, you can adjust your position to be nearer the action while you are teaching or lecturing. The students will hopefully be less inclined to feel "invisible" if you are standing close by!

Alas, I have had to do just that in a few of my seminars with adults! I typically stand to the same side of the room to deliver my talk—my right, your left. Unfortunately, I have had a couple instances when the attendees on the opposite side of the room have felt the need to talk incessantly—at times somewhat loudly—to each other during the presentation. As I said, this has happened a couple of times to me, but I handled it with no embarrassment or accusations to an individual by merely switching sides at break or lunch time. That way, it looked as though I was adjusting simply as a matter of course and not because of any one person or group of people. Nobody got "called out," but all of the folks around the loudmouths breathed a sigh of relief, as the chatting was halted.

Lastly, a nonverbal can be a powerful "signal" to kids who are either nonverbal themselves, young, or perhaps in a situation when the cacophony reaches a fever pitch and you do not have the energy to shout above the din! Many preschool and elementary teachers try to capture the attention of the class as a whole by clapping a rhythm, either the front end of "Shave and a Haircut" (with the students responding with the "Two Bits" part) or a cadence with which the rest of the room is asked to clap along. This method is light, engages all students, and gets everyone focused on you. Parents can use this same strategy, because it cognitively redirects and commands attention in a subtle, nonshaming manner.

I also work with parents and teachers to consider working out a nonverbal "signal"—not unlike how a third base coach would work out a series of signals with the batters on the team. For example, you can say that when you pat your head, the rest of the room must return to their seats and pat their heads. At a family gathering or at church, for instance, a parent can deliver a strong nonverbal that is understood by their child but avoids the shaming intrusion of strangers. As mentioned, this sort of redirection has a little air of levity to it and thus may be more easily accepted by children than a more punitive measure.

A teacher can likewise create a shared signal with just one student. You can work out with Matthew that when you put your finger on your nose, he is doing a great job. If you tug at your earlobe, he is getting out of hand and needs to pull it back together. The rest of the class does not have to know these signals, thus protecting Matthew from being called out repeatedly in front of his peers. What's more, just like the opposing manager in a baseball game, if the class "steals your signals" and starts to figure out the system, you and Matthew can change it up, thereby establishing a rotating series of signals that may stay one step ahead of the class. One or two hands in your pockets, crossing your arms, pushing up your glasses on the bridge of your nose, and even a good old-fashioned wink of the eye can be powerfully subtle signals to help Matthew feel connected and on track.

The other benefit of private nonverbal communication with a student is that the protected nature of the signals establishes a bond with you under which Matthew may feel safe. This is an exceptionally powerful intervention technique for male teachers with their male students, particularly those who do not have a male role model in their life.

Here is another nonverbal that you can teach directly to the kiddo in question: Help the kid to attend to the way the rest of the world perceives *him or her*. Working hard to change subtle body language like eye contact, erect posture, smiling, or even the way the child holds facial expressions, and random acts of politeness can go a long way toward producing a friendly reflection from the folks around that kid. I tell my clients that I am going to fight their war on two fronts with them: I will work cognitively to address some of the elevator music they hear internally but also want to adjust the patterns of reinforcement they pull from the world around them.

Think about it this way: Many kids and teenagers are notorious for maintaining their own misery by thinking that the world rejects them, but then go out of their way to put on a sour-puss face, or dye their Mohawk blue, or wear aggressively oppositional clothing. In turn, the world rejects them harder, and they are off to the races. Changing the level of acceptance they invite externally can produce changes internally by opening possibilities of their relationships.

Here's another one for you: There is a pool of research (Tenenbaum, 2010) that indicates that the feedback loop between the musculature of the face and the emotional centers of the brain actually runs both ways. In other words, most of us know that when we feel happy, we smile. That makes sense, right? But this research showed that when we smile, we can actually *cause* ourselves to feel happier! The expression we wear can impact our mood!

Think about the angry or defiant kids we encounter. They wear a sour puss most every second of the day, right? That sour puss can drag their mood into the tar pits of depression, anger, or lethargy. So help them to be more accountable when taking inventory of their facial expression—nothing could require less effort that wearing a smile. Heck, even a neutral expression can transform some of the bad feelings they may be self-inducing.

4. Behavior Shaping

This concept is fairly straightforward, as it means to work on reinforcing a complicated set of behaviors one step at a time, or, as in the movie *What About Bob?*, we have to move in "baby steps." In psychobabble, we use the term *successive approximations* (Peterson, 2004) to describe this process. As the kiddo takes baby steps toward changing a behavior, each step is rewarded to help keep the kid on track toward the ultimate goal of learning a new behavior.

In other words, remember the oil tanker and freight train metaphors. Rome was not built in a day and neither were these troublesome kids. They have been shaped by their world to behave in a certain manner to get their needs met, and they will continue to struggle against changing their strategy as you work toward a different solution. So it will take time, energy, and patience on your part, but hang in there! Making progress one step at a time with those who feel like a burden will always feel more satisfying than moving along the kids who are a joy to have in the room!

5. Catch Kids Doing Well

Here is another one of those idioms you end up hearing in every seminar on behavior management, in every fireside chat about parenting techniques, and in many other "rah-rah" venues. The problem is that this is a concept we all *know*, but it is a very difficult one to actually put into motion! In fact, once families are in trouble, this is among the first concepts to fly out the window!

When I am consulting with a parent or a teacher, I often throw out the old "catch 'em being good" standby. Typically, this elicits a reaction of barely contained frustration, as the adult fires back with some version of, "Are you *nuts?* If that bear is hibernating, I'm not going to go over and kick it in the head!"

In other words, when the child happens to be quiet or working or just—by pure happenstance—has randomly decided to sit still on the couch and watch *Scooby Doo*, the adult tiptoes in the other direction. We have all done this and then embraced the warm tranquility that ensued. That moment or two of peace and quiet becomes a brief port in our stormy day, for sure.

But think about what you are teaching that kid when you do this (remember Skinner?) — that when he is being appropriate, you leave him about as alone as possible because you don't want to irritate the coiled snake. But if he begins to misbehave again, you are probably back on top of him, and maybe with added vigor because he stepped all over your brief nirvana.

Remember, *the worst student in your classroom or the worst child in the home is not bad 100% of the time!* It just doesn't work that way. Yes, he is misbehaving at a greater pace than perhaps any kid in the history of civilization … but there are times of peace throughout the day or throughout the class period. Find those times, and reinforce them rather than leaving the kid alone. Make it better for that kiddo to be good than to not be good.

Remember, too, if attention-seeking is the goal of the bulk of a kid's misbehavior, see if you can make attention be the reward he works toward (i.e., lunch with the teacher, running to the store with Mom or Dad, a brief sit-down with you, time to entertain the class, etc.). If it is power, then give a little power (let the kid be a special helper, do work in the principal's office, act as playground monitor, etc.). In other words, using M&M's®, stickers, homework passes, and other tangible rewards may be effective, but tailoring a reinforcement system to the specific needs of the child can have a more powerful hold on him. Remember diplomacy? Reach behind the misbehavior and tend to the issue that is breathing life into it.

6. The Premack Principle

The Premack Principle (Premack, 1959) is a term that you probably recognize on some level. It seems to ring a distant bell related to your Intro to Psych curriculum. Again, this is a term you memorized for the midterm and then promptly replaced in your memory with some sort of sports statistic, bundt cake recipe, or the uncanny ability to discern between "kind of dirty," "still wearable," and "torch this thing with Napalm" when sifting through the clothes on your dorm room floor (I have a feeling I am only talking to the guys here).

To refresh your memory, Premack refers to the idea of placing a low-priority behavior before a high-priority behavior. In other words, you earn the right to do what you want to do AFTER you do something that you don't want to do. The high-priority behavior (eating ice cream) becomes the re-enforcer to the low-priority one (eating broccoli). As Pink Floyd said (about a hundred years ago, I'm afraid), "How can you have any pudding if you don't eat your meat?"

If you can set up similar contingency-based plans with your kids, you may find that this works. In the end, the kid(s) are not working to avoid a negative consequence but rather are working to earn a good one. If they do not all get the math worksheet in on time and thus do not earn the re-enforcer, there's no harm, no foul. You can try again tomorrow.

Let me add a therapeutic caveat by once again mentioning Jay Haley (1993). Haley was interested in designing methods of therapy that utilized a client's natural resistance to change. In other words, none of us *really* relishes the thought of changing— even though the behavior in question may not be healthy or desirable. So in clinical work, Haley figured that our energy could be better spent if we used the client's resistance rather than fought against it. Remember the class clown example? Using the talent and energy instead of squashing it was the key to unlocking the student's success.

191

For now, I am going to refer to Haley's technique as the "anti-Premack." This is my name, not his, but the technique is all Haley. Remember that the Premack Principle requires that a high-priority behavior reinforces a low-priority behavior. Haley stands that concept on its head and recommends contracting with the client (see #7 below as well) so that if he or she performs a high-priority behavior, the client then agrees to engage in a low-priority behavior that is a healthier or more desirable choice.

For example, say a client wants to give up smoking (or cussing, or hitting his little brother). You make a contract (and the client agreeing to participate is critical) that whenever he smokes, he will then do 25 push-ups or run around the block or to the corner and back—you get the picture. As an aside, Haley was also keenly interested in the beneficial effects of exercise on physical and mental health and therefore liked to work it into his therapy. Be that as it may, Haley's technique puts the client into a no-lose scenario: Either he or she stops smoking to avoid the low-priority behavior (an example of aversion therapy?), or else he or she continues to smoke but adds healthy changes to his or her lifestyle.

The low-priority behavior does not have to be exercise—it can be cleaning the bathroom, dusting the living room, making dinner for one's spouse, or whatever. Haley felt strongly that the low-priority behavior, if repeated, would eventually replace the high-priority behavior. In other words, the two behaviors would switch on the priority continuum.

7. Contracting

Contracting is an interesting technique because on the surface, it does not seem to carry a lot of weight. When I bring this up in seminars, many of the participants raise an eyebrow and then check to see if maybe I drank my lunch.

I am here to say that signing a contract *does* seem to carry a lot of weight with kids—especially with males and particularly during their teen years. There is still some "honor among thieves," as agreeing to a behavioral contract can add a dimension of self-control that just discussing behavior may not. But don't limit your usage of contracting to older males; this technique can work with boys and girls of all ages.

Contracting can be a powerful tool. To bring this back into the home or classroom, utilize contracting with your junior high or high school kids to make concrete an agreement you are willing to forge with them. Of course, your sticking to your end of the bargain is of utmost importance, but creating a tangible record of the deal gives you a document to return to should the teen ever cry foul. It also gives the kid the feeling that you respect him or her because you felt he or she had the dignity to honor a contract.

Another concrete record I secure quite often with clients has to do with diet. I (as a matter of course during the intake process) ask all of my kids, teens especially, to give me a quick rundown of the things they have eaten and drunk over the past 3 days. Some folks call this a "food log" or a "food journal," but I am not nearly that formal with my data collection. I just want to know (a) what they are putting into their body and (b) how much caffeine are they drinking.

I don't think any of us would argue that diet can significantly impact mood and behavior, but losing valuable sleep will have a similar effect. The worse one's diet is and the more caffeine one consumes, the worse one's behavior and sleep will be. For these reasons, I will point out how lousy a kid's diet may be and ask that he or she commit to reducing the amount of caffeine and increasing at least one of the four basic food groups. We eventually settle on a dietary contract and sign it to seal the deal. I often have to remind kids that Jalapeño Cheetos do NOT count as a serving of vegetables.

Contracting can be powerful. And to be frank, if kids don't sign an informal contract with you, they could be in for other, more seriously binding contracts that have serious consequences when broken (i.e., suspensions, legal actions, failures).

193

8. Creating Opportunities to Serve Others

As I mentioned in the section on bullies, creating situations in which kids can earn respect from others in extraordinary situations can be powerful and provide incentives for behavior change. Think about it this way: Some of the kids who drive you bananas are ones who have learned to get their respect needs met in a variety of misguided ways. The respect they garner in these negative scenarios may not always be exceptionally gratifying, but in the mind of the "bad kid," it's all he or she has to get that need met. The behaviors are always hooked with stress though, because the "respect" is ill-gotten.

For example, a high school sophomore may suddenly get into Satan worship because it elicits a shock or fear reaction from peers and adults. You add to this a delightful array of piercings, black fingernail polish, outrageous clothing, and other assorted body art, and now the kid elicits a similar response from strangers who may not know about the Satan worship. This reaction will give the kid a brief, intense, sense of satisfaction, but it is inadequate when compared with other behaviors that may not have stress or negative consequences associated with them.

Opening new opportunities for respect to be earned in conventional (read as: HEALTHIER) situations can begin to turn the oil tanker. However, once kids choose the ill-gotten path to seeking respect, they are likely to become exceedingly pessimistic that the usual way will work for them.

I am being a bit wordy in this section, but suffice it to say that true respect will strike a different chord in these kids than fear, shock, or other fleeting forms of pseudo-respect.

By the way, some kids who have been on a bad path for a long time may actually behave worse once they are put into a healthy situation, as they begin to feel either 1) pressure to keep behaving well—something they do not believe they are capable of doing—or 2) anger at whoever or whatever dealt them the hand they have been given. So, while misbehavior may spike temporarily in these instances, stick with the kiddo and offer as much support and guidance as you are able.

All right ... we're in the middle of the 7th inning here, and we have yet to describe any plans that are structured and systematic in their approach. In the next couple of chapters, I do exactly that, so fear not! The relief core has been warming up in the bullpen, so let's grab a hot dog and a beer while we embark on the seventh-inning S-T-R-E-T-C-H. Anyone care to sing "Take Me Out to the Ballgame" in the voice of Harray Caray? Let's go, Cubbies!

Chapter 11

A Bit More Involved
Teaching Old Dogs New Tricks

Moving forward, we transition our ballgame into later innings by thinking about some strategies that involve a bit more in terms of time and attention. Still, while these strategies may ratchet up the level of commitment on your part, they may also ratchet up the impact on the targeted kids. I cover a few old standbys but put a different spin on them to facilitate user friendliness!

In this section, I describe the Good Behavior Game, time-out, and perhaps the senior member of our eldest dogs club: taking away of privileges. I then reserve an entire chapter to cover token economies (see Chapter 15), because this technique, when properly applied, can reap enormous benefits. I explain further and offer ideas for adaptation to different situations later.

For now, lower the protective eyewear, snap the rubber gloves into place, and get ready to get down and dirty with me!

1. The Good Behavior Game

Versions of the Good Behavior Game have been around since the days of the Cro-Magnon. This is evidenced by recently discovered ancient cave drawings depicting classrooms whereby teachers, clad in stylish yet comfortable mammoth skins, are seen doling out Skittles® and Tootsie Rolls® to third grade students with thick, slanted foreheads and hairy, muscled forearms (the students, that is, not the teachers). On the chalkboard, we can make out the outline of a crudely drawn stick figure of Jon Bon Jovi (popular even before music was invented)—he is missing both legs and one arm. The missing appendages were cause for initial concern to the archaeologists who unearthed this particular cave painting, but when they put the scene into the context of the Good Behavior Game, it all suddenly became perfectly clear.

The power of the Good Behavior Game is not in the name, but in the opportunity it provides to incorporate a warning system (or, some "mulligans") directly into your behavioral strategy. Plus, you can build a sense of community and accomplishment into a classroom, as the system relies on social monitoring for success. Everyone pulls on the same rope, so to speak. However, this system is not only germane to teachers and school systems; I have taught many parents to use the same system at home, only we use a dry erase marker and the refrigerator door rather than the board at the front of the classroom (a whiteboard or grease board can be used at home if the parent balks at writing on the fridge).

Returning to schools for a moment, the Good Behavior Game is the standard recommendation for classrooms with two or three or four (or so) acting-out students. To begin, let's assume we only have one student or one child in the classroom acting out then expand into more. In describing the game, I use a lot of words and a number of pages, but bear in mind that this is actually a very simple strategy to implement. As I explain the pieces involved, I also sprinkle in a couple of real-life examples, too, to illustrate how the components work in perfect harmony. Here's how the game works (loosely adapted, and including Dr. Steve's own spin, from its original creators, Barrish, Saunders, & Wold, 1969):

First, you make a drawing on the board or fridge. I talk about situations involving high school kids later on in this section but open the discussion with younger kiddos. In this case, the drawing on the board can be somewhat rudimentary: a thermometer, for example. There are countless other possibilities, limited only by the imagination of the adult and/or kids. But let me stick with the thermometer example for the sake of continuity and clarity.

You draw the thermometer on the board with a reservoir at the bottom, then five graduations of temperature running up the side of the tube. Each graduation (i.e., temperature, or "degree") is clearly marked as counting down to the "zero" point, which will be the reservoir itself.

For the rules of the game, take your target behavior—let's say it is yelling out in class without raising your hand first. (Any .com behavior will work here in the home or classroom.) Explain to the class that when you hear a student yell out, you will do one of the following things:

a) Issue a warning. After the warning, you will then either proceed directly to step "b" or issue a second warning. And to repeat, the number of warnings will depend on the general nature of your room (or home). For students who are well behaved overall, you may issue a single warning to give them a chance to pull it together. For kids who tend to be more on the rambunctious side, you may give a couple warnings. In any case, you will either issue a warning, or proceed directly to the next option.

b) Erase the "5 degrees" mark off of the thermometer. When you erase the "5 degrees" mark, you can either lop off the number alone or obliterate the entire part of the tube that sticks up past "4 degrees." As you can probably anticipate, with each repeated transgression, you erase another and another graduation ("degree"), until finally, the reservoir at the bottom gets erased, and the prize is not granted for that period of time. If there is still mercury in the reservoir at the end of the pre-determined length of time, the kids earn the prize.

As I mentioned previously, it is vital that you "set the hook" as early in the process as possible. Kids need to know that they have the capability to succeed, so building in an assurance of initial success is important. Therefore, if the kids burn through the thermometer too quickly, you have a couple of variables to adjust to your situation and ensure success. They are 1) *the latency of reset* and 2) *the number of degrees.*

These two variables play off of each other and need to be considered in tandem to maximize the potential of the game. The level of variation again depends on the general nature of the kid(s), as you will eventually settle onto a point of *equilibrium* with them. In this instance, equilibrium means that you hit a point whereby your kids have the right combination of *latency* and *degrees* to be able to earn the reward. This equilibrium will give the game some traction, as it will allow the students to reap the benefits and "get it." Over time, the goal will be to push that wall back, but I explain that later. There sure are lots of big words and complicated-sounding concepts and rules! Here is how to think about each of these concepts and put them into motion:

The latency of reset refers to the amount of time the game goes on before the clock gets reset and the thermometer goes back to five degrees. It is also the amount of time required for the kids to either earn or not earn the pot of gold at the end of the rainbow. In school, if you have the students for only a set amount of time (e.g., 52 minutes per day if you teach a course in middle or high school), then your time is pretty much determined for you. No need to mess with the natural schedule of the day, unless you have a room that is remarkably out of control, in which case you will work to reset the clock more frequently. Again, the goal is to reach equilibrium.

If you have your class all day, you can either go the entire day on one thermometer, split the day into "pre-lunch" and "post-lunch," or move to reset after each subject is taught or even hourly if that is an easier method for the kids to digest. The determining factor will be how well they are able to wrap their brains around the concept and also how well they are able to succeed. Plus, keep in mind that smaller, shorter-term goals are generally more effective than longer-term, bigger ones. This is particularly true with younger kids who are not as accurate at envisioning longer time frames.

At home, many parents split their time with the kids into (a) the period between arriving home from school until dinner and (b) from dinner until bedtime. This sytem works well and can be used effectively unless the kiddo quickly burns through the thermometer and feels like a failure. In such cases, the latency can be adjusted downward until the equilibrium is achieved and the child feels successful. In fact, in seriously out-of-control households, I tell parents that they are going to have to make a huge time commitment because we are going to begin by resetting the clock and redrawing the thermometer every 15 minutes. I want the kids to earn positives and force the parents to catch them being good as often as possible. After a week or so of that, we will go every 30 minutes. After a week of that, we switch to every hour, and so on. We "push the wall back" and force the kids to maintain better behavior for longer stretches of time.

Let me take a brief sidebar here to talk about rewards. I know I left our last concept a bit fuzzy, but I return to it and clarify it for you later.

If you would like to use a bigger goal as the carrot on the stick, you will need to help the kids move toward it slowly. For a step-wise progression toward a bigger goal (like a field trip or a pizza party or a special trip or attending a friend's birthday at Chuck E. Cheese—something remarkable in terms of time and expense), then have the kids earn points along the way. This way, they can feel as though the immediate goals are well within reach. This system also builds in some flexibility to allow for bad days to take place without sinking the ship of the entire operation. For example, make each day that the kids have mercury left in the reservoir worth 10 points, but make the trip to the Science Museum worth 200 points. Then, you can use a graphic representation of a *big* thermometer, with graduations of 10 that you can slowly fill all the way up to 200. This system maintains hope even through some bad-behavior days. Plus, if you can keep the date of the trip flexible, it can depend solely on the behavior in your room or home. The better behaved the kids are, the quicker they can earn the trip.

In this example, I made the successful completion of the short-term game (i.e., keep the reservoir until the end of the time period) worth 10 points for a reason. If it is worth 1 point and the trip is worth 20 points, you limit your own flexibility. If the mercury is worth 10 per day, you have the capability to throw in some bonus points along the way for exemplary behavior or for other projects that may be fun to add to the mix. You can now throw in 3, 5, or 7 points at random intervals to drive home the point that good behavior is *always* going to be more beneficial than bad behavior.

So, the *latency of reset* is all about how to determine reset time. In explaining the *number of degrees*, we again must consider the general behavior of the kids. If the kids behave well, you may only need three or maybe even two degrees. A classroom with lots of troublemakers or a son or daughter that is more ill-behaved may need six or seven. Again, the point of deciding how many degrees you will need is so you can keep focused on helping the kids achieve the goal to help you set the hook. In a nutshell, you need fewer mulligans for better-behaved kids and more for those who need a little extra help to reach their goals.

How these two concepts play out together requires a little ingenuity on your part. With a situation that feels somewhat more out of control, you can either add more degrees or you may wish to shorten the latency to help the kids get some grip on the game. In the end, you want the right combination of degrees and latency to ensure success.

Before I go on, I know I keep emphasizing that the child has to feel successful, so it is imperative that you find that equilibrium point in setting up the game. The reason that success in the short run is so important has to do with some of the "bad kids" in your home or classroom. These are kids who have generally been perceived as bad throughout their entire life and may not realize that success is even within their grasp. They get good at losing, and of course, perception is reality. Getting the oil tanker turned requires that they begin to redefine the opportunity as "possible" rather than "impossible."

As I alluded to earlier, once you have reached that point of equilibrium and your targeted kiddos begin to earn the pot of gold, you can begin to tinker with degrees and latency to push the children to maintain good behavior for longer periods of time and with fewer warnings as you "push the wall back."

For example, after 2 weeks you may decide to make the latency 90 minutes instead of 60. The number of degrees will remain the same, but the kids will be required now to hold it together for a longer period of time with the same five degrees. Or, you can keep the latency at 60 minutes but shorten the number of degrees to four or three instead of five, thereby requiring that the students have fewer "yelling outs" within the same period of time to earn the pot of gold.

Another way to monitor this "pushing the wall back" would be to reward better behavior with higher point values or keeping some mercury in the reservoir. Thus, if it used to be 10 points for not burning through five degrees in a 52-minute class period you can lower the number of initial degrees to four (from five) or make the successful completion of the class period worth 12 points instead of 10. You create a system of greater reward for greater behavior.

This system will keep its grip if you follow through on the longer-term payoff, then immediately establish a new reward system. It's sort of a *quid pro quo*: If the kids let you do your job as a great mentor/parent/teacher, you will let them do their job of being screwball kids and teens!

Here is an example of how to adapt the game for older kids. Let me return to a school for an illustration. If you teach high school, a thermometer on the board may seem a bit hokey, which may derail your attempt to establish roots with the game. Here is how I used the Good Behavior Game to help a high school chemistry teacher in a pretty rough inner-city school begin to regain control of her classroom. In her case, the kids would begin to shout insults to one another, which would (of course) escalate until a fight broke out. In general, we tend to frown on fights breaking out in a fully stocked chemistry lab—know what I mean?

Same rules apply as already described but with a twist: I told the teacher to ask the students to come up with a pop icon who could, in essence, represent the thermometer. In that case, the class liked a rapper named Lil Wayne. So, fine … let's use Lil Wayne.

The teacher drew a picture of Lil Wayne on the board, but in a particular manner. I told her to draw his head with all the details (i.e., eyes, ears, nose, smiling mouth, hair), then the rest of him as a stick figure. The stick figure had a trunk, two legs and two arms—in other words, five appendages ("degrees") and one smiling face ("reservoir"). Now, the system was set up whereby she would erase one body part of Lil Wayne each time she heard an insult, with his face being the last part to go. Thus, if Lil Wayne was still smiling at the end of the class period (i.e., there was still mercury left in the reservoir), she gave the class a tally on the board. And for the first wave of the game, three tallies would equal a reward (which the class worked out with her).

Over time, I advised her to increase the number of tallies required to earn the reward but to also work with the class to increase the value of the rewards. Better behavior leads to better rewards, right?

Also, the teacher had the flexibility to add hands and feet to Lil Wayne in her attempt to find the point of equilibrium. If the class could not initially manage to get through chemistry without burning through all five body parts, she could have added a few more until she found the point whereby they could hold it together and start forward progress in the game.

Before moving on, let me address what happens when there are a number of kids involved in this process—something that obviously happens in classrooms a lot. Again, let me state that the success of the entire class rests on their ability to pull the troublemakers under control. This system gets difficult when there are four or five students acting out, as they may band together, making their bad behavior nearly impervious to the efforts of the rest of the room to contain them. If this is happening in your classroom, then divide the class into, say, four teams (based on the number of troublesome students). Put one of the students with a behavior problem on each of the teams. This will eliminate the cumulative effect of the four together and thereby make each team responsible for reigning in only one of the acting-out peers rather than all four.

You can then reward each team individually for keeping mercury in their reservoir, have each team contribute points into the BIG thermometer, or use some combo of both. The beauty of any good behavior plan for behavior management is in its ability to be adaptable across a number of developmental levels and situations!

Incidentally, the only way that the Good Behavior Game will completely fail at school is if you have a student who enjoys the power of being able to derail the train of the entire classroom (or team). If this happens, you can try to put the troublemaker on a team with some of his or her stronger-willed classmates in an effort to give them a chance to rein this student in, or else you may have to set up a plan to deal with him or her individually. More examples to follow!

2. Time-Out

Time-out is perhaps the most ubiquitous of the behavior programs with a specific name. Time-out could have its own wing in the Parenting Hall of Fame. I have been sitting here for several minutes, drinking a soda and trying to think of any other behavior plan that has achieved such widespread acclaim.

Needless to say, I can't. Pretty much anyone who a) has kids, b) has spent a lot of time around kids, c) lives somewhere within 53 miles of a kid, or d) has ever been a kid themselves, has heard of time-out.

The technique and term were first coined by a behavioral psychologist, Arthur Staats, in 1958 but really came to the forefront in 1970 (Staats, 1970). So, while time-out's long history gives it an advantage, in that the rules of the procedure are generally understood without too much explanation, it also serves as a major weakness. What I mean by that is everyone has a preconceived notion of time-out. And I don't just mean that they know the rules; rather, everyone has an opinion about the utility of time-out. They either love it or hate it, and their opinion is generally set in stone.

Let me explain a couple issues I deal with when I consult with parents or school personnel. First, I assess their mindset toward the program and then see what rules they understand to be "the truth" when it comes to implementing time-out. I have to do this because the success or failure of my role as consultant seems to hinge on my ability to break on through their preconceived notions and essentially "re-teach" time-out in a more useful way.

Having said that, I am quite certain that you, dear reader, also have your own ideas of how to do time-out and whether it is worth your effort. I implore you: Please shelve these ideas for a few minutes and read on with an open mind.

Before I wade into the quicksand (by the way, whatever happened to that "death by quicksand" that was so popular on TV in the 1950s?), let me back up a step and say a couple things. First, some of you school folks work in an environment where you have a formalized time-out procedure. If you are in a self-contained classroom or an alternative school or other structured setting, there is probably a documented, step-by-step process you must follow. If this is the case, then carry on. The bottom line in *any* employment setting is that you have to do what your boss tells you to do. My guess is that the procedure is in place for your safety as well as the safety of your students.

Second, in some settings, time-out in any form may not work. Whenever you attend a seminar or read a book like this one, you will bump into a lot of different ideas that may or may not be applicable to your specific situation. Nothing gets more bothersome to me in a live seminar than when I introduce an idea, and then someone in the back raises his or her hand and says some version of, "Yeah, but … I am doing (fill in the blank), and that won't work in my situation."

I am never sure what exactly they want me to say in that case, so I usually just reply with a polite, "Uh … okay." So let me reiterate: If it won't work, then don't do it!

Here's the deal: I am not going to teach you the nuts and bolts of time-out. If you really want to know those nuts and bolts, I am sure there are volumes of text already written on the topic. Rather, I am going to help you re-think the notion of time-out so that it becomes a more effective tool for behavior management. Let me take it out of the archaic and transform it into a slick and shiny "new and improved" version. I may even throw out the term *space-age polymers* to show just how unbelievably glamorous this new product is. Heck, I may even get a cool celebrity endorsement to begin a groundswell of support and to lend credibility to the program!

To begin this sojourn, let's review the two purposes of time-out. To put it another way, why do we even have time-out? I am sure most of you could hit this softball out of the park, but let me answer this semi-rhetorical question myself. Time-out is meant to

a) Separate a kid from the herd: Remove the child from whatever the situation is that is causing overstimulation, distress, or anxiety.

b) Give the child time and a space to cool off—and I really meant to write it that way. Practicing the skill of "gaining control" is important for kids.

Most everyone knows that already, but the most pressing problem (as I see it) involving time-out is that it becomes another venue for a power struggle to develop between student and teacher or child and parent. Taking some of the sting out of time-out could encourage higher levels of compliance and thereby remove some of the fight that often happens when time-out situations arise. In other words, I want to help you—and the kids—see "calming down" NOT simply as a punishment but as an opportunity for kids to get settled back down to earth. Heck, many adults joke, "I wish *I* could get a time-out once in a while!"

You know why grown-ups say this? It's because we don't see time to *chill* as a bad thing! We have the ability to self-select, and thus we interpret "time away" as a positive rather than a noxious event. Here are a few ideas to tweak the time-out concept, to take out some of the punch, and to make it more user-friendly.

a) Name Change. The first order of business is to change the name. *Time-out* tends to be a loaded—and somewhat antiquated—moniker. As I said, everyone has an opinion or attitude toward time-out, so let's not call it that anymore. When many people think about time-out, they imagine the kiddo will have to sit like a wooden soldier in some preordained time-out spot to fulfill whatever the time-out requirements happen to be.

Parents sometimes tell me that that is how they picture time-out, and they ask how to "make" the child sit in time-out. The scenario tends to *create* rather than *diffuse* tension in the home.

For these reasons, I recommend a name with less toxic implications. I often suggest calling the procedure *quiet time.* Calling it quiet time implies that, once the child is in quiet time, he or she will only be allowed to engage in quiet activities. Thus, the kid may not necessarily have to sit still on a chair, but he or she certainly can if he or she elects to. Alternatively, the child could be able to read a book, draw, do homework, or just chill out. The rules you create can slowly change the program from being overtly punitive to providing an opportunity for the kid to calm down before getting back into the swing of things.

We can also use more "hip" names, like "chill out time" or "cool out time" or some other tag that has a positive spin. Choose something to which the kids can relate, as they are the ones affected by your choice.

b) Self-Selecting. An additional way to take some of the punch out of situations in which *you* tell a kid what to do is to offer an opportunity for him or her to *self-select* chill out time. For example, if you create a space designated solely for "chilling out" and allow kids to enter that space on their own accord, it becomes a more functional option when they begin to feel out of control.

To pull this off, take a corner of the classroom or a low-traffic space at home and decorate it in a fashion that is conducive to chilling out. If you don't want to call it the chill out space, you can give it some other name that hooks onto something the kids are studying at the time. I have heard of teachers calling that area "Antarctica" or "Australia" (to coincide with something learned in geography class). The point is, make a space that is set apart (both physically and via décor) from the rest of the classroom.

What you want to eventually develop is a situation in which kids are allowed to enter that space when they feel like they need to get away for a few minutes, when they need to calm down some, or whenever something leads them to want to be alone for a while. With some kids who tend to push the boundaries, you may also need to have a time limit—or an actual timer—for the chill out zone.

The option of self-selection makes the zone a less confrontational set-up when you have to direct the child into it.

Another artifact of this idea is that the chill zone in your home or classroom will begin to develop a personality of its own, with its own rules of engagement! The kids will know how to act when they enter the chill zone and will react accordingly. Plus, they will begin to refer to that part of the room as though it were another character in the big Broadway play of their life, rather than just a formerly empty corner of a cinderblock classroom.

I heard a great suggestion from a teacher at a tough private school. He had created "The Wall" in his classroom (an obvious tip of the hat to Pink Floyd, I'm sure). When students were on The Wall, they were on penalty, and the severity of the offense determined where on The Wall they would be placed. In the end, The Wall had its own persona, and the students all knew the score of the game if one of their peers was seen at any point along The Wall.

As these examples demonstrate, with a little buoyancy, a version of time-out can be folded more neatly into your day instead of creating a disruption in it.

c) "Get Out of Class Free" Cards. Another idea for an alternate version of time-out is one that we use through our office with many of our clients with Asperger's. With these kids, we work out a deal with the school whereby they are allowed, once per day, to be given a "get out of class free" card. With this card, they are afforded an opportunity to self-select 10 minutes to go to their safe place (more on this in a minute) to calm down.

This program needs to have a couple pieces in place before it can be pulled off successfully, but in general it works for these kids because it affords them an opportunity to recognize escalation and then to practice de-escalation, control, and containment.

The pieces that need to be in place are as follows: First, we teach the kids how to recognize escalation. Our lesson is grounded largely in physiological reactions to stress, as students with Asperger's are somewhat more prone to disconnecting from the emotional aspects of becoming upset. Therefore, we teach these kids that if you feel your fists clenching up or your belly beginning to tighten or your jaw clenching or any number of other common reactions, then that means you are beginning to grow upset or escalate.

Next, we work out the safe place. Typically, this tends to be the office of a counselor we are working with. It may also be the vice principal's or principal's office. The location depends largely on who has a positive working relationship with both our office and also the student in question.

Finally, we may arrange for an escort if the student needs some guidance in getting to the safe place. We don't want to have a student running amok in the building if we can possibly avoid it! Usually, the younger students may need some assistance to get themselves situated.

We may also help the teacher coach the rest of the class in how to address this issue, as there may be some "sibling rivalry" evolving among classmates who would like the same courtesy extended to them. In this situation, we can either make it a class-wide program (although for other students, the safe place will have to be moved to a location within the room to avoid a stampede on the poor guidance counselor!). Incorporating the get out of class free program with the chill out zone (referred to previously) is an effective means for dealing with any possible rivalry/jealousy. Another option when other students in the class are jealous of the kids with Asperger's getting to go to a safe space is to get the others on board when it comes to helping the students with Asperger's. Letting the class know they will be instrumental in helping a fellow student out may elicit a different reaction than being indignant.

In any case, once these pieces are in place, we begin the program with our client. It's a good idea to open by telling the kid that *any* ongoing abuse of this system will result in the privilege being taken off the table. As stated previously, this allows the kid a chance to practice the skill of lassoing the horse and dragging it back into the barn. As you might recall, helping children develop this skill was also recommended for reducing the number of tantrum outbursts, as it provides an alternative to the feeling of hopeless and unbridled escalation.

d) A Few Additional Thoughts on Time-Out. I thought it prudent to talk about a couple other ideas I have heard from folks around the country. One involves a time-out technique of having the child engage gross muscle groups to encourage calming while he or she is having a time-out.

I'm not sure if any of you have seen the new-fangled time-out chairs that are being manufactured, but they essentially look like a seat on top of a half of a Pilates ball. The way these seats work is to create an unstable base at the bottom—something akin to making the child into a life-sized Weeble®. The kiddo has to concentrate on shifting his or her weight constantly in reaction to the movements of the ball base. The basic idea is that if the kid is forced to focus on *sitting*, he or she will be less inclined to direct his or her efforts toward acting out.

Another feature of these chairs is that they are soft and squishy underneath, which allows the child to engage in gross motor movement by forcing him/her to maintain balance by keeping a constant center of gravity with their legs. This can also detract from acting out energy. Some chairs, come with little legs on the bottom to stabilize the ball, thus allowing for some bouncing capability without the danger of the chair falling over sideways.

Now, before you dismiss this as another flash-in-the-pan idea that will fade away like other fads have, I can say that there is anecdotal evidence for the utility of these seats. I have heard from teachers and therapists around the country that they have used them with success.

e) Deep Tissue Pressure. Here's another idea, particularly for kids on the autism spectrum. Just as gross muscle involvement (mentioned previously) can work to de-escalate a lot of kids, according to the research of Temple Grandin (2008), deep tissue pressure also helps.

Temple Grandin became "the cow lady" (my words, not hers!) through her famous work in the 1980s. She was hired by a meat packing plant to help them with the slaughter process; they were having difficulty keeping the cattle calm while they were being walked to slaughter. Grandin, being an adult on the autism spectrum, had devoted her life's work to (a) a Ph.D. in animal science from The University of Illinois and (b) understanding and helping her deal with her condition. Through her work, Grandin eventually invented the hug machine and applied it to hypersensitive kids and adults everywhere. She found that, paradoxically, for children and teens who could otherwise not be touched lightly, deep pressure elicits a calm-down response instead of a reactive, agitated response.

Parents and teachers may be able to better relate to Grandin's ideas if they think about swaddling a baby. Wrapping a baby tightly can soothe it, because the pressure mimics the pressure of the womb. The pressure equals security and comfort, thereby helping the baby settle down and de-escalate when it is upset. For many kiddos on the autism spectrum, the same principle applies: A strong hug or a (literal) swaddle with blankets can soothe. I have instructed parents and teachers to get a carpet remnant and roll the child up in it or lay the child on a softly carpeted floor, place a bean bag chair on top of him or her, and slowly lean into the bean bag chair. However possible, create pressure.

They do make fancy hug machines for kids. They look a little bit like the wringer from an old-fashioned clothes-washing machine. The kids pull or push themselves through the wringer and literally "roll" themselves to comfort! There are also weighted vests, weighted throw blankets, and bed-sized blankets that come in several different weights—some have pockets sewn in so that the net weight can be adjusted for different-sized folks. All of these items are designed to calm when escalation begins. Each of these can speed the efficiency of time-out because they trigger a parasympathetic response and create calm from the storm.

f) Conclusion. The final idea I have for teachers and parents is one to which I alluded briefly earlier in this book. This is an idea that goes back to taking a bit of the power struggle out of the time-out situation. If you are having trouble having the kids sit like wooden soldiers in their time-out place, then back down some on that requirement. As already stated, adding a bit of buoyancy will help float some of those kids who are regularly in very heavy situations. In these cases, maybe just put a square of masking tape down on the floor around the time-out spot and tell the kid that he or she doesn't have to sit perfectly still, but must 1) be quiet and 2) remain within the square.

This will be particularly effective with younger kiddos who may have the intention, but not the ability, to sit perfectly still for 3 minutes!

To summarize time-out, remember that offering the child or teen a replacement behavior for the offending one can 1) build a relationship as you two take some one-on-one time to work this out and 2) give an alternative to the bad behavior. Learning takes place in times of calm—such as during and following the time-out—not in times of distress. So, de-escalate and then teach by subsequently reinforcing the kid's application of the new, positive behavior option.

3. A Few Therapy-Oriented Ideas—Even for Non-therapists!

a. Journaling. One very basic intervention we use as therapists involves journaling, through which the client can gain mastery over bad feelings and negative impulses by expunging themselves of the "ick." In technical terms, this is called *catharsis*, but it is actually a bit more involved than that.

For example, when a teenager writes out how she feels, two important processes are happening for her: (a) she is putting to words all of the ambiguous, and perhaps ambivalent, thoughts and feelings she has had floating unchecked through her brain, and (b) she is organizing these thoughts and feelings on the paper, which can diminish the impact (or power) they have over her. Nothing ever seems quite as heinous once it can be understood and expressed. Think about the last time you talked though something that was bothering you. It may have been over coffee and with a close friend, but once in the open air, the terrorizing thoughts probably lost a lot of their steam.

Generally, this technique works best with kids who enjoy writing and have a somewhat simple time expressing themselves in this manner. For some kids, writing down how they feel each night will be a nearly impossible, and therefore frustrating, chore. For them, there are a number of alternate means for allowing themselves the freedom of expression. For example, you could have the younger kids (who may not be able to write all that well in the first place) draw a picture representing how they feel.

One of my favorite ways to structure this exercise (if you would like to add some structure) is to have the child draw himself or herself (or his or her mother, father, or other significant person) as something *other than* a person. It is interesting to see what animal or inanimate object a child may select to represent himself or herself or another person. You can also chart progress over time by seeing how a child's representations morph into more positive or less positive depictions.

For teens, you may want to consider having them draw, write music, put together a self-shot movie via their cell phone, splice together film scenes from Hollywood productions (if they have the software and know-how to accomplish this—it amazes me what kids know how to do these days), or create a reality TV–type "confessional." To pull this off (and most kids think this is a pretty cool exercise), have them record themselves using their computer's built-in camera or their cell phone's movie mode. The kid should speak extemporaneously to the camera, just as if he or she were a reality show contestant commenting on his or her life. The teen can go through some of the crises of the day, revel in his or her accomplishments, or wax philosophic about anything that strikes his or her fancy.

In the end, it is about taking what is janky and wicked on the inside and getting into open air.

b. Games with Rules. Let me now describe one of my favorite interventions—using games that have rules. I like this one because it's fun AND it teaches many of life's most basic rules. Playing games helps to teach sportsmanship (i.e., how to be a gracious winner *and* a good loser), controlling levels of frustration, anticipating an opponent's thought process and potential next moves, planning ahead and strategizing your own moves, impulse control (especially in games which require patience), and "driving between the lines" (or, put another way, following the rules).

Games for kiddos with impulse control problems include Slap Jack, Jenga®, Operation® (the Hulk® version is my favorite because my big fingers can actually maneuver the pieces), and Don't Break the Ice®. You can make Jenga® a more therapeutically oriented game by either purchasing the therapy edition or by taking a marker and writing sentence stems and/or feelings stems on the sides of the blocks. Then, when each player takes a block out, he or she must respond to the stem. For a good selection of therapy games for children of all ages, go to the Self Help Warehouse website, http://www.selfhelpwarehouse.com/games.html.

Most games require some combination of skill and luck (e.g., Trouble®, Connect Four®, Sorry®). As you play, you and the client can process your thoughts and reactions openly so the kid can learn from an adult's perspective.

Some games, such as Candyland® and Chutes and Ladders®, tend to be governed by luck-of-the-draw. When playing a game that is not determined by luck alone, there exists the issue of deciding who wins the game. For example, if you are playing checkers with a 7-year-old kid, I am pretty sure that you will win 10 times out of 10 if you play the child straight up. To get around this, and also to help the client feel more empowered, I usually structure the game by asking on the front end, "How old do you want me to play today?" That way, if he wants to win, he tells me to play like I'm a 2-year-old. If he gets a little more confidence, he may ask me to play him head-to-head like a 7-year-old. And if he strolls in a little cocky that afternoon, he may ask me to play like somebody my age (which, in his eyes, is about 95, I'm afraid). This way, the kid is put in charge of the level of competition, thus allowing for his needs to be met by my participation. Trust is built, and he can learn to handle the weight of winning or losing.

Let me share a couple of closing thoughts. Perhaps the most-utilized game in my office is actually one of the simplest. I have a Nerf® hoop hanging on the back of my door, and almost every kid tromping through likes to take at least a shot or two. For many kids, therapy is a dry, irritating experience. A kiddo may feel like he or she is in the "spotlight dance" if he or she has to sit on the couch and I stare across the room at him or her. Shooting hoops puts us shoulder to shoulder, refocuses the child's anxiety, and allows some of the nuttier clients the room to be active and get out some energy. When a kid is active, he or she is far more likely to open up and talk to me than if the kid is sitting and listening to the clock ticking in the background.

Video games can be fun too and can take the pressure off the kids to fill empty space by talking; however, beware of getting hustled. Some of the doggone games require all 10 of your fingers, six of your toes, and your tongue to properly work the controller. (Ever count the number of buttons on a video game controller???) More than a couple teenage boys have laughed like hyenas while they smoked my grits playing Madden® football. Revenge is a dish best served cold, so I dust off my old Candyland® game and crack my knuckles menacingly.

c. Minuchin's "Make It Happen." This is another simple technique but one that can be quite effective in fortifying (and defining, in some cases) a parent's power base. Salvador Minuchin writes about his "make it happen" technique in a couple of his books (see Minuchin & Fishman, 1981). Its intent is to shore up what he refers to as the "executive subsystem." In other words, if a 3-year-old is running the house, he or she has to be standing on the shoulders of an adult. Arranging the subsystems to reflect a healthier hierarchy (the parents on top, the children below) we can then work to restore balance.

To illustrate this technique, Minuchin gives an example of a single mom who came to his office with a hyperactive 4-year-old daughter. The girl bopped wildly around the office, singing to herself and touching everything within reach, while the depressed, overwhelmed mother sat on the couch like a pile of dirty laundry.

Minuchin asked her, "What would you like to have happen?" The mother (of course) indicated that she would like for her daughter to sit down on the couch next to her and be quiet.

Minuchin simply replied, "Make it happen."

The mother began to protest, "What? I can't do that! Don't you see what she's doing in your office right …"

Minuchin interrupted her, "Make it happen."

The mother began again, "Did you hear what I said? I said that …"

"Make it happen."

The mother, now frustrated, got up in a huff, grabbed the daughter, and sat her 4-year-old fanny on the couch next to her. The daughter remained in place for about 8 seconds and then sprang up and resumed canvassing Minuchin's office. Rather than acquiesce to defeat, Minuchin used those 8 seconds to reinforce the power that Mom forgot she had. He said, "Excellent! That was great, Mom!" When the daughter sprang up, he said, "Now do it again."

That entire session was spent reinforcing Mom's control in a situation in which she felt none to begin with. Dethroning the daughter was going to be a long process, but it had to begin with a single step, and the 8 seconds of compliance was just that.

4. The Taking Away of Privileges

This little nugget is so engrained in the management strategies of parents and teachers that there is not much I can reasonably expect to add! However, I do have one thing for you to think about when implementing the taking away of privileges.

If you have a repeat offender—a child who keeps doing the same old same old to get into hot water—it's easy for a pattern to develop whereby the child no longer cares if you remove the privilege. In other words, if recess or video games get taken away over and over, the impact of the loss lessens over time. Plus, you begin to erode the kid's hope of ever having a week of success!

In most cases, the kid does the crime, he or she does the time, and then the privilege gets reinstated right away. In other words, there is no further contingency. With most kids, this strategy works. You yank recess for most screwball students, and they feel it. However, with the repeat offenders, we should change up the game plan. Here is what we can try with the few who *don't* feel the pain of having privileges taken away:

Rather than automatically reinstate a privilege after the appropriate sentence has been served, create a contingency for reinstatement. For example, let's say Gregory loses two recesses because of some transgression. He serves his time away from recess, but rather than have him go on his merry way the next day, create a system of restitution, and if you can make the restitution fit the transgression, then you have an ideal situation. For instance, if Gregory has broken something of yours in the classroom, he should serve the two recesses and then "work off" his debt by cleaning the room, helping you with a project, serving others, and so on. The amount of time required to reinstate recess would depend on the relative value of the thing that was broken. Only after he has "undone" the offense can he return to normal recess.

This strategy can also work well in the home, particularly for kiddos whose parents have a hard time recognizing when a punishment is over and for kids who have lost a lot of self-esteem because they are *always* getting into trouble, breaking stuff, and messing up. With high-impact, high-stress, high-energy kids with ADHD, both conditions are usually present.

If one such kiddo breaks something at home that costs, say, 12 bucks, Mom can swing a deal whereby she pays him a fair wage, and he gets to work it off. She could pay 5 dollars an hour to rake leaves or pick up rocks or weed the flowerbed. (Active restitution activities are best for high-energy kids, plus it gets them out of the house!) When he has completed 2.5 hours of the task, he has made good on the transgression, and all is dropped—and that concept is *key*. The parent has to agree to let it go once the child makes good on the transgression, otherwise the restorative power of dignity will be lost. The parent has a clearly defined endpoint, and the child has the satisfaction of knowing that he or she can mend a broken fence.

In many cases, there will not be a direct 1:1 correlation between transgression and ideal restitution. However, you can still set up a scenario whereby the child pays back time, money, or stress (!). The point is, value gets placed on the return of the privilege instead of their just being an automatic re-up. Placing a minor barrier to reinstatement can deepen the impact of the loss, build empathy by furthering the child's understanding of the relative worth of the asset sullied by his or her behavior, and allow your plan to progress down the path of making it better to be good than to not be good.

Those are a few of my ideas for structured means of gaining control over behaviorally challenged kids and teens. As you move through these plans, you can begin to identify those children who are truly atypical and may not have the capability to respond to your management techniques. I discuss those kids later. I have devoted the entire next chapter to a system that has been shown to be very effective for gaining control of the home or classroom—token economy. I know many of you are already using some version of token economy, but I hope I can add to the ideas you carry and/or create a new avenue for those of you who are not utilizing this idea.

Chapter 12
The Token Economy
Setting the Stage for Living

Let's move into talking about a great, adaptable, flexible system called token economy!

Let me begin this discussion with a definition. I realize that most of you have at least heard of the term *token economy*, but unless you are using such a system in your home or classroom, you may not know exactly what it is. In a nutshell, a token economy is a system whereby kids earn tokens for good behavior (more on what tokens are in a minute), and then over time, they have options related to how they use or "spend" their tokens. This system was first developed in Florida by a fellow named Teodoro Ayllon in the 1960s and came to prominence when he and a colleague published a watershed book on the topic (Ayllon & Azrin, 1968). You can get really specific ideas from Ayllon's series of books on the subject, and he is still alive and hard at work writing and teaching at Georgia State University. In this chapter, I draw on his theories and present some ideas on how to apply them.

So, the token economy in the home or classroom works almost like using currency. You earn, you spend, and you revel in small victories. This is why I subtitled this chapter "Setting the Stage for Living": We teach kids valuable life lessons about earning, spending, and managing their finances through this process. In fact, the lessons can be amazingly direct, but let me table that for now. Rather than confuse matters with a cumbersome narrative on all the options available within token economy, I set this chapter up like an FAQ (Frequently Asked Questions) page on a website. I have kept it relatively manageable by limiting it to 10 questions.

In the spirit of the Internet sites on which this section is modeled, I list the questions first and then get into the responses. I only wish I could make them clickable links to save your eyes the strain of actually having to read each one, but life goes that way sometimes. Here we go …

1. How do we get started?
2. What do we use for tokens?
3. What do we use for rewards?
4. How do I know what to make everything cost?
5. Can this program be adapted for older kids or in situations where I have six or seven classes of 30 kids each moving through my classroom every day?
6. Can this system be used class wide rather than for individual students?
7. I have a student/child who gets very angry because he or she always feels outperformed by a classmate/sibling. Is there either a way to deal with this situation or perhaps a different method to dole out rewards for token economy?
8. Do I also take away tokens for poor behavior?
9. What is "response cost"?
10. What are your closing words of wisdom?

1. How Do We Get Started?

The first step is to sit the child or the class down and let them know the deal. If you are a teacher, you will either be implementing this program from the starting line in August or

September, or you will be implementing it mid-stream. Either way, the directions/rules should be laid out in a manner that the targeted kids can understand.

Then, you'll need to put the nuts and bolts into place, including figuring out the type of tokens you will use, the goals for appropriate behavior, and the relative "cost" for each goal. Let me hit each of those questions separately.

Furthermore, keep this in mind as you begin this program: The power of this program with some of the kiddos who have worn the "bad kid" label throughout their entire life is to have them *start to feel successful*. Remember the point I brought up a chapter or two ago that the *worst*-behaved kids in the joint are not bad 100% of the time. There is just no way. During those brief respites when they are sitting still and paying attention, you have to hustle back and catch them being good. Change the rules of how they see themselves and make it better to be good than to not be good, but also let them know that they can (at least in your room) be successful.

2. What Do We Use for Tokens?

This is a great question! Parents and teachers have suggested all kinds of tokens for use with this system. At times for teachers, the choice really is not up to them—their institution may have a school-wide program that tailors its tokens either to the school mascot (e.g., "Paw Prides," "Jaguar Bucks," "Happy Monkeys") or a more generic ideology ("Catch 'Em Being Goods," "Atta Boys/Girls"). If you implement the token economy system within your room exclusively, you have options. Perhaps the most common token I have heard is using the raffle tickets that you can purchase by the roll. These tend to be popular because a) they are available at any Wal-Mart®, b) they are relatively inexpensive, and c) you get about 35 million per roll, making them plentiful enough to last for a while.

I have also heard of using poker chips, marbles, kidney beans, pennies, and different forms of play money. Monopoly-type paper money is commonly used because it affords you some flexibility with regard to denomination, but there are many types of play money available at toy stores, or you could use faux jewels or gemstones, *Pirates of the Caribbean*® doubloons, or other play coins.

Occasionally, I run into a more enterprising teacher who makes paper money on the computer with *his or her own face* on the bills. That is a pretty cool idea, and it has the advantage that the tokens won't get mixed up with tokens used in other classrooms, as the currency is clearly specific to that particular teacher.

When I think about those classroom situations, I tend to suggest tweaking the program some if the teacher has the knowledge, time, and motivation to do so. For example, you can still make paper money on the computer, but rather than using *your* picture, put a picture of *each student* on the money. Obviously, you would have to have a reasonable number of students to pull this off (it's not for the high school teacher who sees 135 students per day!), but there are a couple benefits to doing it this way. First, the kids will feel a sense of pride because they have money with their face on it. But on an even more practical level, this method will keep the nerds from getting rolled in the bathroom for their cash—nobody can spend it except them!

While I'm on that subject, an advantage of *not* personalizing the tokens to each child is that generic tokens would allow them to pool their resources to show a bit of altruism to their classmates or siblings. They could offer up a few bucks to help a friend pay a classroom fine or get a privilege he or she had been working toward or make an empathetic donation to a brother who was not able to earn it himself.

The rule of thumb, as with any program, is to keep it interesting, enjoyable, and most of all, *doable* for you! No program will bear fruit if it gets uprooted from the word "go."

3. What Do We Use for Rewards?

There are a few schools of thought when it comes to determining the rewards available to the kiddos in return for their good behavior tokens. Perhaps the easiest method is to just sit down and ask *them* what they would like to have as "menu" items for the token economy. Of course, that does put the wolf in charge of the henhouse just a bit. However, remember that you as the grown-up are not always as tuned in to what the kids these days like or do not like!

I should also mention that the prizes (or goals, rewards, etc.) do not need to be material goods. Parents often look resentfully at me when I suggest raising the stakes by making each successive prize more valuable—the parent mistakes "value" for "more money." Time, attention, and privilege can all serve the same purpose without the parent spending a dime.

I always bear in mind that another of the little secrets of teaching (that I am not certain anyone outside of the teaching profession understands) is the answer to the following question: "Who *pays* for all of that stuff in your classroom?" It is *you!*

Thus, for those of you who come from school districts or systems where the teachers are *not* paid well, it is especially important think in terms of time, rights, or privilege just like parents do. Computer time, free time, homework passes, extra credit on a quiz, lunch with the teacher (okay, this one may not be as alluring for high school students), leading the line to the lunchroom, and "cut" passes for lines to the water fountain can all be used. Once again, you are only limited by your imagination when it comes to nontangible rewards in a token economy.

When you are consulting with a full classroom of kids to figure out the menu items, there is a good way to pare down the laundry list that the students are sure to generate. For instance, you can create your own list of 20 or so items, then pass it out as a forced-choice checklist and ask the students to check the top five or seven things on the list. You then basically proceed as if this exercise is an election and count the votes on all of the "ballots." Have the class agree to keep, say, the top 10 items in terms of number of votes each item earned.

A twist on this idea is to personalize the menu for each individual student and have each kid write down five or seven things toward which he or she would like to work. Obviously, this system will begin to fall apart if you have a lot of students each day, but if you maintain roughly the same class for the entirety of a school day, you may be able to keep up with your group. This system seems to work best for parents because it affords the child a sense of control.

Once the menu has been created, be sure to make it visible alongside your house or class rules. The more prominent the external system available to the kids, the less you have to be thinking on your feet and the easier your job becomes!

4. How Do I Know What to Make Everything Cost?

While this may seem somewhat easy to tackle on the front end, you would be surprised at how often I get asked this question. As adults, we have a strong desire to be effective with our behavior management system and also fair. Of course, "fair" does not mean everyone gets treated the same; it means that everyone gets what they need! Have you heard that one too many times yet? In any case, make certain there is some wiggle room when it comes to setting price points in a token economy.

The starting point will be to spitball some ideas with the kids, but bear in mind that you must maintain ultimate veto power with the ideas that come out of such a gathering. Your best guess at the outset is probably the best starting point, but there are two reasons why you need to have some flexibility.

First, as the game evolves, you will get a better feel for how much "earning power" the kids have. If the menu items are either too cheap or too expensive, work with the kids to adjust them accordingly. Once again, this is a life lesson for the kiddos—small things may be easier to afford, and larger things take more effort. Talk through the process so they get a good feel for financial management.

Second, the governing law of supply and demand economics comes into play: Things that everybody wants may go up in price! On the flip side, if there are menu items that seem to be ignored by the children, then either drop the price or get rid of them entirely and replace them with rewards that are more in demand.

On a related note, I have heard some creative ways to hammer home the idea of *economy* in the token economies. For example, some teachers charge students for every privilege you can think of—from renting their desk (if they miss a payment, they sit on the floor until they can afford to get the desk back), to being able to write with a ballpoint pen (for younger students), to being allowed to get a drink or go to the bathroom outside of regular class visits to the water fountain or restroom. I have also heard of parents writing "tickets" for infractions and making their teenagers pay a fine for bad behavior.

Those parents and teachers may take the token economy idea to an extreme, but they do demonstrate the level to which you can roll with the system to maintain order. Try setting up a financial committee that will hear grievances about the system and work toward setting prices to avoid gouging.

Incidentally, I have often heard teachers ask a question about how to deal with students who excessively ask to go to the restroom or get a drink. In these cases, I recommend adopting a *hardliner* economizer's philosophy. While you cannot deny reasonable restroom breaks to students, you *can* have one of the menu items be "extra restroom pass," or "extra water fountain pass," thereby effectively putting a price tag on the privilege to go to the restroom or get a drink outside of the usual ebb and flow (pardon the pun) of the regular classwide breaks.

5. Can This Program Be Adapted for Older Students or Situations Where I Have Six or Seven Classes of 30 Kids Each Moving Through my Classroom Every Day?

Absolutely! I'm sure you guessed my answer for this one. If you are like most middle or high school teachers, you are not just dealing with one group of 23 students on any given day—you may have six or seven classes of 23 (or more!) filtering though your room. Keeping track of a cumulative program like token economy for 150 or 175 students can be quite cumbersome. Furthermore, if you hang charts, graphs, or systems around the room to aid with keeping track of all this stuff, your room is going to end up looking cluttered.

For those of you in this kind of situation, I suggest "wiping the slate clean" after each class period, thereby eliminating the chore of maintaining a cumulative system. In other words, you would throw out the notion of building toward longer-term, bigger goals.

For this system, get yourself a few of those small pads of sticky notes to use as tokens. They are usually available in wildly obnoxious fluorescent colors. Their colorfulness works to your advantage, because they are very visible at a glance. Let's say you are teaching ninth grade Earth Science. If there are a couple students in the back who talk all the time during class (that never happens, right!?), keep right on going with your lecture on the value of igneous rocks to the ecosystem, and while you are speaking, make your way unobtrusively around the room and smack a sticky note on the desk of those students who are actually paying attention.

As an aside, this approach also addresses two common questions I get asked. First, I am often asked, "Doesn't a token economy rip off those students who always do what they're supposed to do anyway?" Nope, this system actually rewards everyone who is doing what they are supposed to. The second common question is, "What do I do when I have a couple of students who are talking all the time?" You reinforce others who are behaving around them to ease them into compliance.

Anyway, you give a sticky note with the proviso that everyone is to keep them on their desk until the end of class each day. You may want to use a different color of sticky notes each day so the enterprising youngsters cannot cheat by bringing their own sticky notes to confuse the issue!

The strength of such a system rests in your ability to hustle back and smack a sticky onto the desk of the students who had been talking amongst themselves but then decided to pipe down and start to pay attention. Give them traction with the game and change the rules to reflect their ability to earn reward.

Instead of making the sticky notes worth a trip to the treasure chest, you can make them worth bonus points on the next quiz. If the class is being extra good or if you are feeling extra charitable, you can say that if anyone earns, say, five stickies in a class period, he or she gets a homework pass for that or the next day.

Whatever the reward, remember two things: First, make it something that will be a targeted priority for everyone in the room, and second, the prizes are based on daily performance rather than an accumulation. Thus, when class is over, we cleanse the palate. Everyone grabs their sticky notes and deposits them either in your awaiting hand or into a predetermined garbage can. You don't want them to "accidentally" find their way onto the black market to assist the students in your classes later that day.

6. Can This System Be Used Class-Wide Rather Than for Individual Kids or Students?

I already addressed this question somewhat in the answer to #5, and I include a bit more about it in the next answer, too. No need to fill valuable space with redundancy.

7. I Have a Student/Child Who Gets Very Angry Because He or She Always Feels Outperformed by Classmates/ Siblings. Is There Either a Way to Deal With This Situation or Perhaps a Different Method to Dole out Rewards for Token Economy?

This situation is actually one that occurs with relative frequency in larger groups (such as in classrooms or families with several kids) and results in some of the better-behaved kids getting pestered when you are not around. What happens is that the kids who have a hard time maintaining a consistent income (if you know what I mean) grow weary and jealous of the kids or sibs who seem to always be at the top with good-behavior points. So, they act out against the well-behaved chess club kid who *always* wrecks the curve.

In this case, rather than play the game straight, we can adjust the rules to maintain hope for those who struggle compared with the rest of the children. Such kids may never gain the purchase power to get some of the larger-ticket items if they feel frustrated and hopeless in the system. Instead of linear pricing for the rewards, juggle the system to resemble a raffle.

What I mean is that we make the tokens resemble something other than money; for example, chances dropped into the hat to be pulled out for the rewards. This way, even if you only get a couple of tokens in any given period of time, you still have a shot at hitting the reward. Obviously, the better behaved the kid, the more chances he or she has to enter into the raffle. However, here is a secret from me to you that will help distribute the wealth: *You are completely in control of who wins each round!* Unless there is a nosey kid peering over your shoulder when you pull the winning ticket out each afternoon (or whatever the timeframe happens to be), you can "miraculously" choose the ticket of one of the more poorly behaved kiddos once in a while.

This keeps all the kids engaged and reduces the level of tension. Everybody wins sometimes. You keep the well-behaved kids on the line but also set the hook for some of the more troublesome ones. In keeping with the spirit of this system, the better behaved the kids become, the more they have a chance of winning. Just have them do the math (which can also serve as a wonderful tie-in to the algebra you are trying to teach).

A second idea is to randomly draw a couple of names at the beginning of the time period or the start of the day—these will be the secret "students of the day" who win all the good-behavior points or a prize. Seal the names in an envelope and attach it to the blackboard or refrigerator for all to behold. To use this approach, you will have set up a system whereby points are awarded to the group as a whole for their behavior. At the end of the day or class period, open the envelope and allow everyone to see who will be credited with the group's points or the prize for the day.

In this system, the kids are motivated to maintain good behavior because, presumably, they each have an equal chance of being selected as "student of the day" or "mystery kid" or whatever clever name you wish to assign. As an added bonus feature, you can play a role in making necessary "adjustments" to who wins each day (i.e., "rigging" the results!). So, if any particular student has been repeatedly snubbed due to dumb luck or random chance, you can delight in "discovering" his or her name in the envelope the next day and declaring that student as the winner.

8.   Do I Also Take Away Tokens for Poor Behavior?

Ah, this question often inspires spirited debate. Let me defer initially to a statement I made earlier in the book: If you are doing something that works, keep doing it! With this in mind, I always recommend that teachers or parents who begin a token economy *not* take away tokens for bad behavior. In other words, once the kiddo earns a token, it is his or hers to keep.

The reason for this recommendation is that with some of the roughest kids to manage, for every token they earn, they are probably going to lose many more—so many, in fact, that by the end of the second week, they actually owe you *money* because there are not enough tokens to possibly cover the markers they have with you. Bang—gone is the hope for success and motivation along with it.

With hope goes the game. To repeat, these children are good at losing and don't expect they can win in the first place. Thus, it is particularly important with these kids to use the token economy as a system of positive reinforcement. This way, you drive home the point that once they earn a token, it is theirs to keep. From there, they can spend it, they can keep it, they can sell it on eBay—it really doesn't matter what they do with their earnings, when you say that their winnings are *theirs*.

Having said that, I do understand that some situations require some sort of consequence system to be in place. I speak more about this in Chapter 16, where I discuss dealing with the really poorly behaved kids. For now, let me preliminarily offer an alternative: We can shift from a token economy, which works solely as a system of positive reinforcement, to a system called response cost.

9. What Is "Response Cost?"

There are a number of ways to pull off a response cost sytsem. Response cost is a system we can dovetail with token economy to address the need for consequences. With response cost, we use the same rules as for token economy, but we come from the opposite perspective.

In token economy, everybody starts out with *nothing* and then earns for good behavior. In response cost, everyone starts out with *something* and then loses for poor behavior. When you combine the two systems, at the end of whatever period of time you designate, everyone goes back to the baseline amount of tokens, except that any tokens a kid has earned become token economy tokens—they are now that child's to keep and will not be taken away.

Let me give an example. Let's say you teach a self-contained class of 12 students. You determine that everyone is going to start the day with 20 tokens and that you reset the clock twice a day—after lunch and at the end of the day when the students are preparing to go home. (Or, if the end of the day tends to be chaotic, maybe you should save the reset until the following morning.)

Whichever the case, you arrange your "menu" of token values and rewards, but you add a third page dealing with transgressions. Obviously, not every rule violation costs the same amount—some are worse than others; for example, we pay different fines if we get caught doing 15 versus 25 miles per hour over the speed limit.

You could decide that talking out of turn in class is worth 1 token, missing homework assignments is worth 3 tokens, slugging someone on the playground is worth 10 tokens, and you're off to the races. You get the drift.

In the home, you can be very concrete. For instance, you might begin the week with a stack of 20 quarters. Each infraction costs your child a predetermined number of quarters. Anything left at the end of the week becomes their "allowance"—it is now theirs to keep—and we begin the next week with another stack of 20 quarters.

Recall the discussion earlier about how often you reset the clock. You may begin doing it twice a day. Or, if you have kids who are going to burn through those tokens fast, you may want to reset every hour. Reach a point of equilibrium, and then begin to pull back.

You can combine both programs *if* you have kids who will not over-burn their cache. In other words, you can make the number of tokens a child has in his or her possession somewhat fluid, giving for good, taking for bad, but only if you do not encounter a scenario whereby a deficit occurs and the kids begin to lose hope. As I've stressed, success is imperative, especially for those who have learned they will not succeed.

10. What Are Your Closing Words of Wisdom?

I've addressed two of the three most common points of feedback I typically field when I present this information, but there is a more interesting philosophical discussion that occasionally arises. This discussion usually occurs with the adults who tend to think deeply about their approach to things, and their concern merits a bit of space in this chapter.

The point they bring up has to do with intrinsic versus extrinsic motivation. In simpler terms, they wonder if we are merely training our children to respond solely to rewards provided by the environment and not to "do the right thing" just because it is the right thing to do. Shouldn't the drive to perform an appropriate action come from within?

That is a great question and one for which I do not have a rock-solid response. Most behavior management plans you encounter in seminars or staff development trainings tend to rely exclusively on external rewards for good behavior. In fact, in our business, rewards typically are, by definition, elements provided by the environment.

To dig further into this, even a reward that triggers a sense of pride, such as a compliment or appreciation, is necessarily provided by external sources (i.e., in this case, the adult—parent or teacher). Can we foster intrinsic motivation in a system that centers on external rewards?

My answer to this question relates to the origin of intrinsic motivation in any of us. Are we born with it? Is there a class or a TV show that teaches this to us? Does it come as the surprise in a box of over-sweetened breakfast cereal?

Here is my point: Intrinsic motivation is not something inscribed directly into our DNA. It is planted and nurtured by the adults in our lives who teach us to become the wonderful human beings we are today. These adults accomplish this task not only by building our sense of worth and esteem but also by emphasizing and shaping (i.e., *teaching*) the interpretations we make to ourselves when we engage in either nice or naughty behavior.

Let me try again: Intrinsic motivation can be taught alongside any other behavior modification plan if the instructors do a couple things (which, frankly, you may already be doing): First, use praise and compliments to reward effort and positive behavior. When doing this, you should also underline for the child the intrinsic message of prosocial behavior. For example, "That was really cool, Taylor. You not only helped Melissa, but you also made her feel grateful for the helping hand. That feels good."

In this example, you gave an external re-enforcer (praise) and handed Taylor a way for her brain to interpret that behavior as striving for that external reward. In addition, you highlighted two other things: First, you helped Taylor develop empathy by making an interpretation of Melissa's behavior, and, second, you put a name to a potential intrinsic motivator—feeling good about helping others. Incidentally, you also sent a message to Taylor that she can gain your approval or attention by conducting herself in a similar manner in the future.

What I just described is one thing you can do to build intrinsic motivation. The second is something I already touched on earlier in the book when I spoke of pushing the wall back as the kiddos gain mastery of self-monitoring/self-management. Using this technique to build intrinsic motivation requires that positive behavior goes on for longer periods of time before the reward is doled out. During these extended periods of self-management and prosocial behavior, you can continue to hammer home the point that, although these kids are not being rewarded extrinsically for the good behavior, they are still maintaining because they are learning to do things out of respect for themselves and those around them.

You will still have some kids who take umbrage with this point, insisting that it's the pot of gold at the end of the rainbow driving them. Even with these kids, it remains important to consistently and verbally emphasize the intrinsic value of doing good, because they still have the potential to learn the "right thing to do."

This is a tough issue. For some kids and teens, teachers really are like surrogate moms and dads. In fact, teachers may find themselves playing that role more than they wish. If kids are not getting these lessons at home, they certainly will need to be introduced to them in a safe and nurturing environment, as opposed to in the justice system or by their equally problematic buddies! I think it is absolutely vital for educators to teach not just the basics, but also, other ways of thinking or interpreting life.

I know a lot of folks who think differently—they believe that teachers are there only to teach the three "R's" and nothing else. They argue that life's lessons are learned in the home, and that other points of view should be discouraged instead of encouraged, stating that they only serve to confuse kids and, thereby, create dissonance and rebellion.

I understand that position and will *always* urge parents to take an active role in teaching kids how to fish rather than just giving the fish to them. However, I also believe that mental and emotional flexibility are the underpinnings of success far more often than are rigidity and an unwillingness to adapt. Thus, I think it absolutely imperative that teachers (and parents!) reinforce exploration, questioning, and responsibility for one's actions. Should we be trying to help kids develop intrinsic motivation? You bet! But along the way, they can still enjoy and feel motivated by extrinsic delights such as Tootsie Rolls®, stickers, extended recess, and bonus points on a midterm.

Chapter 13
Tips for Dealing with Maximally Problematic Children
Helpful Hints to Consider

What do we do with the kids who make it almost impossible for the approaches described in this book to work?

This chapter is divided into sections based on the type of child you are dealing with. Before I get into detail about the types of kids, bear the following points in mind. First, these kids are truly the oil tankers: Nothing will work immediately, and progress will be measured slowly. Second, the ideas I recommend here are not intended to be "magic wand" cure-alls, but rather, are additional ideas to aid in turning said tankers. Third, these ideas should be used in *conjunction* with a structured behavior management plan, not *instead* of one.

As you know, the best behavioral plans are meant to provide a choice (e.g., through warning and mentoring systems), focus on the present and the future (e.g., by avoiding dwelling on the past or holding a grudge), and instruct and guide kids (e.g., through providing alternate behaviors, talking through, and debriefing). When any of these elements of a plan begin to falter because a child has deeper issues or neurochemical problems, we need to move into alternative programming.

As I stated in a previous chapter, this book may not give you exactly what you are looking for. You may have a specific scenario in mind and would like to know *exactly* what to do in said scenario. I can only suggest general recommendations with the caveat that you adapt them to your setting, to your unique personality, and to your specific group of kiddos.

Before I get more specific, let me provide a few general thoughts for dealing with these children and teens. Let me also say that whatever you decide to do behaviorally will work most of the time with about 80% of our kids. Most of them are pretty good. They will grow up, get good jobs, have good families of their own, and pay their taxes. Unfortunately, we tend to lose sight of that sometimes when we have difficult kids, because the 5% of our kids who act up consume 90% of our energy!

1.   Drop the Authoritarian Techniques

If any part of your being leans toward the "authoritarian" end of the scale (i.e., more rigid, less flexible, believing "might makes right"), you are going to have to take it down a notch. Remember the "hunting dog" (or "tug toy") kids? They will *not* respond well to rigidity or to an inflexible structure you may try to impose on them. I discussed this earlier, but it is worth repeating because there is no better set-up for failure than allowing a defiant child the opportunity to maintain locked horns with you.

One of you is going to blink first, and since *you* are the grown-up, you are better equipped emotionally to pull off the maneuver. Give some slack, offer a choice, and allow the child the opportunity to choose compliance rather than have it thrust on him or her.

2.   Remain Emotionally Neutral

This is another rehash but an important one: Remember to take energy out of a situation rather than add energy to it. Your getting "amped" up is going to serve as jet fuel to the escalating situation and may actually make it worse. What's more, when you lose your cool, you are essentially taking your "clarity of thought" and "goodness of judgment" out of the equation, as you cannot think as well when you are in a state of escalation.

3. Recognize the Function of the Behavior

Another recap! This is starting to feel like a summary of the book, but reviewing this point is helpful in setting up the rest of this chapter.

Remember the notion of diplomacy. You will be in the best position to diffuse bad behavior if you understand what is behind it, pushing it and energizing it. The better you are able to recognize the need being met by the behavior or the message that is intended to be communicated by it, the more successful you will be in determining how to help that child achieve the need or message in a way that is more appropriate.

4. Focus on Positives Embedded in Negative Behavior

Once again, I implore you to find the cool aspects of the "bad kids." This will not only help you connect, but also will provide you with a more genuine and effective compliment than a generic one that comes out of "trying to find something good to say." In working to change the rules for how these kids see themselves, do your best not to throw their good qualities down the garbage disposal because they are "just the bad kids."

Leadership was one quality I mentioned earlier as a potential good quality "bad kids" may have. There are a number of other strengths these kiddos may exhibit. For example, class clowns may have really fast processors in their brains—maybe they can turn a phrase quickly or are good at manipulating language, or perhaps they can tie together different aspects of a situation to make it funny. Those are strengths if they are applied in a positive way.

Kids who shout insults back and forth may be fantastic at conjugating swear words in ways you never thought possible. Well, okay … that may not in itself be a very flattering characteristic, but it does belie an underlying intelligence, right?

This point was brought home to me a couple of years ago in Nashville. It must have been a slow news day, because the 5 o'clock newscast had a live breaking story about two teens who were being taken to jail for spray painting graffiti on an office building. The news cameras were there, of course, and eventually panned over to show the graffiti.

I remember sitting there in my easy chair, staring idly for a minute at the office building being shown on my 32-inch, garage-sale TV and then thinking to myself, "Hey … *that's pretty good!"*

Those kids had some real artistic talent. I wondered if anybody else had noticed or if there was an adult who took an interest in these guys because, despite their being "bad kids" who defaced private property, they actually had some talent. They were remarkably creative and artistic. If this strength was pointed in a positive direction, it could genuinely pay off for those kids.

But alas, who would be the grown-up to step up and foster the talent of those teens rather than throw it away because they were "bad kids?"

5.   Respond With Care

Let me give you something to think about: If a child gets you to react with anger and resentment, he or she has effectively made you into a copy of every other significant adult in his or her life. How can change happen if these kids are allowed to recreate their own warped world over and over? Change the rules!

It's easier said than done. Tuck away in the back of your mind that doing the same thing over and over while expecting different results is the definition of insanity—*or childhood*. It is up to grown-ups to help our kids learn a different means of meeting their needs.

6. Remember the "Golden Rule"

If you become frustrated when a child misbehaves, you may inadvertently treat the offending kiddo harshly. If this happens, you'll get no judgment from me—it's a tough job to be a therapist, parent, or teacher! But occasionally take a step back and think about whether you are treating that kid how you would like to be treated. Making yourself proactive rather than reactive can help diffuse tension, both in that situation and in your mind!

I have covered some general tips. Now, let's traverse into the minefield of dealing with some specific types of utterly resistant kids. In no particular order, here are *the big three:*

a) Kids Whose Self-Image Is Threatened. These are the kids and teens who have a reputation to maintain or who are trying to save face in front of their buddies. A few ideas to consider:

Set them up for success. The more you can somehow adjust your interactive style to meet the needs of your particular kids, the better behaved they will become. That is not to say that they will be angelic by any stretch, but as I said previously, the more you can do to make life less of a disaster for them, the more likely they are to behave well for you.

Think about it this way: If you feel constantly attacked, you will circle the wagons and start to shoot back. In the classroom, the students who are not the best academicians may feel school is a constant barrage of information and demands that they will never be able to comprehend; same in a therapy office setting. Thus, they are faced with the option of looking bad in front of their buddies or just feeling like a *"bad kid."*

Basically, I am recommending that you be sensitive to the interactive or learning styles employed by your kids. The less the kiddos feel plowed under by your teaching style or invasive therapeutic voice (oh, come on, we all have one!), the less likely they are to act out or to punish you.

Also, bear in mind the advice I gave early on in the book regarding how to deal with some of the angry kids in the room. I advised you to temper your approach. The more you come on strong in letting them know how wonderfully they have been performing, the more pressure they will feel, and the harder they will work to undo the compliment. I say more on this in the discussion of the third type of tough student.

Reframe language to promote a sense of control. With students or clients who self-handicap (i.e., those who would rather not try at all so as to not look as if they gave their best effort and then failed) or who generally cut their own legs out from underneath them in order to protect themselves from looking bad, you really have no leverage at the outset.

In a classroom setting, if a student decides that he or she is not going to do an assignment, can you *force* them to do it? Can you hit them with a blow-dart loaded with sodium pentothal and then brainwash them into doing their work?

Probably not. If a student stubbornly refuses to do something, they have absolute power. This can also happen in the home, particularly when a parent feels powerless. Frankly, if a kid wants to get kicked out of the classroom or kicked out of school, he or she will also do just that. In fact, getting kicked out of school is relatively easy if you really put your mind to it.

For the kids and teens who are on that track, we have to make hay while the sun shines. Work at relationship building when they are present and participating. For the kids who self-handicap, the same principle applies.

If a student decides to not do a homework assignment, help him or her understand that this is a choice he or she is making rather than buy into whatever the excuse happens to be (e.g., "I don't know how," "I can't do it").

If you reflect on a moment when you know he or she *did* perform the operation, then suddenly the task in question goes from being *externally controlled* to being *internally controlled.* Put another way, the task moves from being something the kid has no control over to something that he or she is *electing* to avoid. If the kid *can't*, there is no reason to try. However, if he or she is making a *choice*, there is at least the *possibility* of a different outcome.

Using this language has a very different spin than language that allows a kid to believe he or she is powerless to change the outcome. The child may still choose not to do the assignment, problem, task, or test, but now it is not because he or she is unable.

Avoid being overly positive. I touched on this point earlier when I introduced oppositional defiant disorder (ODD). I elaborated a bit then, so this section remains brief.

Remember that, at times, a teacher or therapist's natural tendency is to want to "make up for" or "balance out" a rough home life or upbringing. You may make an approach that is so far weighted to the positive that the kiddo has no idea how to incorporate the concept into the paradigm of how he or she sees himself or herself.

Let me again state that this type of kid probably has a pretty negative self-image. Add to that the fact that he or she has a well-established reputation to maintain with his or her buddies, and you have yourself a student who will not be able to handle you saying he or she can be president some day.

What's more, if you slap a remarkably positive label on a really difficult kid, you put pressure on him or her to perform to the standards of that label. I have been preaching that typically, we need to raise standards to let kids know they are indeed capable of adjusting their game in our school systems, but the more you make that overt with the angry kids, the less likely they are to want to participate.

A better approach would be to temper your positive labels and remain more data focused. For example, saying, "Dexter, you got an 88 on the last quiz. That was among the highest grades in the class," is a better alternative to, "Dexter, what a great job! You are one of the brightest kids in here this year!" The first sentence lets Dexter save face *and* feel pride at the same time. The second one requires him to wriggle out of the positive label so he doesn't have to explain himself to his friends or carry the weight of living up to the label.

Prepare kids for positive feedback and then make a quick retreat. Obviously, giving compliments and positive feedback is a vital part of building relationships and raising self-image. The problem is that the angry kids—teens in particular—are not going to be able to tolerate the compliment, particularly if you hang in their emotional space afterwards!

For example, if you walk over to Antonio and say to him, "Antonio, that was really cool what you did," and then you hang around and maintain eye contact with him, his anxiety is going to spike. For that moment, he feels like you are requiring him to say something nice back to you, and that creates an untenable situation—particularly if his buddies are nearby. Now, they are all looking to him to see how he handles the situation, and they sure don't want to be put into a similar bind.

So, Antonio will invariably do one of two things: 1) He will punish you for putting him into that situation in the first place or 2) he will work double time to undo the compliment so that you *never* put him in that position again.

The only shot your compliment has to soak in for Antonio is if he has to sit with it, and he will *not* do that if you hang there with him. So, when you compliment or praise an angry kid, my advice is to hit it and then keep on walking. He may shout something at your back as you move away, but what you are essentially doing is taking the battle away from him.

There may also be times when you make an emotional interpretation of something your student, child, or client goes through. For example, you may see Juan embarrass Carlton, so Carlton slugs him. While walking Carlton to the principal's office, you can drop into the conversation, "Whew ... that had to be embarrassing, brother. Sorry about that."

This interpretation is important for Carlton, because it will help him to open up other internal emotional possibilities. Carlton is good at being angry—he spends most of his life being angry. What he lacks is the awareness to help him interpret his experience any other way. You can help develop the ability to differentiate and identify feelings in him, but he will (once again) fight you on it if you hang there with him.

To think of this pragmatically, consider how boys and men interact. There is not a lot of emotional "sharing" that goes on, right? Monosyllabic grunts, maybe, but usually very little in the arena of emotional dissection. So, when you make the interpretation, just hit it and move on. Let it soak in by not forcing it to soak in.

b) What to Do If There Is Open Conflict Between Child and Adult in the Home or Therapy Office or Between Student and Teacher in the Classroom. This brief section presents a few things to keep in mind when you encounter a situation with a student whereby the two of you end up like a couple of mountain goats with your horns stuck together. In other words, occasionally there arises a relationship with a student that is founded solely on negative interactions—you two cannot escape each other's orbit, and it creates a negative synergy.

Most teachers would read the preceding paragraph and chuckle to themselves. Essentially, that chuckle would indicate about 5% sympathy, 10% familiarity, and 85% outrage. "I cannot believe the temerity of such teachers!" some of you are shouting at the open pages of your book. True, we cast aspersions on teachers who give a bad name to the rest of us, but I want to remind you that most of these teachers began their career with the best of intentions. Eventually, many teachers find themselves in this predicament.

Really, it is sort of human nature to keep searching for a bigger and bigger stick with which to hit the student until we finally figure out how big a stick it's going to take for him or her to actually listen to us. Unfortunately, when this happens, you

245

paint yourself into a corner, and there seems to be no way out for either of you!

Here are a few pointers to file in the back of your mind.

Recognize that the student has been hurt, does not trust, and is trying to prevent future hurt. This was discussed in the section on ODD, but it is worth repeating here to keep your hope alive.

It is extraordinarily difficult to focus on the genesis of ODD when you are locked in battle with the student. Still, recall that the positive behavior support approach is founded on both positive reinforcement and also the relationship you forge with the child. When kids with ODD are fighting you every step of the way, you fall into their trap of making sure that they don't have to like anybody—particularly you.

Changing the rules involves your understanding what's going on inside the children you encounter. Remember that once you are in the locked-horn position with a kid, he or she has got you. When this happens, they have put you into the same role as every other grown-up in their life, have you off balance, and can manipulate your emotions.

Avoid coercive statements and sarcasm. Again, human nature leads us to act and react differently when we are royally frustrated and angry. I know none of you wake up in the morning with a sinister plot to tear down the esteem of a frustrating child or teen through coercion, but those sorts of behaviors can eek into your dealings with kids as you get more hopeless in your role as mentor.

This frustration leads to toxic interactions, and while acting out may give you some guilty pleasure if you are dealing with a kid who constantly irks you, you will erode the relationship. Trust cannot build in an atmosphere poisoned by negative complicity—these kids are skittish enough as it is. As you grow more coercive, you are adding credence to the kid's notion that relationships and trust cannot build.

This is particularly true if sarcasm is a part of your interactive style. I know this was covered previously as well, but let me tell you this: If you use sarcasm as a regular part of your interactions with these kids, you will be drawn into using the sarcasm in negative ways when you get frustrated. As your stress and anger builds, back off the sarcasm or you will cross the line between tasteful jocularity and egregious coercion.

Finally, remember the "tug toy" and "hunting dog" kids. These are the ones who will push back twice as hard when they bump up against a coercive statement or direction. The more you say, "Oh, yes you will," they will be shouting back, "Oh, no I won't!" And then where will you both be? Relax, breathe, and reapproach in a manner that will allow for your message to penetrate.

Avoid toxic or overbearing penalties. Probably the most common question I used to get during my seminars was some version of, "Dr. Steve … can you please give me a consequence I can lay on the kids that will actually work?"

Behind that question is a story of frustration and of two mountain goats that started to tumble off the side of the cliff because they could not disengage from each other. With really difficult kids, adults will punish, then up the ante, and then ratchet the intensity up even more, all in an effort to find that big stick that will work. In the end, you use the biggest board in the shed, and the kids are still not compliant.

Unfortunately, a couple things begin to happen when you are stuck in the cycle of consequence-avoidance as a means of behavior management: First, the child in question now has control. He or she is not going to let you know if your consequences have any impact because either they really don't, or if they do, the kid's lack of emotional response frustrates you, and that is fun for him or her.

Remember, that some of the kids wearing the "bad" label are good at being punished. For some of these kids, your consequences really *do not matter*. Frankly, in this situation, nothing you can do to them is going to faze them one way or another. This is particularly true of those kids who come from a disastrous home life. In school, consequences pale in comparison to those in the world they have to survive when they go home at night.

There really are some kids who are saturated with punishment and truly do not care what else you do to them. To illustrate this point, I am reminded of Judd Nelson's character in the movie *The Breakfast Club*. In this film, Judd's character had Saturday detention until he was 41 years old. Does he really care if you add another three Saturdays? No! He is maxed out with penalties and really could care less if anything more gets heaped onto the pile.

For these kids, hope is not only fading; it has been obliterated. A lack of hope always inspires bad behavior, because consequences become irrelevant to the decision-making process. If you don't get hurt by blows to the head, are you really afraid to join in a fistfight?

In these situations, I can almost guarantee you that there is a notable absence of positive interactions between you and the other mountain goat. Those horns have been locked for far too long, and you two have not had enough distance between you to see the light of day. A breath and a step back are vital, but so is a gesture toward building positive reinforcement. Remember PBS (positive behavior supports)?

Let me also say this: It is sometimes hard to help adults change their mindset away from behavior management via consequence avoidance and toward that of behavior management via goal attainment. In other words, kids will wear you out trying to find the "ultimate consequence" of noncompliance— especially kids who are accustomed to losing, good at being punished, and starkly devoid of hope. Their lives are lived from a consequence avoidance point of view. *There is power in not caring.*

Change the rules and offer the gift of hope. It sounds a bit rah-rah and a little like empty rhetoric, and I realize it is difficult to wrangle with some of these lovely kiddos day after day. You can fall into the trap of allowing them to make you feel utterly hopeless. But ultimately, frustration leads nowhere.

Use "symptom estrangement." Let me briefly address hope one more time. Remember the analogy of "bad kid … or bad behavior" with the shirt and the ketchup stain? Let me reiterate the point of that metaphor: If you feel hopeless (i.e., that you are dealing with a "bad kid" rather than a kid with bad behavior), then your approach will be more negative and more consequence-based and will feed the cycle of hopelessness.

As best you can, try to see these kids and teens as harboring bad behavior—not being intrinsically bad—in an effort to keep hope alive. Letting frustration build can result in burnout for *you*, and that is not a fun place for you to be.

Don't take it personally. This is another phrase you hear repeated as part of the rhetoric in every seminar on behavior management and in every book you pick up on the topic. This is one of the mantras we tell you to repeat to yourself like a mini version of the Alcoholics Anonymous Serenity Prayer, leading to some cynicism on your part, because it is easier for seminar leaders and book authors to make statements like these when we are not stepping into the line of fire like you are every day in your home, office, or classroom.

Remember that a kid's "angry defiant attitude" is not about *you*. The kid is reacting toward you in a venomous manner because you fill the stencil in his or her mind. You have stepped into the role of authority figure or grown-up, and these are roles that have traditionally driven the kid nuts.

It is doubly hard to keep this point in mind because these are the kids who will work double time to make it seem as personal as they possibly can. They are trying to push buttons and keep you emotionally off balance.

Never give up on a kid. This is definitely a little bit of true rah-rah, but remember that sometimes the change you effect in the difficult kids may not become apparent until years later. Sometimes these kiddos will return to your classroom or office and tell you about an event from the eleventh grade when you did something they never forgot—something you could have never predicted would have an impact. Maybe it was even something you had no recollection of ever doing because it wasn't intended to be profound! I guess I want to warn you to not underestimate the power you have in the lives of most of your kids.

Think about some of the angry ones who do have a rep to keep—they will never let you know if you get to them! That makes them too vulnerable, and they cannot tolerate this position. Plug away at the issues and change the rules. Be the change you wish to see in your kids!

c) For Teachers Specifically: What to Do If a Student Has a Fear of Failure. These are the students who share features in common with those in section A. They have probably grown into sharing space on your radar screen with those in section B. The characteristic that sets these students apart is the shame they are feeling due to a sense of inadequacy—perhaps due to an undiagnosed learning disability or some other problem with learning. For example, perhaps they were passed through earlier grades without clearing the academic hurdles necessary to provide a foundation for future learning, thus setting them up for continued failure and frustration. When this happens, the students create diversions, or smoke screens, to cover their tracks and not let others into their "secret."

Discreet note-writing. Actually, this can be one of the most powerful interventions you can initiate with a student who has a profound fear of failure. Whether or not he or she has a behavior problem, the student may still harbor "the secret."

I recommend dropping a little note to the student. For example, let's say you have a fifth or sixth grade boy in your class named Connor who is struggling to read. Imagine you are doing one of those exercises in your class whereby everyone reads a little bit out loud and then passes off to another classmate to carry the torch.

You, being an astute student of human behavior, notice that Connor is starting to crouch like a puma because something has got to give. He is going to cause some disruption in the room so he does not have to feel stupid in front of everyone. When you see this tension begin to rise, stroll by and—as subtly as you can—drop Connor a quick note that says something like, *"Do you want some help?"* and then just keep on walking.

By the way, never write, "Do you *need* help," as the word *need* has a very different spin in Connor's already defensive mind. Basically, Connor will think you believe he really is as "stupid" as he already thinks he is.

Stick with allowing him the grace and dignity to dictate what happens next. After a minute or two, catch his eye, and if he gives you a look that seems to indicate the door may be slightly open to the idea, or if his eyes or face seems to cautiously say, "I don't know … what do you have?" then pass by and drop him another note as surreptitiously as possible. This note can say something like, *"Do you want it to be from me or one of your classmates?"*

Once again, the point is to dole out the rope. Put Connor in command of the pace and the direction in which this exchange is about to sail. If he decides not to pursue it, don't push; he has spoken for now. Still, you have opened the door in as nonthreatening a way as possible under the circumstances.

On a deeper level, your note is extraordinarily important to Connor because it essentially says two things. First, it tells him that you get it—there is an elephant in the room, and his name is "You don't read so well." You are not going to ignore the elephant any longer, nor are you going to judge or ridicule Connor despite having this information.

Most importantly, your note says something that speaks to Connor in his language. Your note also conveys that you will protect him from the rest of the class if he wants you to. Despite calling out the elephant, you are not going to embarrass Connor in front of his buddies or his girlfriend or the rest of the room. This secret is between two people—you and him. If he wants some help, you can make sure to provide that free from shame or judgment.

Private notes can have all sorts of different spins to them. For example, you could write one that says, *"Dear Nolan: It's lonely in here without your homework. Signed, Your Folder."* A note like this one can take some of the punch out of what has probably been a series of tense exchanges between Nolan and every other teacher he has experienced. Leave him with the dignity of knowing that you are certainly not ignorant of what is going on with him, but also that you understand the circumstances that may exist in his life that distract him from being able to keep his eyes on the finish line. Take the punch out, and he will be more likely to discuss options with you than if you come straight at him from a consequence-based viewpoint.

There are probably some students in your room who are wound tighter than a Swiss watch and will freak out if they miss a homework assignment. For them, taking the seriousness out of an occasional misstep can be a powerful intervention, as it conveys to him or her that life does not depend on a specific assignment. In essence, you are saying, "Relax, and let your natural ability flow."

Finally, I am certain many of you also send good, positive notes home to Mom and Dad. This can be a powerful intervention because parents who have had the"bad kid" for several years get tracked in when they deal with the school system. Some even get to the point that they immediately jump to the defensive if the phone rings and the caller ID reads, "School." They avoid answering all together. In any case, they start asking themselves what their child did now.

Before I continue, I want to let you know that I understand the issue with sending good notes home regularly. In a nutshell, I know that the parents who are most likely to show up for parent/teacher conferences are those who want their kids to do well. They are the parents of the "good kids"—those who *want* their children to read and write and behave.

Every once in awhile, you will have a situation whereby little Ethan is acting out and you have no idea what's going on with him. Then Mom and Dad walk in, and it's all suddenly clear. However, that is usually the exception, not the rule. For the most part, if you have a "bad kid," you will probably have a difficult time maintaining contact with the parents. If you line up 100 "bad kids" and give each of them a note to give to their mom or dad, maybe 15 or 20 notes will actually find their way in front of a parent's eyes.

Still, those 15 or 20 exceptions represent an important group to help, because good notes going home can have a couple of advantages. First, when parents get these notes, it can begin to change the rules at home for these students. If a parent has had a "bad kid" for 6 or 7 years, it is probably difficult for him or her to conceive of the child doing anything other than acting out and getting into trouble. Cracking the door in that parent's mind just a smidge to let some light in could help the student.

Second, sending good notes home gives you a little credibility in the mind of the parent, because you are not immediately set up as the antagonist in the drama that the parent anticipates is certain to unfold between August and June. If you can show you will offer a balanced view of his or her child, you may diffuse some of the parent's defensiveness.

Scaffolding. Scaffolding implies that you get your kids started with help and support or help them to break an assignment down into smaller, digestible bits but then allow them the opportunity to complete the task by themselves. In other words, you provide just enough support to ensure success, but you stop short of basically doing the task for them. Allowing a certain level of struggle or frustration can help the student to learn if the struggles and frustrations do not reach too high a level and don't exceed the student's ability to manage or cope.

It's like teaching a youngster to tie his or her own shoes. If you keep tying the shoes for the child, he or she will never learn. Left completely to his or her own devices, the kid will never learn it either, as shoe-tying is a complicated operation. A good parent will guide and support—while the whole time having the child go through the motions on his or her own. Teach the child to fish, and you feed him or her for life!

Be prepared to modify the teaching style or work requirements. I don't mean to suggest the entire class be held hostage by the learning style of one or two students. Rather, modifications can be made on a person-by-person basis for those students who may have a learning style not reflected by traditional classroom techniques or who may need to focus on effort and take *baby steps* rather than huge strides toward the finish line.

An example would be if one of your students needs to use a MP3 recorder or laptop computer to help with "getting" all of the information from you or to get work back to you. Having a processing deficit or a problem with reading or writing may necessitate this step. Having some flexibility also works to help scaffold the student enough that he or she is able to keep up and not feel snowed under by the pace set by the rest of the class.

Occasionally, a teacher will ask me how to handle the classroom dynamic that may arise if you handle one student differently or if the rules are slightly different for one student. When such a dynamic arises—and remember, students have a very quantitative sense of justice—you will have to hit it head on to avoid disgruntlement among the masses.

My first piece of advice is to take the emotional valence out of the circumstances. Model a sense of normalcy for the rest of the room. If the students get the sense that you are also feeling a little guilty or unsure about what is happening, they will smell blood in the water and begin to circle like piranhas. They need to be assured, on some level, that this is *normal*. So, state the situation (whatever it happens to be) with this particular student in as matter-of-fact a tone as you can. Say it just like you are ordering lunch—no emotional spin whatsoever. Yes, there are special rules for one of the students, but you are not put off at all by that.

You can also point out that the class makes special accommodations for students who have specific needs all the time. Remind them of when Carly broke her leg, and she was allowed to pull up an extra desk on which to rest her cast. Or, remind them of when Joanna's grandpa died, and you let her make up the work after the funeral and giving her a little respite to mourn. Fair does not mean everyone is treated the same; rather, it means that everyone gets what they need.

Whatever the circumstances, your job is to make sure the class helps out each student. For example, if students start to harass the one kid who needs a special accommodation, you need to nip that type of behavior in the bud immediately to avoid fostering the shame already present in the heart of the struggling student.

A town hall meeting is the perfect venue in which to inform everyone of the new set of rules and emphasize that they are not going to affect the way you continue to deal with your students.

Implement cooperative learning. Set students up for success by creating group projects. Include students with lower, middle, and higher academic abilities in each group and let students help each other. Or, create a project where students can contribute from a point of strength rather than weakness.

The bottom line for any plan with students who are hiding their struggles is to let them know that you will do your best to ensure better experiences. Ultimately, each student can decide not to do the work or not to learn. Relationship building is your only chance with them at that point. The consequence of failure weighs much more heavily on them than any consequence you can conceive.

Show these kids that the academic experience does not have to lead to failure, even if you are just one life raft in a flood of bad experiences.

Epilogue

Well, here we are. I have followed the basic flight plan of behavioral change and led you down paths related to the understanding and behavioral management of problematic kids and teens. Hopefully, I have made a case for changing your perception of "bad kids" to "badly behaved kids." Through knowledge, we build understanding; through understanding, we build relationships; through relationships, we change the world one child at a time. If you don't understand *why* you are doing something, you will have difficulties making adjustments—you will learn only one way and have nowhere to go if you begin to falter.

I want to thank you for reading this book and hope you have found it constructive and a "fun read." I will close by offering you an email address where you can contact me if you have thoughts, comments, questions, additions, deletions, or "over-the-top" raves about the book: dr.steve.o@hotmail.com. You can visit my website at www.doctorstevetherapy.com.

Try to reserve my inbox for thoughtful comments only. I don't want to sift through the wreckage I may receive if you fall into one of the following categories:

Someone who hated the book

Someone who hated me

A St. Louis Cardinals fan

Anyone who has ever dated Heather Locklear

A person with no detectable sense of humor

Diehard Trekkies

Anyone who has ever attended an opera
… and understood it

A parolee who has homicidal impulses toward good-looking authors

Cat people

Psychotic ex-girlfriends (you know who you are)

Folks who don't love Bon Jovi

Acura NSX owners (lucky dogs)

Anyone who has ever served hummus to guests without issuing a strong warning first

Extremist wackos on EITHER side of an issue

Competitors who masquerade as interested fans

Bankers

The morally intrusive

Administrators at Marquette University

Anyone who has broken my nose
(there are two of you out there)

People who aren't home during trick-or-treat

Critics who have never risked getting into the ring themselves

Whiners

People who pretend to like vegetarian hot dogs

Low talkers

Blow-hard know-it-alls

Anyone who has heard of Tony Stewart yet won't cheer against him

Those who expect the world to be handed to them

Weirdos (scratch that—some of us are pretty cool)

The guy who stole the stereo out of my car in 1987

The easily offended

Men who use the word *galoshes*

People who can't sing but still love to do karaoke

Anyone who bowls worse than I do

Every girl who has ever broken my heart

Those who've never felt the freedom or the ability to have an original thought of their own …

… and anyone with a list longer than mine!

Be well,

 Dr. Steve

References and Further Reading

Allen, J. S., Damasio, H., Grabowskia, T. J., Brussa, J., & Zhang, W. (2003). Sexual dimorphism and asymmetries in the gray-white composition of the human cerebrum, *NeuroImage, 18*, 880–894.

Allyon, T., & Azrin, N. (1968). *The Token Economy*. New York: Appleton-Century-Crofts.

American Academy of Child and Adolescent Psychiatry (June, 2009). Children with oppositional defiant disorder, *72*. Retrieved March 16, 2011 from the American Academy of Child & Adolescent Psychiatry website: http://aacap.org/page.ww?name=Children+with+Oppositional+Defiant+Disorder&section=Facts+for+Families

American Psychiatric Association. (2002). *Diagnostic and Statistical Manual of Mental Disorders*, 4th ed., Text Revision. Washington, DC: American Psychiatric Association.

American Psychiatric Association. (2010). Temper dysregulation disorder with dysphoria. Retrieved October 31, 2010 from American Psychiatric Association website: http://www.dsm5.org/ProposedRevisions/Pages/proposedrevision.aspx?rid=397

Aristotle (2001). *"The Nichomachian Ethics": Classics of Moral and Political Theory*, 3rd ed. Morgan, M. L. (Ed.). Indianapolis: Hackett Publishing Company.

Barkley, R. (1997) *Attention-Deficit Hyperactivity Disorder: A Handbook for Diagnosis and Treatment,* 2nd ed. New York: Guilford Press.

Barrish, H. H., Saunders, M., & Wold, M. M. (1969). Good behavior game: Effects of individual contingencies for group consequences on disruptive behavior in a classroom. *J Appl Behav Anal, 2,* 119–124.

Batsche, G. M., & Knoff, H. M. (1994). Bullies and their victims: Understanding a pervasive problem in the schools. *School Psychol Rev, 23*(2), 165–174.

Beck, A. T. (1979). *Cognitive Therapy and the Emotional Disorders.* New York: Plume Publishers.

Beck, A. T. (1987). *Cognitive Therapy of Depression.* New York: Guilford Press.

Benson, H., & Klipper, M. Z. (1976). *The Relaxation Response.* New York: HarperTorch/HarperCollins.

Brown, R., & Gerbarg, P. (2005). Sudarshan Kriya yogic breathing in the treatment of stress, anxiety, and depression: Part I—Neurophysiologic model. *J Altern Compliment Med, 11*(1), 189–201.

Burns, J. M. (1978). *Leadership.* New York: Harper and Row Publishers, Inc.

Cahill, L. (2005). His brain, her brain. *Scientific American, 292*(5), 40–47.

CBS News (2007). The plague of sexual misconduct in schools. Reported October 20, 2007. Accessed March 16, 2011 at CBS News website: http://www.cbsnews.com/stories/2007/10/20/national/main3388380.shtml

Cherry, E. C. (1953) Some experiments on the recognition of speech, with one and with two ears. *J Acoustical Soc Am, 25*(5), 975–979.

Chess, S., Thomas, A., Birch, H. G., & Hertzig, M. (1960). Implications of a longitudinal study of child development for child psychiatry. *Am J Psychiatr, 117,* 434–441.

Coe, F. (Producer), & Penn, A. (Director). (1962). *The Miracle Worker* [Motion picture]. United States: United Artists.

Cohen, S., Kessler, R. C., & Gordon, L. U. (1995). Strategies for measuring stress in studies of psychiatric and physical disorders. In Cohen, S., Kessler, R. C., & Gorden, L. U. (Eds). *Measuring Stress. A Guide for Health and Social Scientists*. Oxford: Oxford University Press.

Cunning, K. "Individualized Education Program (Conference Summary Report)." Special Education and Support Services. Illinois State Board of Education. Web. <http://www.isbe.state.il.us/spec-ed/html/forms.htm>.

Dekaban, A. S., & Sadowsky, D. (1978). Changes in brain weights during the span of human life: Relation of brain weights to body heights and body weights. *Ann Neurol, 4*, 345–356.

Descartes, R. (trans. Cottingham, J.; 1984). Meditations on first philosophy. In Cottingham, J., Stoothoff, R., & Murdoch, D. (Eds.). *The Philosophical Writings of Descartes*, Vol. II. Cambridge: Cambridge University Press.

Disability Online (2004). www.disability.vic.gov.au/dsonline/dsarticles.nsf/pages/Receptive_language_disorder?

Dworkin, S. (1939). Conditioning neuroses in dog and cat. *Psychosomatic Medicine*, 1(3), 1–9.

Freud, S. (1949). *The Ego and the Id*. London: The Hogarth Press Ltd.

Gardner, H. (1983). *Frames of Mind: The Theory of Multiple Intelligences*. New York: Basic Books.

Geller, B. (2003) Neurochemistry of ADHD and its medications. *J Watch Psychiatr*, April 9, 2003.

Grandin, T. (2008) *The way I see it: A personal look at Asperger's and Autism,* 2nd ed.). Arlington, TX: Future Horizons.

Greenberg, J. S. (1999). *Comprehensive Stress Management*, 6th ed. Boston: McGraw-Hill.

Haley, J. (1993). *Uncommon Therapy: The Psychiatric Techniques of Milton H. Erickson, M.D.* New York: W. W. Norton & Company.

Hargreaves, D., & Colley, A. (1986). *The Psychology of Sex Roles*. London: Harper & Row.

Hendrix, H. (2007). *Getting the Love You Want: A Guide for Couples*, 20th Anniversary ed. New York: Henry Holt & Company, LLC.

Herzog, D. B., Greenwood, D. N., Dorer, D. J., Flores, A. T., Ekeblad, E. R., Richards, A., Blais, M. A., & Keller, M. B. (2000). Mortality in eating disorders: A descriptive study. *Int J Eat Dis, 28*(1), 20–26.

Holland, J. G., & Skinner, B. F. (1961). *Analysis of Behavior*. New York: McGraw-Hill.

House, R. J. (2004) *Culture, Leadership, and Organizations: The GLOBE Study of 62 Societies.* Thousand Oaks, CA: SAGE Publications.

Ingersoll, G. M., & Benson, K. (1996). What is your classroom management profile? *Teacher Talk, 12*(1).

Johnson, F. J. (2006). *Effective Classroom Behavior Management.* Louisville, KY: Butler Books.

Johnson, F. J. (2006). *Proactive Discipline for Reactive Students: A Guide for Practicing.* Louisville, KY: Butler Books.

Kaplan, R. M., & Saccuzzo, D. P. (2005). *Psychological Testing: Principles, Applications, and Issues*. New York: Thomson Wadsworth.

Kindlon, D., & Thompson, M. (2000). *Raising Cain: Protecting the Emotional Life of Boys*. New York: Ballantine Books.

King, S. (2008) *Bag of Bones*, 10th Anniversary ed. New York: Scribner.

Kolb, D. A., & Fry, R. (1975). Toward an applied theory of experiential learning. In Cooper, C. (Ed.). *Theories of Group Process*, London: John Wiley.

Kotler, L. A., Cohen, P., & Davies, M. (2001). Longitudinal relationships between childhood, adolescent, and adult eating disorders. *J Am Acad Child Adolesc Psychiatr, 40*(Dec): 1434–1440.

Lahey, B., & Loeber, R. (1994), Framework for a developmental model of oppositional defiant disorder and conduct disorder. In Routh, D. K. (Ed.) *Disruptive Behavior Disorders in Childhood* (pp. 139–180). New York: Plenum Press.

Logan, B. K. (2002). Methamphetamine—Effects on human performance and behavior. *Forens Sci Rev, 14*(1/2), 142.

Maccoby, E. E, & Jacklin, C. N. (1974) *The Psychology of Sex Differences*, Palo Alto, CA: Stanford University Press.

Maslow, A. H. (1943). A theory of human motivation. *Psychol Rev, 50*, 370–396.

Mattingly, G. (2010). A prodrug stimulant for the treatment of ADHD in children and adults. *CNS Spectrums, 15*(5), 315–325.

McFarland, K. L. (2000). *Specific Classroom Management Strategies for the Middle/Secondary Education Classroom*, ERIC Document ED437340. Accessed March 16, 2011 from Education Resources Information Center: http://www.eric.ed.gov/ERICWebPortal/search/detailmini.jsp?_nfpb=true&_&ERICExtSearch_SearchValue_0=ED437340&ERICExtSearch_SearchType_0=no&accno=ED437340

McPartland, J., & Klin, A. (2006). Asperger's syndrome. *Arch Pediatr Adolesc Med, 17*(3), 771–788.

Medical Education Online (2011). Male/female brain differences. Retrieved April 27, 2011 from http://medicaleducationonline.org/index.php?option=com_content&task=view&id=46&Itemid=69

Minuchin, S., & Fishman, H. C. (1981). *Family Therapy Techniques*. Cambridge, MA: Harvard University Press.

Mitchell, Carissa. "Current Forms - SPED." Sevier County Schools Special Education Current Forms. SPED. Web. 2004. <http://www.seviercountysped.com/current-forms.html>.

National Assessment of Educational Progress (NAEP, 2011). *Standardized Testing Statistics*. Accessed April 27, 2011, from http://www.educationbug.org/a/standardized-testing-statistics.html.

National Health Interview Survey, (2003).Retrieved April 16, 2008, from http://www.cdc.gov/nchs/nhis.html

National Institute of Mental Health (2000). *Child and Adolescent Bipolar Disorder: An Update From the National Institute of Mental Health*. Accessed March 16, 2011 from National Institute of Mental Health website: http://www.nimh.nih.gov/health/publications/child-and-adolescent-bipolar-disorder/summary.shtml

Pavlov, I. P. (1927). *Conditioned Reflexes: An Investigation of the Physiological Activity of the Cerebral Cortex*. Anrep, G. V. (trans. & Ed.). Oxford: Oxford University Press.

Peterson, G. B. (2004). A day of great illumination: B. F. Skinner's discovery of shaping. *J Exper Analysis Behav, 82*, 317–328.

Premack, D. (1959). Toward empirical behavioral laws: I. Positive reinforcement. *Psychol Rev, 66*, 219–233.

Redl, F. (1972). *When We Deal With Children: Selected Writings*. New York: MacMillam Publishing Company.

Roth, M. (September 27, 2010). For many with autism, reading facial expressions is a struggle. Pittsburgh Post-Gazette. Retrieved March 16, 2011: http://www.post-gazette.com/stories/life/lifestyle/for-many-with-autism-reading-facial-expressions-is-a-struggle-265665

Roth, T., & Roehrs, T. (2004). Insomnia: Epidemiology, characteristics, and consequences. *Clinical Cornerstone, 5*(3), 5–15.

Ruble, D. N. (1988). Sex role development. In Barnstein, M. H., & Lamb, M. E. (Eds.) *Developmental Psychology: An Advanced Textbook*, 2nd ed. Hillsdale, NJ: Erlbaum.

Sernyak, M. J., Leslie, D. L., Alarcon, R. D., Losonczy, M. F., & Rosenheck, R. (2002). Association of Diabetes Mellitus with use of atypical neuroleptics in the treatment of schizophrenia. *Am J Psychiatr, 159*, 561–566.

Shaffer, D., Fisher, P., Dulcan, M. K., Davies, M., Piacentini, J., Schwab-Stone, M. E., Lahey, B. B., Bourdon, K., Jensen, P. S., Bird, H. R., Canino, G., & Regier, D. A. (1996). The NIMH Diagnostic Interview Schedule for Children Version 2.3 (DISC-2.3): Description, acceptability, prevalence rates, and performance in the MECA Study. Methods for the Epidemiology of Child and Adolescent Mental Disorders Study. *J Am Acad Child Adolesc Psychiatr, 35*, 865–877.

Simmons, R. (2002) *Odd Girl Out: The Hidden Culture of Aggression in Girls*. New York: Harcourt Press.

Simpson, K. (2001). The role of testosterone in aggression. *McGill J Med, 6*, 32–40.

Staats, A. W. (1970). *Learning , Language and Cognition*. London: Holt, Rinehart & Winston.

Stein, M. A., & Weiss, R. E. (2003). Thyroid function tests and neurocognitive functioning in children referred for attention deficit/hyperactivity disorder. *Psychoneuroendocrinology, 28*(3), 304–316.

Stossel, J. (1998). *Boys & Girls Are Different: Men, Women, and the Sex Difference.* ABC News Special, January 17, 1998. The Electric Library.

Tenenbaum, D. (2010). *Can Blocking a Frown Keep Bad Feelings at Bay?* Retrieved March 16, 2011 from University of Wisconsin News website: http://www.news.wisc.edu/17602

Thomas, A., & Chess, S. (1977). *Temperament and Development.* New York: Brunner/Mazel.

Thorndike, E. L. (1898). Animal intelligence: An experimental study of the associative processes in animals. *Psychol Rev, 2*(4), 1–109.

Treffert, D. A., & Christensen, D. D. (2005). Inside the mind of a savant. *Scientific American, 293*(6), 108–113.

Viadero, D. (1998). AAUW Study finds girls making some progress, but gaps remain. *Education Week*, October 14.

Viorst, J., & Cruz, R. (1987). *Alexander and the Terrible, Horrible, No Good, Very Bad Day.* New York: Aladdin Paperbacks.

Walsh, B. T., Roose, S. P., Glassman, A. H., Gladis, M., & Sadik, C. (1985). Bulimia and depression. *Psychosom Med, 47*(2), 123–131.

Wood, T., & McCarthy, C. (2002). *Understanding and Preventing Teacher Burnout.* Eric Digest. Washington, D.C.: ERIC Clearinghouse on Teaching and Teacher Education.

Wood, W. & Eagly, A. H. (2002). A cross-cultural analysis of the behavior of women and men: Implications for the origins of sex differences. *Psychological Bulletin, 128*, 699-727.

Yapko, D. (2003). *Understanding Autism Spectrum Disorders: Frequently Asked Questions.* New York: Jessica Kingsley Publishers.